BASEBALL IN AMERICA & AMERICA IN BASEBALL

EDITED BY

DONALD G. KYLE & ROBERT B. FAIRBANKS

INTRODUCTION BY RICHARD CREPEAU

With Contributions by

BENJAMIN G. RADER, STEVEN A. RIESS, SAMUEL O. REGALADO, DANIEL A. NATHAN, MARK DYRESON, AND DAVID VAUGHT

Published for The University of Texas at Arlington

by TEXAS A&M UNIVERSITY PRESS *College Station*

First edition
This paper meets the requirements of ANSI/NISO
Z39.48–1992 (Permanence of Paper).
Binding materials have been chosen for durability.

Library of Congress Cataloging-in-Publication Data

Baseball in America and America in baseball / edited by Donald G. Kyle and Robert B. Fairbanks ; introd. by Richard Crepeau ; with contributions by Benjamin G. Rader . . . [et al.]. — 1st ed.

p. cm. — (The Walter Prescott Webb memorial lectures ; no 38)

ISBN-13: 978-1-60344-023-3 (cloth : alk. paper)

ISBN-10: 1-60344-023-2 (cloth : alk. paper)

1. Baseball—United States—History. 2. Baseball—United States—Miscellanea. I. Kyle, Donald G. II. Fairbanks, Robert B. (Robert Bruce), 1950– III. Rader, Benjamin G.

GV863.A1B387 2008

796.35770973—dc22

2007037685

CONTENTS

PREFACE

The annual Walter Prescott Webb Lecture Series, held on March 9, 2006, focused on the theme of "Baseball in America and America in Baseball." The theme is especially relevant for a university in a city home to a professional baseball team and its stadium, and the series coincided with first World Baseball Classic and spring training of Major League baseball.

The intention of the series was to invite noted historians of American sport to investigate the historical development of baseball in America and explain the rich symbolism of baseball for the players, spectators, and America. From rustic sandlots to monumental stadiums, from Little League to the World Series, baseball has long been an institution in American culture and society, but what does baseball mean in American history, and what is American about the game? Why are millions of fans, rich and poor, urban and rural, male and female, devoted to a game that is always long on strategy and sometimes short on action? How did baseball emerge historically from an archaic children's game to become a pervasive national symbol and a vast commercial enterprise? What is the significance of baseball in the history of leisure, business, labor, immigration, race, and urbanization in America?

Although Professor Webb became famous as a historian of the frontier, and early volumes reflected his orientation, recent volumes have been innovative in approaches and themes. After our announcement of baseball as a theme, a retired faculty member who studied with Webb informed us that Webb also was a knowledgeable baseball enthusiast, and so the lecture series in his honor has come full circle.

The co-editors, whose research concentrates on ancient sport and urban history, do not profess to be experts in the history of baseball, but we invited four of the very best baseball authorities to present papers and contribute essays to the series: Benjamin G. Rader, James L. Sellers Professor of History at the University of Nebraska-Lincoln, who gave the keynote; Steven A. Riess, Bernard J. Brommel Distinguished Research Professor at Northeastern Illinois University; Samuel O. Regalado, California State University, Stanislaus; and Daniel A. Nathan, Skidmore College. We applaud these experts for their scholarship, their lively and impressive presentations, and their collegial interaction with the large and engaged audiences in attendance. It is worthy of note that these fine scholars have all also made essential contributions to the growth and success of the North American Society for Sport History and to the maturation of the field of sport history. This volume also includes the essays of the co-winners of the annual Webb-Smith Essay Competition: Mark Dyreson of Penn State University, and David Vaught of Texas A&M University. Chosen from an unusually large number of excellent submissions, their essays complement the lectures and expand the volume.

We recognize Dr. Richard Crepeau, University of Central Florida, himself an expert on baseball and American sport, for introducing Dr. Rader as our keynote speaker, and for contributing an insightful and articulate introduction to the volume. We thank Dr. Stephen Maizlish, from the Department of History at UT Arlington, for presenting Dr. Regalado's paper when he was unable to attend due to an emergency. Our thanks also go to Carol Lehman of University Publications for her assistance with publicity materials, and Susan Sterling and her staff for their attention to a myriad of details involved in the lecture series and this publication. We also greatly appreciate the assistance of the publication team at Texas A&M University Press. Finally, we recognize Dr. Joyce Goldberg, Chair of the Webb Lecture Committee, for her careful planning and coordination of the academic and social events.

◆ This volume is dedicated to the memory of Clay Gould (1971–2001), an inspirational baseball player and coach who became the University of Texas at Arlington's fourth baseball coach in 1999 at the young age of 27. He grew up in Arlington, Texas, and was an All-State third baseman for Arlington High School. He played baseball at UT Arlington and went to the NCAA tournament twice in his four years. The Southland Conference named him its 1993 player of the year and he was nominated for the prestigious USA Baseball's Golden Spikes award. After graduating he played professional ball for two years for the Tyler Wildcatters in the Texas-Louisiana League. He started his coaching career in 1994 as a volunteer assistant coach at UT Arlington, and he became a full-time assistant coach following the 1996 season and then head coach three years later. From the beginning he focused on making the university's baseball program one of the best in the nation. He out-recruited perennial baseball powers Mississippi State and Oklahoma in his first year. The next year his team won the Southland Conference Championship and claimed their first-ever NCAA tournament victory with a dramatic 7–6 win over the University of Houston.

Midway during his first year as head baseball coach, Clay underwent surgery for cancer. Despite this, he missed only three weeks of the 2000 season. Although doctors were optimistic about his recovery, he had a relapse the following year and exploratory surgery that May found that the cancer was spreading rapidly. He died on June 23, 2001, leaving behind Julie, his wife of 19 months, and a 10-month-old daughter, Logan Soul. UT Arlington and baseball lost a great coach and a very decent human being.

Donald G. Kyle
Robert B. Fairbanks

BASEBALL IN AMERICA & AMERICA IN BASEBALL

INTRODUCTION

"Baseball in America and America in Baseball" was selected as the topic for the 2006 Walter Prescott Webb Memorial Lectures, one of the notable traditions of the academic calendar. For those of us who have been part of the growth in the field of Sport History and the subfield of baseball history, the choice is both inspired and highly gratifying. Those chosen for this singular honor as lecturers are representative of the best scholarship devoted to the proposition that the history of the national pastime can illuminate the history of America in valuable and unique ways.

The writing of baseball history goes back into the nineteenth century with the likes of Henry Chadwick and Albert Spalding, but the writing of baseball history as an academic discipline is more recent. The two great pioneers in the field were David Voigt and Harold Seymour, whose multivolume histories of the game were among the first baseball histories to be regarded as serious academic endeavors. They were also, to my knowledge, the first baseball histories to be reviewed in the professional history journals.

Since then there has been an explosion of academic material published on the history of the national pastime in books and in articles in the leading history journals. In addition there are several journals devoted to sport history and to the history of baseball. By the middle of the 1990s, many job applications in the field of American History carried academic presentations and publications dealing with baseball or sport history as part of the professional vita. Only a scant few history departments still withhold recognition of the legitimacy of baseball history and sport history as part of the academic enterprise.

Baseball history has gone through an internal explosion and development. General histories of the game are still produced, but more and more research has focused on particular aspects of the game. The history of the business side of baseball has become a minor growth industry. These efforts take the form of large economic histories and franchise histories, and include the dynamics of the economic interaction between teams and communities. Serious biography examines the role of the hero and illuminates issues of class, race, and values. The intersection of baseball and politics is another rich area being examined.

Larger issues of race have attracted considerable scholarly attention from baseball historians. Baseball is studied as a window on culture and values and as a transmitter of ideals, as well as a means of acculturation for immigrants. The relationship between the growth of baseball and the growth and development of all forms of media goes back into the nineteenth century with the emergence of a sporting press. In the twentieth century, radio, television, film, and the information transformation have all impacted the game.

In point of fact, all the great forces that have shaped the American experience have also shaped baseball from the local sandlots to the modern stadiums. All the great forces that shape the human experience and the development of human personality impact baseball, and vice versa. Baseball is often a mirror or symptom illuminating the larger society, and on occasion it becomes an agent for change.

◆ This volume, resulting from the 2006 Walter Prescott Webb Memorial Lectures, is a collection of six essays offering a window on the variety and quality of baseball history being produced within the halls of academe. They represent the work of three generations of baseball historians. Each brings a unique perspective to the game; each focuses on a different but equally important aspect of baseball history; each represents the high quality of historical research and writing that has become the hallmark of the field.

In his contribution to this volume, David Vaught cites the now too often quoted line from Jacques Barzun, "Whoever wants to know the heart and mind of America had better learn baseball." However, Vaught points out that if you read on to the end of the sentence Barzun offers further direction: "and do it by watching first some high school and small town teams." Historians have until recently paid scant attention to the latter part of Barzun's advice. In this collection, David Vaught, Sam Regalado, and Dan Nathan offer essays that redress that shortcoming.

David Vaught's " 'Our Players Are Mostly Farmers': Baseball in Rural California, 1850 to 1890" takes us into California's Central Valley where the towns of Davisville and Dixon developed a strong baseball rivalry. Vaught addresses several questions: Were the players mostly farmers? How rural were these towns? Why did baseball become popular at this time and place? Why have historians, both baseball historians and rural historians, missed this phenomenon, which was such an important aspect of community life?

Vaught, as both a baseball and agricultural historian, is particularly well equipped to seek answers to these questions. He makes use of a wide variety of materials and paints a fascinating picture of life in rural California in the second half of the nineteenth century. The changing economic and demographic conditions of the time and place, the natural disasters that hit these communities, and the daily round of life, including the patterns of recreation, are among the details that Vaught explicates in this gem of an essay. There is also a short examination of the evolution of the game at this grass roots level, including the impact of separate visits to the region by Alexander Cartwright and the Cincinnati Red Stockings.

Vaught concludes with a call for more histories of baseball at the local and the nonprofessional level. He calls on his fellow historians of rural life to reexamine their assumptions about baseball and its role in the lives of people on farms and small towns across America.

Samuel Regalado, in "'Invisible Baseball': Japanese Americans and Their Game in the 1930s," offers another slice of baseball history at the local and regional level. Regalado, too, focuses on the nonprofessional game. What he gives us here is an examination of the Japanese American community through the lens of baseball, and this community's interaction and lack thereof with the larger American community. Geographically he concentrates on California although he does venture into the communities of the Northwest.

Regalado's primary interest is in the Nisei generation who came of age in the years of the Great Depression and who faced massive discrimination in California and throughout the West. The Nisei were isolated from the larger community and were frustrated by the desire of the Issei that the Nisei serve as a bridge between cultures. As with their Euro-American contemporaries competition was a central value and sport was one means to instill that value.

The Japanese Americans operated in a sporting tradition conveyed through athletic clubs, and Regalado examines that tradition in America. Baseball was an integral part of the sporting culture that the Issei brought to the United States, and for them it was a significant part of their community recreational life. However, it failed to offer a bridge to the larger American community.

Faced with discrimination, the Japanese Americans, as so many others have done, turned inward. Baseball was played in isolation, and the larger community took little notice. Japanese American baseball had a golden age in the 1930s but remained largely invisible to the outside world. This is a fascinating story well told, and in the end there is little mystery as to why Regalado opens his essay by quoting from Ralph Ellison's *Invisible Man*.

Indeed the African American community had its baseball communities and leagues that were just as invisible as that of the Japanese. Dan Nathan, in "Chasing Shadows: The Baltimore Black Sox and the Perils of History," relates the history of one such invisible team that in 1929 won the first and only pennant in the American Negro League.

Little is known or remembered of these talented representatives of the city of Baltimore. By 1933, the Black Sox franchise was out of business and few now recall them or their achievements. As Ellison says, and anyone who has ever compared the white and black press knows, African Americans were nearly totally invisible to the white society. It is as if the black press and white press in the same city were reporting on activities on two different planets.

In this thoughtful essay, Dan Nathan not only attempts to piece together the story of the 1929 Black Sox, but he also raises significant questions about memory and history. What is it that individuals choose to remember? What is it that society chooses to remember? Who decides what will be remembered and how it will be remembered? On what basis are these decisions made? For historians, these are central and troubling questions, especially if as a historian you are trying to write a history of one of those invisible groups.

Speculation on these questions and other matters leads Nathan across many fields, baseball and otherwise, and across a century or more of baseball history. He takes us through the 1929 season with the Baltimore Black Sox and, in the end, offers a panoramic view of the Sox and their contemporaries. Nathan places the team within the community and shows the centrality of Negro League baseball to the isolated African American communities.

Last but not least, Nathan returns to the questions of memory and history. He examines how historians work their way around and through the historical evidence and the gaps in that evidence, patching and filling, to finally produce what has sometimes been called a "useable past." Nathan's trip through memory is also a trip through his own personal past showing how one historian is moved toward a topic through a myriad of influences in his own history.

These three essays form one pod in this collection. The other three are more discrete entities, and although they could be tied together, such a connection would be forced and serve no purpose.

Steven Riess, in "The Profits of Major League Baseball, 1900 to 1956," tackles another kind of baseball history and one that defies all historians who are wedded to hard and accurate evidence. What Riess attempts to do is make a reasonably accurate assessment of the profitability of baseball in the first half of the twentieth century. The difficulty of the task is due largely to the fact that most baseball owners have treated the hard data of profit and loss as a state secret.

Riess ferrets out the facts of profitability and seeks to explain the factors that contribute to it. These factors include the size of the city; the quality of the ballpark; the presence or absence of Sunday baseball; and the quality of the team, which often correlates with salaries. Riess analyses value, selling price, and the comparative economic return on investment. He charts the ancillary income from other ventures such as stadium rental to Negro League teams. The analysis is broken down by decade and by league.

The essay is rich in information and analysis, it offers important insights, and it is written with clarity. Riess knows the questions to ask and the angles to pursue, including what owners were doing with some of their profits. There are also a few surprises along the way.

In the end, the most impressive achievement of this essay is the painstaking research required to gather and verify the data and to make certain that the data are comparable across the spectrum of major league baseball. Once that is accomplished, Riess is able to draw meaningful and important comparisons between teams, leagues, and circumstances. He deftly shows what can be done with some dogged and creative research, and the rewards that can be reaped from simple hard work. This is a model for historical research and writing.

Mark Dyreson's "Mapping an Empire of Baseball: American Visions of National Pastimes and Global Influence, 1919 to 1941" offers yet another example of the insights into American history to be gained from baseball history. This essay is based heavily upon research done in the records of the U.S. Department of Commerce. As well as explaining the symbolism of the game for Americans, Dyreson clearly demonstrates why baseball people believed the game was a significant force in promoting American economic expansion around the globe.

The years between World Wars I and II are often characterized as a period of "isolationism" in the United States. To a great extent this was a popular myth focusing only on public opinion polls and selected political rhetoric. The fact of the matter is these decades were a period of considerable global expansion for American business and economic influence.

What Mark Dyreson has done in his contribution to the Webb Lectures is lay out one small part of the American economic expansion as tied to baseball and to the sporting goods industry. It is fairly well known that American sport accompanied American military forces and American missionaries as they pushed America's imperial destiny across the planet. What is not so well known is the way in which the U.S. government promoted American commerce globally in the interwar period; and what is even less known is the role sport, baseball, and the sporting goods industry played in that process.

To paraphrase Yogi Berra, you can learn a lot by just looking, and that has never been any better demonstrated than by Steven Riess and Mark Dyreson in these two excellent pieces of historical research.

If the history of baseball can illuminate the history of America, it is also true that the work of American historians can illuminate aspects of baseball history. In his thoughtful essay, "'Matters Involving Honor': Region, Race, and Rank in the Violent Life of Tyrus Raymond Cobb," Benjamin Rader draws on the work of a number of historians of the South to explain the personality and actions of Ty Cobb, the Georgia Peach.

One of baseball's first superstars, Ty Cobb had a reputation as a man who played baseball to the hilt and as a person of violent temper. He was considered a "dirty" player by many of his opponents. His reputation was earned in the series of violent episodes that marked Cobb's life on and off the field of play. Rader's essay opens with a description of some of these incidents, and Rader then provides a chart of twenty-four cases of Cobb's violent behavior.

In seeking to explain the violence that dogged Cobb's life, Rader turns to Bertram Wyatt-Brown's *Southern Honor: Ethics and Behavior in the Old South* as well as a number of other works on the subject of southern violence. Honor was central in the violent southern backcountry as it was in the more ritualized world of Southern gentlemen. Rader sees in Wyatt-Brown's work a key to understanding the violent behavior of Ty Cobb, who was a product of the southern backcountry. As such, Cobb was hypersensitive to the denigration of his region and imbued with the protocols of race. He was also aware of the significance of status in the stratified Southern society.

Honor, race, and status carried an underpinning of violence, both individual and group, ritualistic and spontaneous. Rader interprets the incidents of violence in Cobb's life as reflective of these values, with honor as the centerpiece.

Operating from this perspective, Rader offers a very different portrait of Ty Cobb than the one that has marked the conventional explanations of Cobb's behavior. This is a very interesting rendering and one that nicely illustrates the interconnected world of historical research and interpretation across disciplines and subdisciplines. Rader's creative use of the work of Southern historians shines a new light on Cobb's troubled life and reveals the peculiarities of the history of his region.

The six essays that you are about to encounter represent some of the best work by contemporary baseball historians. They will introduce you to the wide variety of approaches to baseball history as well as the ways it can inform and be informed by the larger field of American History.

Enjoy.

Richard C. Crepeau
University of Central Florida

DAVID VAUGHT

"OUR PLAYERS ARE MOSTLY FARMERS" BASEBALL IN RURAL CALIFORNIA, 1850 TO 1890

On a hot Sunday evening in June 1887, the Davisville Oletas and the Dixon Etnas played the fifth of fourteen ballgames between the two rivals that summer. Several hundred fans crowded around the diamond at "the Y," a triangular-shaped grounds bounded by the three railroad lines that converged at the Davisville depot. Sitting on grocery boxes, empty kegs, rocks, and small benches under the broiling sun, the spectators—"highly desirous of witnessing the contest," as the local scribe put it—waited anxiously for the first pitch. The game did not meet their expectations, however. "The local nine played listlessly" and lost by a score of 18 to 7. The Etnas took home the one-hundred-dollar purse, and the betting in the stands amounted to hundreds of dollars more. Fortunately for the "disappointed" Oletas fans, another game was already scheduled for the following Sunday at Driving Park in Dixon, where their team would have a chance to "redeem themselves." Sure enough, the Oletas returned the favor, beating the Etnas on their diamond and sending the Dixon fans home equally disheartened. By season's end, the two teams split their summer series evenly, with fans from both towns "mourning the defeats" and cherishing the victories.[1]

The excitement that baseball generated in these two small towns in the lower Sacramento Valley was by no means unusual. The game (an earlier version of it) was introduced to rural California during the Gold Rush, gradually gained a stronger foothold over the next two decades, and then caught fire in the 1880s, when farmers and townspeople began spending a great deal of time watching, playing, and reading about the sport in the local newspaper. By 1885, according to the same reporter, they had become "devoted to the game"—so much so that on the rare occasions when a Sunday evening in the summer went by without "their accustomed amusement," life became "unbearably dull" for players and fans alike. The scheduled games, well-established venues, large crowds, newspaper coverage, fierce rivalries, high-stakes gambling, and close bonds between teams and residents all reveal that baseball—heretofore regarded by historians as a largely urban phenomenon—had become deeply rooted in the region's rural culture. One farmer went so far as to say that attending church on Sunday—or, more specifically, "seeking the salvation of our immortal souls"—had become "a matter of secondary importance."[2]

The farmers' devotion to the game in the 1880s raises three sets of interconnected questions—two historical, the other historiographical. First, just how "rural" was baseball in towns such as Dixon and Davisville? Were the players themselves farmers? Did the game that they played evolve differently from the one played by their urban contemporaries? Second, why did baseball become so popular in rural California at precisely this time? What was it about the 1880s—socially, culturally, and/or economically—that compelled rural residents to embrace the game so wholeheartedly?[3] Finally, why have historians in large part missed this rather startling phenomenon? For at least three decades now, practitioners of both the new rural history and the new sport history have emphasized culture and society, but the two subfields have rarely intersected.[4] We know much about agriculture and rural life during this period and a great deal about baseball's development from a primitive game into a profession and, indeed, "the national pastime." Why, then, do we know so little about baseball in late-nineteenth-century rural communities such as Davisville and Dixon?[5]

By focusing on one region, two towns, and a relatively small number of players and fans, this essay can offer a starting point for answering such questions.[6] My examination, however brief and suggestive, adheres to the words of Jacques Barzun, which ring just as true today as when he first penned them in 1954. Historian after historian have quoted the first half of his pronouncement: "Whoever wants to know the heart and mind of America had better learn baseball. . . ." Few, however, have added the rest: ". . . and do it by watching first some high school or small town teams."[7] Barzun sensed that the essence of the game—its widespread popularity and cultural meaning—has always been fundamentally local. The Davisville-Dixon rivalry, therefore, needs to be understood in its rural context—not as a by-product of the developing urban-professional game. "Our players are mostly farmers," wrote the Davisville correspondent.[8] It would behoove us to consider his words seriously. The history of the game in the region, he knew, was interwoven with the history of the region itself.

Were the players, in fact, mostly farmers? The limited literature available would seem to suggest otherwise. Even the few scholars who have prom-

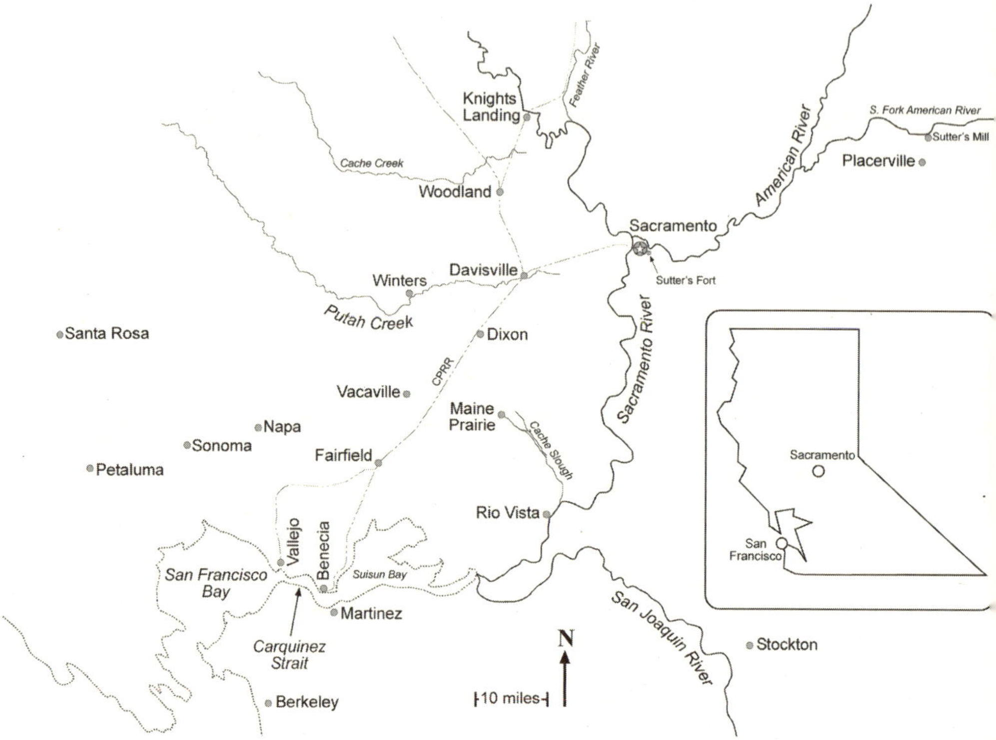

Davisville, Dixon, and Vicinity, Northern California, 1850–1890. Courtesy Ethel Vaught.

ised to emphasize "barn raisin' games" and "down home" baseball in the late nineteenth century rarely focus on farmers themselves. The Miamisburg Actives in western Ohio, the Kalamazoo Champion Base Ball Club in western Michigan, and other such "village" teams in recent studies consisted primarily of local townspeople—clerks, merchants, artisans, bankers, and lawyers, not farmers from the surrounding countryside.[9] Like many of those towns, Davisville and Dixon owed their existence to the railroad, in this case the Southern Pacific Railroad (see map). Both were on the last leg of the first transcontinental line, with Davisville the first depot out of Sacramento, fifteen miles to the west, and Dixon the next stop, another nine miles down the tracks. Both towns had small but fairly stable populations of about five hundred, with more than enough workers and young professionals to fill two teams. Yet, the Davisville correspondent was right. Of the sixty-nine players identified in box scores and feature stories between 1878 and 1895, census records and biographical sources indicate that forty-four of them (68 percent) were, in fact, farmers.[10]

Not that there was much reason to doubt the word of the Davisville correspondent, a longtime resident named Elijah W. Brown, one of the most trusted and in-the-know members of the community. After migrating to the region from Missouri in 1855 via the Isthmus of Panama, Brown had tried his hand at a little bit of everything. He ran a cattle and grain ranch on Putah Creek with his half-brother, Gabriel, for a few years; worked as a bookkeeper for local wheat merchant William Dresbach; owned and operated his own hardware store in Davisville after the town was established in 1868; speculated in town lots from time to time; and organized the Sinclair Windmill Company, which helped promote a local irrigation movement in the 1880s. For most of that decade, he also wrote a weekly "Davisville Doings" column for the *Dixon Tribune* (and later for the *Yolo County Democrat*) under the byline of J. O. N. Brown. He left no subject of local interest unturned, from county politics (he was an avid Democrat), to crop conditions, to community gossip, to baseball. No one knew the history of the region, its farmers, the two towns, their residents, the game, and its players better—or expounded upon such matters more—than him.[11]

That history began in the wake of the Gold Rush. A number of rural communities in northern California proliferated in the 1850s—not in the standard American fashion of settlers moving westward along a broad front, cultivating the land homestead by homestead, but communities nonetheless. Putah Creek, named for the river that ran west-to-east out of the coast mountains across the lower Sacramento Valley, was one such community. Most of the nine hundred transplanted midwesterners who settled it over the course of the decade came not to farm but to seek riches in gold. Those unfortunate to arrive after 1851, however, found that surface deposits had been depleted by the one hundred thousand 49ers who had gotten there ahead of them. Too ashamed to return home, they turned to agriculture and rural life with the same intensity of expectation that brought them to California in the first place. Admitting failure a second time would simply not be an option.[12]

Farming along Putah Creek, though often extraordinarily productive, proved immensely challenging. Using all the latest technology including McCormick reapers and treadmill threshers, farmers cultivated the region's virgin soils to produce bumper harvests of sixty to eighty bushels of wheat per acre—four to five times the average "back home"—most of which helped feed the escalating populations of San Francisco and Sacramento. "The lands of Putah," proclaimed one wide-eyed newspaper reporter in the fall of 1852, revealed "the magnificent results of agriculture under the bold and energetic patronage of its farmers." Yet, not a single one of them made a profit in the 1850s. High production costs at the beginning of the decade and falling prices at the end, the result of the boom and bust of the Gold Rush, never gave farmers much of a chance. Greed and arrogance did not help either. Had they paid even the slightest interest to the human and natural history of the region—in particular how Indians and Mexicans before them had coped with periodic floods and droughts—they might have limited their mistakes and excesses. Nor should the sheer power of seduction be underestimated. The abundance of natural advantages, amazing new technology, gigantic yields, and instant fame—all on the heels of the disillusionment of the Gold Rush—drove these farmers to pursue market opportunities aggressively even though the odds were stacked against them.[13] Their eagerness to keep pumping money into their farms was all the more astounding given the fact that the title to the land itself was in question. Three Mexican land grants engulfed the region, which meant that farmers, under the provisions of the Treaty of Guadalupe Hidalgo and the California Land Act of 1851, had to defend their property rights before federal authorities. Until the mass of litigation was resolved—a process that took almost two decades with one of the grants—no one truly owned the land.[14]

In their haste to succeed in California, farmers committed themselves not only to material pursuits but to community life as well. Neither the legal chaos caused by the land grants nor the seductions of farming in the Sacramento Valley—nor the unfulfilled dreams of the Gold Rush—dampened the community sentiments that they brought with them from the Midwest. In just a few years, residents shared a specific sense of place ("Putah Creek," as they called it), similar patterns of everyday life, common obligations, and a number of public rituals and institutions that pulled men, and eventually women, together as a social unit. They gave names to bends in the creek, crossings, roads, bridges, and other elements of the landscape; gathered together to celebrate holidays, weddings, births, and other community activities; formed strong religious ties; and felt obligated by tradition and necessity to participate in all facets of township and county government.[15]

Putah Creek farmers also shared a favorite pastime—horseracing. Those with southern roots were largely responsible for importing fast trotters and building racetracks, and virtually everyone cheered their favorite horses and reveled in the attention that winners, particularly at the state fair in Sacramento, gave their community. The most celebrated trotting stallion from Putah Creek was "Rattler," who won more races, took more premiums, and earned more in stud fees than any horse in northern California in the late 1850s and early 1860s. When Rattler died in 1863, the *Sacramento Daily*

Union ran his obituary as its feature news story. "The death of this fine animal," the paper bemoaned, "will be regretted by turf men throughout the state"—especially settlers along Putah Creek. The tradition of fine horsemanship, which began among the gentry in colonial Virginia before spreading northward and across class boundaries by the early nineteenth century, took root in Putah Creek and throughout the Sacramento Valley almost immediately and lasted well into the twentieth century. Indeed, horseracing symbolized how quickly rural life in California matured in the decade after the Gold Rush.[16]

Baseball, though not nearly as popular as horseracing at this point in time, also made its way to the Sacramento Valley in the 1850s. Legend has it that none other than Alexander Cartwright, whose reputation for "inventing" the game is second only to Abner Doubleday's, brought baseball with him from New York City by literally carrying a bat, ball, and a copy of the rules of his beloved Knickerbocker Base Ball Club overland to the gold country of California. Although most serious accounts acknowledge that such a feat cannot be attributed to Cartwright alone, if at all, most agree that early Californians did in fact play the game that the "father of modern baseball" (as Cartwright's Hall of Fame plaque in Cooperstown reads) helped create in 1845. Among the twenty rules that the Knickerbockers codified (or at least popularized) that year were the diamond-shaped infield, the inclusion of foul lines, and the insistence that players on the field had to throw to a base to get a runner out rather than hit ("soak" or "plunk") him with the ball. Less well known (and far less documented) is the fact that rural Californians took up the sport in the 1850s just as eagerly as urban Californians. Farmers and farmhands, wearing no uniforms but overalls and black shirts, played informal games on Putah Creek ranches between peak periods of the production cycle as early as 1857—"baseball in the olden time," as Brown remembered it. Three years later, at the state fair, Putah Creek residents were among the two thousand spectators who watched teams from San Francisco, Sacramento, and Stockton play a one-day tournament with the "state title," a silver bat, and $350 in prize money on the line. Baseball, it seemed, had arrived in the Golden State.[17]

While baseball continued to thrive in San Francisco and other Bay Area cities early in the next decade, the game's popularity noticeably declined in the state's rural regions.[18] Farmers along Putah Creek and throughout much of northern California found themselves preoccupied with two of the worst natural disasters in the state's history. In the winter of 1861–1862, a flood of enormous, almost biblical, proportions hit the Sacramento Valley when a series of warm, tropical rains melted several feet of snow in the Sierra Nevada. Rampaging rivers poured out of their channels, filling much of the valley like a bathtub and spreading devastation for weeks on end. Cattle died by the tens of thousands, the cities of Sacramento and Marysville were buried deep in mud, farms and ranches were destroyed, and hundreds of people were swept away to their deaths. Most of the land along Putah Creek was completely under water. "There is nothing to indicate the locality of the ranches but a windmill," observed one stunned resident. The "flood of the century" was immediately followed by another mammoth ecological disaster of the exact opposite nature, drought—the most severe and prolonged ever to hit the state. For close to three years, from the fall of 1862 to the winter of 1864–1865, the rains failed. Hundreds of thousands of cattle perished, and crop loss in the Sacramento Valley was so severe that Californians had to import wheat from Chile to make their bread. The back-to-back disasters postponed the state fair for three years, and baseball diamonds and horseracing tracks lay largely vacant throughout the region while farmers struggled mightily to recover.[19]

Those farmers who persisted through the end of the decade—about 35 percent in Putah Creek—were rewarded for their perseverance. With much of the confusion over land titles finally resolved, and with the return of a more stable weather pattern, farmers resumed wheat cultivation with a vengeance. Their timing could not have been better. By coincidence—the type that seems to pervade U.S. agricultural history—California produced three straight bumper crops after the drought broke in 1865, at the same time that Great Britain and other European nations suffered dangerously deficient harvests. Enterprising grain merchants in San Francisco and Liverpool, including the legendary Isaac Friedlander, exploited the opportunity to the fullest, as did farmers in Putah Creek. Production skyrocketed between 1866 and 1869, with almost three-fourths of their crop being exported to the United Kingdom. Farm incomes more than tripled and land values doubled. Thus began what historian Rodman Paul called "one of the most extraordinary of all agrarian episodes"—California's bonanza wheat era. This dramatic turn of events confirmed all the more the prevailing belief among these farmers that demand would inevitably outpace production. Developments over the next three decades would eventually expose that as folly, but for the time being, farmers had finally struck gold.[20]

The prosperity of the wheat boom helped revive horseracing but not baseball, at least not to the same degree. In the late 1860s and early 1870s, the sport of kings, in fact, became something of an obsession in the Sacramento Valley, with racetracks being built on the outskirts of seemingly every town. Several Putah Creek farmers began training their own trotters and pacers, and raced them at venues up and down the valley. Baseball remained dormant in rural areas for several years, though teams in Sacramento, Stockton, and Marysville resumed play in 1867 on a limited schedule. Horseracing, with its traditional, age-old appeal, weathered the turbulent 1860s much better than baseball. It was, by far, still the most popular spectator sport among rural residents in the Sacramento Valley.[21]

In late September 1869, baseball received an unexpected boost from a distant source. Just four months after the golden spike was driven at Promontory, Utah, marking the completion of the first transcontinental railroad line, the Cincinnati Red Stockings barnstormed their way through California. If not the nation's first all-professional team, the Red Stockings were certainly the highest paid, the best promoted, and the most successful. The team payroll was ninety-four hundred dollars, with four of the ten players making well over one thousand dollars a year; their long road trip that season, through the East and Midwest, as well as California, covered over twelve thousand miles and entertained more than two hundred thousand fans; and they ultimately won eighty-one straight games, disposing of one opponent after another with ease. En route to the West Coast, the Red Stockings, in characteristic fashion, trounced two teams in St. Louis by a combined score of 101 to 18. In late September and early October, three San Francisco clubs and another from Sacramento fared little better in six games, losing 35 to 4, 58 to 4, 66 to 4, 54 to 5, 76 to 5, and 46 to 14 to the visitors.[22]

While the thrashing may have broken the spirit of the losing California teams, the Red Stockings brief tour ignited locals' passion for the game beyond expectations. Newspapers, often on the front page, covered seemingly every movement of the players on and off the field, including gala banquets held in their honor in both cities' finest restaurants. Fans (over two thousand for at least three of the games) marveled at the superior skills of pitching, fielding, batting, and running demonstrated by the Cincinnati nine, gaped at their impressive physiques and dapper uniforms (white flannel shirts, Knickerbocker trousers, and spiked oxford shoes complemented the knee-length stockings), and crowded the Sacramento railroad depot to bid the Red Stockings farewell on October 8. In smaller towns on the Southern Pacific line, including Dixon and Davisville, rural onlookers gathered in droves to catch a glimpse of "the gallant men in stockings red" as their train passed through. Indeed, with their flair for promotion and playing prowess, the Red Stockings whetted northern Californians' appetite for baseball, including thousands who never actually saw them play.[23]

Baseball's surge in popularity proved more lasting in urban, rather than rural, areas. In San Francisco, Oakland, Sacramento, Stockton, and Marysville, heated rivalries developed in the early 1870s that sparked "match play" tournaments and, by the end of the decade, the state's first two professional associations of baseball teams—the Pacific League and the California League (both of them forerunners of the famed Pacific Coast League). The players were well paid and the teams drew large and enthusiastic crowds at their expansive new ballparks. When the Red Stockings returned to San Francisco in 1879 on another grand exhibition tour, they found the competition much tougher and the fans equally excited but not nearly as awestruck.[24] In Davisville and Dixon, however, no one rushed to the depot this time to welcome the Red Stockings back. Baseball continued to be played in the area during the 1870s at picnics and other informal gatherings, but with little of the fanfare, much less the professionalism, exhibited in urban areas. Sporadic efforts to form teams in nearby Silveyville and Woodland went for naught, and there seemed to be no enthusiasm whatsoever for organized play in either Davisville or Dixon. Farmers in the region continued to be consumed by wheat and horseracing. If local newspapers were any indication they read, in considerable detail every week, of developments in the world grain market and of trotting races at the neighborhood track, but the box scores and feature stories that now filled the pages of Sacramento and San Francisco papers seemed of little interest to them. As late as 1879, as Brown later admitted, farmers in the area "knew little more of the game" than they had when it first came west over two decades earlier.[25]

The game had changed considerably over that time. In addition to the standardization of the diamond, the establishment of foul lines, the first grand tour by a professional team, and the organization of ball clubs in cities across the country, the essential elements of the modern game—the rules, fundamentals of each position, rudimentary equipment, and even the language—gradually evolved after much experimentation. With regard to the rules, each side now consisted of nine players; three offensive failures ("outs") compelled a team to relinquish its offensive opportunity to its opponent; each team had nine such scoring opportunities ("innings"); fielders could no longer register "outs" by catching batted balls on the first bounce; hitters lost the privilege of waiting for just the pitch they wanted and instead had to confront a well-defined "strike zone"; four pitches delivered outside that zone constituted a free pass ("walk") to first base; and in the 1880s, overhand pitching (along with the dreaded curveball) gradually replaced underhand, and the modern pitching distance of sixty feet six inches became standard. Players became specialists at one or two positions, with the understanding that the best all-round athletes played pitcher or shortstop, the fastest the outfield, and the "pluckiest" the infield. Catchers donned wire masks ("muzzles" or "birdcages"), fielders put on gloves, and teams everywhere adopted the Red Stockings-style uniform. "Long ball," "hit and run," "bunt," "change of pace," "tag up," "battery," "home plate," and numerous other expressions became part of the lexicon of players, fans, and newspaper reporters alike. Indeed, by the late 1870s, shrewd publishers of the great metropolitan dailies understood well the abilities of baseball writers to sell newspapers.[26]

Although today's fan could recognize the game of baseball in the late 1870s, most contemporary rural residents did not. The available (albeit sketchy) evidence indicates that farmers in Davisville and Dixon, if they played the game at all, had not yet adopted many of the basic conventions of the urban game. Recollections of men who played in such remote areas invariably mention the lack of fielding equipment. Catchers especially, but infielders and outfielders as well, suffered "swelled hands, torn nails, and crooked joints" from playing barehanded. Local conditions often dictated the number of players and the layout of the field, outfielders were known as "pasturemen," and teams played in the clothes on their backs, not in uniforms. With the newer rules and state-of-the-art equipment, city teams generally played relatively low-scoring games of two hours or so in length, but the typical rural game often came to an end only with the onset of darkness. "Two square yards of blackboard were needed to record those scores of 80 to 90," Brown recalled.[27]

While farmers continued through the 1870s to play "baseball in the olden time," big changes in their lives, the magnitude of which they had only begun to realize, lay ahead. They were about to take part in the next great agrarian episode in California, the transition from wheat to specialty crops. Wheat production itself posed few, if any, problems. Five times between 1872 and 1884, in fact, no state grew more wheat than California, which earned the Golden State a new reputation as "the granary of the world." While producing to their hearts' content, however, farmers continued to turn a blind eye to the harsh realities of supply and demand—not only the simple economics of overproduction, but also the fact that farmers elsewhere in the United States and thousands of miles away in Europe, Asia, South America, and Australia were beginning to beat them at their own game, many using techniques and machines (the combined harvester, in particular) imported from California. As prices fell precipitously year after year, farmers along Putah Creek and elsewhere began to ask the question none of them wanted to hear: "Does it pay to raise wheat, our bread and butter for so long?"[28]

Their answer, moreover, split along generational lines. "Old-timers" argued, as early as 1880, that the market had bottomed-out and that wheat would surely "reign king in our district" again. For their sons, however, the question was more complicated. They feared that the bottom had in fact dropped out of the market. Wheat's decline, moreover, came just as they were beginning to emerge from their fathers' shadows. They were determined, as one put it, to look forward with "fresh energy and clear vision." For years, their fathers had tended small orchards and vineyards to supplement their grain incomes. The new generation did not abandon wheat in the 1880s, but turned increasingly to fruits and nuts both as cash crops and to cultivate their own identities. To an even greater degree than their fathers, they would spend their lives struggling to resolve the great paradox of agriculture in the modern economic world: farmers' very identity—their inner drive to produce, produce, produce—invariably gluts the market, brings low prices, and spreads misery and frustration.[29]

There is no doubt, however, that the transition from wheat to fruit eventually took place. As late as 1889, California was still the nation's second-leading wheat-producing state, with almost three million acres harvested and exports totaling eight hundred and forty thousand tons. By 1909, wheat acreage fell to less than four hundred thousand acres, with the state becoming a net importer. Over the same period, California emerged as one of the world's principal producers of deciduous and citrus fruits, grapes, vegetables, and nuts. Though no one could have known what lay ahead back in the late 1870s, farmers and their sons were in the early stages of, as one leading scholar described it, "one of the most rapid and complete transformations ever witnessed in American agricultural history." The shift from wheat to specialty crops in Davisville and Dixon, as elsewhere in the state's rural regions, was slow, uneven, contingent, and fraught with anxiety and conflict from the very beginning. Sons inherited their fathers' dreams of striking it rich in California and pursued them with equal, perhaps even greater, passion. With boldness, hard work, and a little luck (not necessarily in that order), they still believed that they could succeed materially and, just as importantly, bring stability and prosperity to their community. They did indeed transform agriculture along Putah Creek, but they also maintained strong cultural ties to the Gold Rush generation—more so than they cared to admit.[30]

This, then, was the context in which baseball's popularity rose to unprecedented heights. Farmers' newfound passion for the game coincided with a period of far-reaching economic, social, and generational change in rural California. Indeed, had Brown said, "Our players are mostly farmers' *sons*," he would have been even more accurate. Of the forty-four farmers identified earlier who played baseball for the Davisville Oletas and the Dixon Etnas in the 1880s, at least thirty-six were sons of Gold Rush-generation settlers. These were young men, identified by Brown and confirmed by census records, between the ages of nineteen and twenty-eight, who in many cases became key players in the transition from wheat to almonds, the specialty crop of choice in the region. When, for example, the fifteen charter members of the Davisville Almond Growers Association met in 1897 to form California's first nut cooperative, eleven of them were sons of pioneer wheat farmers from the 1850s and 1860s, and eight of the eleven had played several seasons for either the Oletas or the Etnas in the 1880s.[31]

Anxious to be distracted from their arduous daily routines and the uncertainties of the times, these young men found baseball to be the perfect antidote. They might have pursued horseracing, as their fathers had before them, but even those who did found playing and watching baseball even more satisfying. The two sports had much in common. Indeed, the racetrack helped develop rural people's fascination with swift motion and sudden action, which the ball field, located in the middle of the track in Dixon, cultivated to the utmost. Baseball's new rules, however, which local teams began adopting early in the decade, imposed a much more precise, detailed order on its participants than horseracing. On defense, players trotted out together to the same positions every inning and tried their best to hone their specific, individual skills for the good of the team; and on offense, they tried to hit the ball within the foul lines and away from the fielders, run the bases without being tagged out, and parlay their individual efforts into runs, the game's most meaningful measure of achievement. They performed all these actions automatically, without pause for concern, because the game itself dictated it. For young men mystified by the operations of the grain market and wary of what the future held but who, like their fathers, could not admit failure or even the possibility of failure, baseball offered excitement, respite, stability, diversion, mutuality, and gratification—all in powerful, albeit short-term, doses.[32]

Other less tangible factors may also have contributed to the "epidemic of baseball," to use Brown's apt description, which hit Davisville and Dixon in the 1880s. Limited evidence suggests that fathers did not want their sons playing the game, especially when games interrupted work on the farm. Brown reported one instance during the wheat harvest of 1885 when an enraged father, shotgun in hand, stormed the Davisville diamond in the fourth inning and marched his son from his outfield position back to the farm—an action that no doubt reinforced the strong tie between baseball and rebellion in the young man's mind. Members of the Oletas and Etnas also, on occasion, spoke of the game's "manly" qualities—its aggressive, competitive aspects—as did so many young Americans, both rural and urban, of this generation. In addition, baseball may even have helped tame two interrelated ethnocultural conflicts in the two towns. Since the early 1870s, a disgruntled minority, led by leaders of the Davisville Presbyterian Church, had decried the region's lack of respect for the Sabbath and temperance. Baseball games on Sundays served only to fuel the fire, at first, but gradually, even the most militant reformers accepted and even welcomed the idea. "Some of the more thoughtful among the temperance advocates," explained Brown, "prefer to have the crowds at the ballgame rather than the alehouse." Indeed, by the end of the 1880s, the saloon-keepers were the ones grumbling over the game's popularity.[33]

The "epidemic of baseball" spread across racial lines as well in one particularly illuminating instance. Two of the most valuable players on the Dixon Etnas in the mid-1880s, brothers José and Isidro Peña, had roots in the area that extended deeper than any of their teammates. Their grandfather, Juan Felipe Peña, migrated to California in 1841 and two years later became co-owner of Rancho Los Putos, one of the three Mexican land grants in the area. Although the U.S. Supreme Court confirmed Rancho Los Putos in 1857, the grantees remained mired in legal turmoil with squatters, speculators, and lawyers. By the early 1860s, only a small portion of the forty-four-thousand-acre grant remained in the Peña family. The overwhelmingly Anglo community of Dixon treated José and Isidro as social outcasts as they grew up—that is, until both brothers demonstrated that they could hit. The "Peña boys," as Brown called them, became fixtures in the Etnas lineup—José at second base and Isidro in centerfield—and led the team to numerous victories. Though Isidro died in a farm accident in 1894, José took advantage of his prowess on the ball field and growing acceptance off the field to become a successful cattleman. Descendants of the Peña family, moreover, still reside in the area today—not entirely because of baseball, of course, but the game did help them carve out their place in the community. Even baseball, however, could not penetrate the rigid racial barriers between white farmers and Asian immigrants, who increasingly dominated the agricultural workforce in the region. Later in the twentieth century, however, even Chinese and Japanese residents in northern California would form their own teams and become equally devoted to the game, albeit on segregated diamonds.[34]

Perhaps the strongest symptom of the "baseball epidemic" was the widespread gambling that permeated the life of these two rural towns. This was not a new phenomenon. Farmers, by the very nature of their enterprise, were gamblers, "staking their all upon the season," as Brown put it. Every year, they rolled the dice on the weather, the yield of their crop, and on just when to sell their crop to get the optimum price. Most Putah Creek farmers, in fact, came to the Golden State on a gamble. They also bet on billiards, poker, dice games, pitching horseshoes, pigeon shooting, the number of raw eggs one could swallow at a sitting, the outcome of elections, whether or not someone would survive an illness—on just about anything. Of course, gambling was the mother's milk of horseracing. So enamored was one Davisville farmer with gambling that in 1884, he borrowed one hundred dollars to make a bet and then refused to pay it back when his horse lost the race. When his lender took him to court, the bettor insisted that anyone with any sense of honor would have given him another chance to pick a winner, and a jury of his peers agreed with him.[35]

Gambling deepened almost everyone's fascination with baseball as well. The game provided not only an antidote to the uncertainties of modern life, but also an opportunity to bet on the uncertainties of modern life. The new rules gave people their money's worth in more ways than one. The more ordered, rational version of the game allowed for more precise, sustained play, and thus greatly facilitated betting. Wagers could now be placed not only on the final score of the game, but also on whether the next batter would get a hit, the next pitch would be a strike, or the next fly ball would be caught (prompting bettors, on at least one occasion, to fire off their guns to disconcert the fielder and make him muff the ball). The players themselves also were not averse to playing games for substantial, winner-take-all purses; paying "revolvers" or "ringers" from nearby teams of Vacaville and Winters to "beef up" their lineups for especially important games; or even taking bribes to throw games, a practice commonly called "hippodroming." Gambling, for all intents and purposes, was as much a part of baseball as hitting, pitching, and running, and it was every bit as "epidemic" along Putah Creek.[36]

The measure of success was plain in baseball, and in the end that, as much as any one factor, attracted farmers to the game. More so than the various tavern sports and even horseracing, baseball tantalized them with the illusion that they could master reality—that they could reverse their fortunes—by simply courting Lady Luck or, when teams tried to fix games, by manipulating her. There was something inherently liberating about this notion. Win or lose, the outcome of the game (not to mention the games within the game) was clearly defined, in sharp contrast to the difference between success and failure on their farms year after year. Baseball and gambling at the Y in Davisville and Driving Park in Dixon had a cultural meaning to players and fans alike beyond the chance to make money. It allowed them to entertain the same impulse that had failed them during the Gold Rush, the gamble of the century. That impulse, along with the tradition of baseball games on Sunday evenings, persisted well into the twentieth century in Davisville and Dixon. Even as teams changed their names, wore uniforms, and played in more organized leagues, and even as "our National game of ball," as Brown put it, became more firmly entrenched, farmers continued to experience the game first and foremost as a local, and therefore rural, pastime.[37]

Over the years, four players from the Oletas and Etnas made names for themselves beyond the confines of Putah Creek. In the early 1890s, Andy Tufts, whose father was one of the earliest settlers of the region and a longtime elder of the Presbyterian Church, pitched the Oletas to dozens of victories and hundreds of dollars in purse money. "The Artist," as Brown called him, caught the attention of the Sacramento Atlas of the fledgling California League, who made him part of their starting rotation for two seasons. Later in the decade, Frank Lamphere of the Etnas, the best athlete that Dixon ever produced, according to Brown, pitched and batted his way into a short stint with the Atlas as well. In the next generation, Dixon's Ray Rohwer and Davisville's Myril Hoag, both descendants of Gold Rush migrants, played not only in the Pacific Coast League but also in the majors—Rohwer for the Pittsburgh Pirates for two seasons and Hoag for the New York Yankees for six. Hitting .301 for the world champions in 1937, Hoag received a hero's welcome upon his return to the Sacramento Valley that October.[38]

Baseball historians might be better off not knowing the exploits of Tufts, Lamphere, Rohwer, and Hoag. They presumably would be tempted, if the genre's historiography is any indication, to exaggerate the significance of these four exceptionally talented players. From the subfield's own pioneers, Harold Seymour and David Voigt, to its more recent stars, Benjamin Rader and Jules Tygiel, baseball historians have focused almost exclusively on the professional game, if on occasion invoking "the big picture" and "populist baseball." "Much of what passes for baseball history concerns only major league baseball," wrote Larry Gerlach in a landmark essay twelve years ago, "and is presented without qualification as though 'baseball' and 'major league' were synonymous." Even those scholars who have studied the game's history prior to the advent of the Cincinnati Red Stockings have treated its coming of age as but a prelude to the professional game. Steven Gelber, Warren Goldstein, and Steven Riess, among others, have done much to remedy this imbalance by placing baseball squarely within the context of an emerging urban, industrial America. But even Reiss's seminal *Touching Base* offers little to assist our understanding of nonprofessional players and play, let alone in a rural setting. Such a concentration has surely been misleading. As both a spectator and participant sport, baseball in the United States has always been primarily nonprofessional. In Davisville and Dixon alone, for every Tufts, Lamphere, Hoag, or Rohwer who played the game between 1880 and 1930, there were hundreds of amateur players and thousands of fans who were just as passionate about the Oletas, the Etnas, and the game itself.[39]

The fact that sport historians have shown little interest in studying rural baseball stems not only from their emphasis on the professional game, but also and even more so from their fixation on pinpointing the game's true origin(s). This began, of course, when the game's promoters, suffering from an attack of anti-British chauvinism at the turn of the twentieth century, decreed that baseball had been created not in England, but in the village of Cooperstown, New York, by Abner Doubleday in 1839. In the process, baseball acquired an official, if mythical, beginning, a distinctly rural American origin, and a romantic pastoral appeal, all of which were reinforced by its gala "centennial" in 1939, by more than a few Gary Cooper and Kevin Costner movies, and by the words of seemingly every baseball broadcaster on opening day depicting, in nostalgic bliss, the green grass, blue sky, fresh air, and carefree atmosphere of the ballpark. Equally fervent but more empirically minded enthusiasts—from Will Irwin in 1909, to Robert Henderson in 1947, to Seymour and Voigt in the 1960s, to David Block in 2005—have presented irrefutable evidence that America's pastime was neither born in America nor a product of rural life. Its persistence among the general public notwithstanding, no serious student of the game has ever taken the Doubleday tale seriously; but in their zeal to debunk the myth of baseball's rural origins and to expose the propagandists who have long sought to give the sport a pastoral image, historians have all but neglected the very real phenomenon of rural baseball itself. Although the game as we now know it did, in fact, develop most fully in New York City before the Civil War, the corollary, indeed axiom, that baseball "was a city game for city men" for the rest of the nineteenth century and beyond does not stand up to empirical scrutiny anymore than the Doubleday tale itself.[40]

Why then, the question remains, have not rural historians themselves exposed the urban bias as folly? Despite their strong commitment to understanding rural life in all its complexity—to "putting the culture back into agriculture," as Hal S. Barron once put it—they, too, seem to have bought into the assumption that farmers and baseball do not belong on the same field. One searches almost in vain for sustained analysis on the subject. Indeed, the best, most comprehensive survey of the literature, David Danbom's *Born in the Country,* examines rural leisure in some detail—barn raisings, frolics, hunting, and fishing in the nineteenth century, and the impact of radio, automobiles, telephones, and the Country Life Movement's emphasis on organized recreation in the twentieth—but makes no mention of baseball. Part of the problem might be rooted in the central theme of the discipline, the capitalist transformation of the countryside in the nineteenth and early twentieth centuries, precisely the period of baseball's ascent. Rural historians have been so concerned with demonstrating that farm families remained, in Mary Neth's words, "incompletely integrated into the market economy" that they have missed or underemphasized cultural phenomena such as baseball which do not reflect the persistence of traditional values and attitudes as self-evidently as kinship bonds, religious practices, and harvesting rituals. Yet, even studies that examine rural culture from a more modern perspective deem baseball, by its omission, largely irrelevant.[41]

The evidence from Davisville and Dixon strongly suggests otherwise. When farmers played baseball or rooted for their favorite team, they displayed some of the central elements of rural culture in California—competitiveness, materialism, individualism, and mutuality. Baseball offered not only an outlet for the tensions of rural life, but also a means of translating a core set of values, which they inherited from their fathers, into action. Each game was a great social drama, full of excitement, suspense, and opportunity, but void of paradox. Players and spectators could express themselves freely—take risks, even poorly calculated ones—with little regard to long-term consequences. Their very identity—their inner drive to produce, produce, produce—found expression and gratification on the ball field rather than the misery and frustration they so often experienced in their wheat fields. There was nothing magical about the game. Baseball came along at the right time in the right place to satisfy farmers' insatiable appetite for achievement in a world of change and chance. It may have been a source of rural nostalgia for city people, but it was the sport of choice for farmers and a powerful cultural agent. Its history, in the Sacramento Valley and across rural America, has only begun to be harvested.

NOTES

1. *Dixon Tribune,* June 4, 1887 (quotes); June 11, 1887; September 17, 1887 (quote); May 19, 1888.

2. *Dixon Tribune,* October 17, 1885 (quote); October 24, 1885 (quote); November 14, 1885 (quote). Although this essay focuses primarily on Davisville and Dixon, baseball flourished in rural communities throughout northern California, as documented in many local newspapers; see, for example, Frank Herzog, "Early Baseball in Siskiyou County," *The Siskiyou Pioneer* 2 (Spring 1954): 11–13, and the several accompanying articles in the same issue. See also, Harold Seymour, *Baseball: The People's Game* (Oxford: Oxford University Press, 1990), 192.

3. Here, I share the assumptions of baseball scholar Steven A. Riess, colonial historian Timothy Breen, and anthropologist Clifford Geertz that popular patterns of play both influence and reflect social and cultural behavior; see the discussions in Riess, *Touching Base: Professional Baseball and American Culture in the Progressive Era* (1983; revised ed., Urbana: University of Illinois Press, 1999), 3–4; and T. H. Breen, "Horses and Gentlemen: The Cultural Significance of Gambling among the Gentry of Virginia," *William and Mary Quarterly* 34 (April 1977): 239–57.

4. On the new rural history, see David B. Danbom, *Born in the Country: A History of Rural America* (Baltimore: Johns Hopkins University Press, 1995); Hal S. Barron, "Old Wine in New Bottles? The Perspective of Rural History," in *Outstanding in His Field: Perspectives on American Agriculture in Honor of Wayne D. Rasmussen,* ed. Frederick V. Carstensen, Morton Rothstein, and Joseph A. Swanson (Ames: Iowa State University Press, 1993), 48–60; and David Vaught, "State of the Art—Rural History, or Why is There No Rural History of California?" *Agricultural History* 74 (Fall 2000): 759–74. On the new baseball and, more broadly, sport history, see Steven A. Riess, "The Historiography of American Sport," *OAH Magazine of History* 7 (Summer 1992): 10–14 (which laments the dearth of rural sport studies); Larry R. Gerlach, "Not Quite Ready for Prime Time: Baseball History, 1893–1993," *Journal of Sport History* 21 (Summer 1994): 103–37; and S. W. Pope, ed., *The New American Sport History: Recent Approaches and Perspectives* (Urbana: University of Illinois Press, 1997).

5. What little we do know about rural baseball comes largely from biographies—usually brief first chapters—of famous professional players who were born and raised on farms. See, for example, Reed Browning, *Cy Young: A Baseball Life* (Amherst: University of Massachusetts Press, 2000); Henry W. Thomas, *Walter Johnson: Baseball's Big Train* (Lincoln: University of Nebraska Press, 1998); John Sickels, *Bob Feller: Ace of the Greatest Generation* (Dulles, Va.: Potomac Books, 2004); Doug Feldmann, *Dizzy and the Gas House Gang: The 1934 St. Louis Cardinals and*

Depression-Era Baseball (Jefferson, N.C.: McFarland, 2000). Other notable, if scattered, contributions include Carl M. Becker, "Crossing Bats: Baseball in the Villages of the Upper Miami Valley, 1865–1900," *Nine: A Journal of Baseball History and Culture* 10 (Spring 2002): 46–70; William H. Mullins, "The Impact of Rural Culture on a Baseball Career: Carl Hubbell of Meeker, Oklahoma," *Nine: A Journal of Baseball History and Culture* 12 (September 2003): 102–14; Peter Morris, *Baseball Fever: Early Baseball in Michigan* (Ann Arbor: University of Michigan Press, 2003), especially chap. 10; and Seymour, *Baseball: The People's Game,* chap. 13 and 14. In the interest of full disclosure, my own full-length contributions to the new rural history, *Cultivating California: Growers, Specialty Crops, and Labor, 1875–1920* (Baltimore: Johns Hopkins University Press, 1999) and *After the Gold Rush: Tarnished Dreams in the Sacramento Valley* (Baltimore: Johns Hopkins University Press, 2007) are two cases in point. The second devotes all of one paragraph to baseball, while the first makes no mention whatsoever of the game. Not until I turned my attention to my next project on baseball history did I recognize its importance to rural life in California.

6. A more comprehensive, systematic study of baseball in rural America awaits the larger work behind this essay, "Country Hardball: Baseball and Agrarianism in American Rural Culture" (book in progress).

7. Jacques Barzun, *God's Country and Mine: A Declaration of Love Spiced with a Few Harsh Words* (Boston: Little, Brown, and Co., 1954), 159.

8. *Dixon Tribune,* June 6, 1885.

9. Seymour, *Baseball: The People's Game,* chap. 13 and 14; Becker, "Crossing Bats," 47–50; Morris, *Baseball Fever,* chap. 6 and 7.

10. *Dixon Tribune,* February 6, 1875; March 21, 1885; August 29, 1885; September 5, 1885; September 12, 1885; October 31, 1885; July 6, 1889; March 15, 1890; May 31, 1890; March 8, 1895; March 15, 1895; June 21, 1895; June 28, 1895; *Weekly Solano Republican,* May 1, 1878; U.S. Census, Population Schedules for Putah Township, Yolo County, Tremont Township, Solano County, and Silveyville Township, Solano County, California, 1880 and 1900, microfilm (Washington, D.C.: National Archives, 1967); Joann Leach Larkey, *Davisville '68: The History and Heritage of the City of Davis, Yolo County, California* (Davis: Davis Historical and Landmarks Commission, 1969), 143–229; Obituary file, Yolo County Archives, Woodland, Calif. (hereafter YCA).

11. J. M. Guinn, *History of the State of California and Biographical Record of the Sacramento Valley, California* (Chicago: Chapman Publishing Co., 1906), 425; Larkey, *Davisville '68,* 146; *James T. Lillard v. E. W. Brown* (1885), Yolo County, Superior Court Case Files, no. 441, YCA; *E. W. Brown v. Sinclair Manufacturing Company* (1894), Yolo County, Superior Court Case Files, no. 1780, YCA.

12. On migration from the Midwest to the gold fields of the Sierra foothills to Putah Creek, see Vaught, *After the Gold Rush,* chap. 1.

13. Farmers' successes and struggles in the 1850s are richly documented in numerous contemporary lawsuits. See especially, *Charles E. Greene v. His Credi-*

tors (1861), Yolo County, County Court Case Files, no. 107, YCA; *Benjamin Cahoon v. Jerome C. Davis and Isaac Davis* (1867), Sacramento County, District Court Case Files, no. 11590, Sacramento Archives and Museum Collection Center, Sacramento (hereafter SAMCC); *George W. Pierce v. Henry E. Robinson* (1859), California Supreme Court, no. 2329, "Transcript on Appeal," California State Archives, Sacramento; *H. O. Beatty v. R. C. Clark* (1861), California Supreme Court, no. 3223, "Transcript on Appeal," 104–105, California State Archives; *W. W. Brown v. C. E. Greene* (1884), California State Supreme Court, no. 9443, "Transcript on Appeal," California State Archives. See also, *Sacramento Daily Union,* October 8, 1852 (quote); Jim Gerber, "The Origin of California's Export Surplus in Cereals," *Agricultural History* 67 (Fall 1992): 40–57; and David Vaught, "After the Gold Rush: Replicating the Rural Midwest in the Sacramento Valley," *Western Historical Quarterly* 34 (Winter 2003): 447–67.

14. United States Land Case No. 232, Northern District, Rio de los Putos Grant; United States Land Case No. 74, Northern District, Los Putos Grant; and United States Land Case No. 411, Northern District, Laguna de Santos Callé Grant—all in the Bancroft Library, University of California, Berkeley; David Vaught, "A Tale of Three Land Grants on the Northern California Border Lands," *Agricultural History* 78 (Spring 2004): 140–54.

15. Lacking a town center before the founding of Davisville in 1868, Putah Creek was, in essence, what rural sociologists call an "open-country settlement." See John Mack Faragher, "Open-Country Community: Sugar Creek, Illinois, 1820–1850," in *The Countryside in the Age of Capitalist Transformation: Essays in the Social History of Rural America,* ed. Steven Hahn and Jonathan Prude (Chapel Hill: University of North Carolina Press, 1985), 233–58, for an extended discussion. On the social and cultural development of the community in the 1850s, see Vaught, *After the Gold Rush,* chap. 4.

16. *Sacramento Daily Union,* October 5, 1857; April 26, 1860; September 29, 1862; March 13, 1863; April 13, 1863 (quote); *Knights Landing News,* March 24, 1860; "Rattler Mare Account, 1861," Jerome C. Davis Collection, MS box 205, California Room, California State Library, Sacramento; *Transactions of the California State Agricultural Society during the Year 1858* (Sacramento: State Printer, 1859), 84–85, 115, 160, 236–37; *Transactions of the California State Agricultural Society during the Year 1861* (Sacramento: State Printer, 1862), 82–83, 122; "Fine Horses" folder, box 12, James L. Warren Papers, Bancroft Library; Joel Franks, "California and the Rise of Spectator Sports, 1850–1900," *Southern California Quarterly* 71 (Winter 1989): 290–91; Breen, "Horses and Gentlemen," 239–57; Bertram Wyatt-Brown, *Southern Honor: Ethics and Behavior in the Old South* (Oxford: Oxford University Press, 1982), 339–50; Kenneth S. Greenberg, *Honor and Slavery* (Princeton: Princeton University Press, 1996), 135–40; Melvin L. Adelman, *A Sporting Time: New York City and the Rise of Modern Athletics, 1820–70* (Urbana: University of Illinois Press, 1986), 27–89; Paul W. Gates, *The Farmer's Age: Agriculture, 1815–1860* (New York: Harper & Row, 1960), 228–30.

17. *Daily Alta California,* January 14, 1852; *Dixon Tribune,* June 6, 1885; June 28, 1895 (quote); *Weekly Solano Press,* May 5, 1869; Kevin Nelson, *The Golden Game: The Story of California Baseball* (San Francisco: California Historical Society Press, 2004), 2–7; John E. Spalding, *Always on Sunday: The California Baseball League, 1886–1915* (Manhattan, Kans.: Ag Press, 1992), 9; David Block, *Baseball before We Knew It: A Search for the Roots of the Game* (Lincoln: University of Nebraska Press, 2005), chap. 6; Harold Peterson, *The Man Who Invented Baseball* (New York: Scribner's, 1973); Harold Seymour, *Baseball: The Early Years* (Oxford: Oxford University Press, 1960), 15–34; Seymour, *Baseball: The People's Game,* 192–94; Anne Cartwright, "Cartwright's Trip West," *The National Pastime: A Review of Baseball History,* vol. 18 (Cleveland: Society for American Baseball Research, 1998), 14–16; Brian McGinty, "The Old Ball Game," *Pacific Historian* 25 (Spring 1981): 13–17; Natalie Vermilyea, "Kranks' Delight: California Baseball, 1858–1888," *The Californians* 8 (March/April 1991): 32–35.

18. On baseball in San Francisco in the 1860s, see Joel Franks, "Organizing California Baseball, 1859–1893," *Baseball History* 4 (1991): 1–5; McGinty, "The Old Ball Game," 17; and Nelson, *The Golden Game,* 10–14.

19. *Knights Landing News,* January 25, 1862 (quote). The *Sacramento Daily Union* covered the flood extensively. For a concise overview, see its one-year "anniversary" stories, December 9, 1862 and January 10, 1863. On the drought, see especially W. H. Fraser, "Rainfall and Wheat in California," *Overland Monthly* 33 (January 1899): 521–23; Frank T. Gilbert, *The Illustrated Atlas and History of Yolo County* (San Francisco: De Pue and Co., 1879), 40–41; Hazel Adele Pulling, "A History of California's Range-Cattle Industry, 1770–1912" (Ph.D. diss., University of Southern California, 1944), 111–17.

20. Rodman W. Paul, "The Beginnings of Agriculture in California: Innovation vs. Continuity," *California Historical Quarterly* 52 (Spring 1973): 22 (quote); Rodman W. Paul, "The Wheat Trade between California and the United Kingdom," *Mississippi Valley Historical Review* 45 (December 1958): 396; Morton Rothstein, *The California Wheat Kings* (Davis: University of California, Davis, 1987), 3–5; Vaught, "After the Gold Rush," 465–66.

21. *Sacramento Daily Union,* August 13, 1860; April 13, 1863; September 8, 1870; *Yolo Weekly Mail,* March 9, 1871; *Davis Enterprise,* October 8, 1970; Joann L. Larkey and Shipley Walters, *Yolo County: Land of Changing Patterns* (Northridge: Windsor Publications, 1987), 37–38; Larkey, *Davisville '68,* 23, 192, 194; Joseph A. McGowan, *History of the Sacramento Valley,* 3 vols. (New York: Lewis Historical Publishing, 1961), I: 164–65, 263–64, 279.

22. Stephen D. Guschov, *The Red Stockings of Cincinnati: Base Ball's First All-Professional Team and its Historic 1869 and 1870 Seasons* (Jefferson, N.C.: McFarland and Company, 1998); Joseph S. Stern Jr., "The Team that Couldn't Be Beat: The Red Stockings of 1869," *Cincinnati Historical Society Bulletin* 27 (Spring 1969): 25–41; Robert Knight Barney, "Of Rails and Red Stockings: Episodes in the Expansion of the 'National Pastime' in the American West," *Journal of the West* 17 (July 1978): 61–70;

Spalding, *Always on Sunday,* 10; McGinty, "The Old Ball Game," 17–24; Nelson, *The Golden Game,* 16–19; David Q. Voigt, "America's First Red Scare: The Cincinnati Reds of 1869," in *America through Baseball* (Chicago: Nelson-Hall, 1976), 29–41; Warren Goldstein, *Playing for Keeps: A History of Early Baseball* (Ithaca: Cornell University Press, 1989), 101–19.

23. *Daily Alta California,* September 24, 26, 28, 29, 30, 1869; October 1, 2, 3, 4, 5, 6, 1869; *Sacramento Daily Union,* September 28, 1869; October 1, 2, 3, 6, 1869; *Weekly Solano Herald,* October 2, 1869; *Weekly Solano Press,* October 20, 1869; Spalding, *Always on Sunday,* 10; Barney, "Of Rails and Red Stockings," 64 (quote). The *San Francisco Chronicle, Examiner,* and *Call* all covered the story of the Red Stockings in California as well.

24. *Sacramento Daily Union,* May 16, 1870; June 13, 27, 1870; September 10, 15, 1870; Vermilyea, "Kranks' Delight," 38; Franks, "Organizing California Baseball," 3–6; Spalding, *Always on Sunday,* 11–13; Nelson, *The Golden Game,* 21.

25. *Weekly Solano Press,* October 20, 1869; *Weekly Solano Herald,* October 16, 1869; *Yolo Weekly Mail,* May 11, 1871; May 8, 1879; April 8, 1880; May 6, 1880; *Dixon Tribune,* April 17, 1875; June 23, 1877; August 25, 1877; August 28, 1879; June 28, 1895 (quote).

26. *Dixon Tribune,* June 6, 1885; Seymour, *Baseball: The Early Years,* 61–65; John P. Rossi, *The National Game: Baseball and American Culture* (Chicago: Ivan R. Dee, 2000), 33; Gunther Barth, *City People: The Rise of Modern City Culture in Nineteenth-Century America* (Oxford: Oxford University Press, 1980), 159–61; Joel Zoss and John Bowman, *Diamonds in the Rough: The Untold History of Baseball* (Lincoln: University of Nebraska Press, 1989), 5–8, 70–76; Benjamin G. Rader, "Introduction," *Early Innings: A Documentary History of Baseball, 1825–1908,* ed. Dean A. Sullivan (Lincoln: University of Nebraska Press, 1995), xviii–xix; Browning, *Cy Young,* 32–33; Voigt, *America through Baseball,* 8; Vermilyea, "Kranks' Delight," 37.

27. *Dixon Tribune,* February 14, 1885; October 10, 1885 (quote); March 15, 1895; June 28, 1895 (quote); Seymour, *Baseball: The People's Game,* 193–94; Frank Herzog, "Bats and Balls," *The Siskiyou Pioneer* 2 (Spring 1954): 25; Vermilyea, "Kranks' Delight," 37.

28. *Dixon Tribune,* August 9, 1884; January 3, 1885 (quote); November 14, 1891; *Yolo Weekly Mail,* November 12, 1887; *Pacific Rural Press,* January 21, 1885; *Wheat: An Illustrated Description of California's Leading Industry* (San Francisco: Commercial Publication Co., 1887), 35, Bancroft Library (author unknown); Horace Davis, "Wheat in California: A Retrospect and Prospect," *Overland Monthly* 32 (July 1898): 60–63; Davis, "California Breadstuffs," *Journal of Political Economy* 2 (September 1894): 530–32; Alfred Bannister, "California and Her Wheat Culture," *Overland Monthly* 12 (July 1888): 67; Rothstein, *The California Wheat Kings,* 2 (quote); Paul Rhode, "Learning, Capital Accumulation, and the Transformation of California Agriculture," *Journal of Economic History* 55 (December 1995): 773–800.

29. *Dixon Tribune,* November 14, 1891 (quote); *Yolo Weekly Mail,* January 1, 1892 (quote).

30. George Robertson, "Statistical Summary of the Production and Resources of California (1850–1910)", in California State Board of Agriculture, *Fifty-eighth Annual Report for 1911* (Sacramento: State Printing Office, 1912), 119–21, 400–401; Rhode, "Learning," 773 (quote). For a full, detailed analysis of the new generation's emergence during the transformation, see Vaught, *After the Gold Rush,* chap. 11.

31. *Dixon Tribune,* September 12, 1885; U.S. Census, Population Schedules for Putah Township, Yolo County, Tremont Township, Solano County, and Silveyville Township, Solano County, California, 1860, 1880, and 1900; Davisville Almond Growers Association, Constitution and Minute Book, January 23, 1897, Board of Directors File, Predecessor and Concurrent Organizations, box 1, California Almond Growers Exchange Records, SAMCC.

32. *Dixon Tribune,* July 14, 1877; August 28, 1879; September 5, 1885; November 7, 1885; August 28, 1886; October 23, 1886; March 15, 1895; Ronald Story, "The Country of the Young: The Meaning of Baseball and Early American Culture," *Baseball History from Outside the Lines: A Reader,* ed. John E. Dreifort (Lincoln: University of Nebraska Press, 2001), 19–33; Barth, *City People,* 151.

33. *Dixon Tribune,* October 26, 1878; May 27, 1880; June 6, 1885; July 4, 1885; November 14, 1885; December 19, 1885; April 10, 1886 (quote); February 5, 1887 (quote); August 6, 1887; February 11, 1888; February 18, 1888; April 6, 1889; March 15, 1895 (quote); May 17, 1895; *Yolo Weekly Mail,* February 8, 1877; May 8, 1879; May 6, 1880; Clare L. Childers, transcriber, "Presbyterian Church of Davisville, California: Minutes of the Session and Register of Communicants, 13 November 1873–14 April 1918," 1997, 3–40, YCA; Sullivan, *Early Innings,* 21–22; Goldstein, *Playing for Keeps,* 43–63; Michael S. Kimmel, "Baseball and the Reconstitution of American Masculinity, 1880–1920," in Dreifort, *Baseball History from Outside the Lines,* 47–61.

34. *Dixon Tribune,* March 21, 1885; April 11, 1885; September 12, 1885; *S. H. Cowell v. Lydia T. Armstrong* (1930), California State Supreme Court, no. 4341, SAC, "Transcript on Appeal," 292–367, California State Archives; Larkey, *Davisville '68,* 198–99; 219–21; Wood Young, *Vaca-Peña Los Putos Rancho and the Peña Adobe* (Vallejo, Calif.: Wheeler Printing and Publishing, 1971), 11–29, app. N; Nelson, *The Golden Game,* 65–66, 73, 106–107, 168–72, 207–14; Samuel O. Regalado, "Sport and Community in California's Japanese American 'Yamato Colony,'" *Journal of Sport History* 19 (Summer 1992); 130–43. See also Regalado's essay in this volume.

35. *Dixon Tribune,* December 12, 1874; February 6, 1875; October 27, 1877; November 24, 1877; May 9, 1885; July 4, 1885; November 14, 1885; February 12, 1887 (quote); April 2, 1887; March 9, 1889; April 12, 1890; July 26, 1890; *Yolo Daily Democrat,* March 5, 1875; *Woodland Daily Democrat,* November 15, 1892; *Sam N. Chantry v. William W. Montgomery* (1885), Yolo County, Superior Court Case Files, no. 463, YCA; Barth, *City People,* 156–57; Nelson, *The Golden Game,* 18.

36. *Dixon Tribune,* March 21, 1885; April 18, 1885; May 16, 1885; May 23, 1885; June 20, 1885; April 3, 1886; July 6, 1889; April 19, 1895; June 7, 1895; June 28, 1895;

Seymour, *Baseball: The People's Game*, 206–207; Seymour, *Baseball: The Early Years*, 51–53; Nelson, *The Golden Game*, 18–19; Larkey, *Davisville '68*, 121–22.

37. *Dixon Tribune*, September 5, 1885; March 12, 1887; July 6, 1889; July 5, 1895; September 17, 1897; April 1, 1898; April 21, 1899; Jackson Lears, *Something for Nothing: Luck in America* (New York: Viking, 2003), 1–24, 147–86; Larkey, *Davisville '68*, 121–22.

38. *Dixon Tribune*, July 6, 1889 (quote); March 15, 1890; June 16, 1893; July 3, 1896; July 10, 1896; Childers, "Presbyterian Church of Davisville," 3–40; Pete Palmer and Gary Gillette, eds., *The 2005 ESPN Baseball Encyclopedia* (New York: Sterling Publishing Co., 2005), 308, 576; John E. Spalding, *Sacramento Senators and Solons: Baseball in California's Capital, 1886–1976* (Manhattan, Kans.: Ag Press, 1995), 9–12; Larkey, *Davisville '68*, 121–22, 177, 217–18.

39. Gerlach, "Not Quite Ready for Prime Time," 107, 129–30 (quote 129); Story, "The Country of the Young," 21. In addition to the works of Seymour, Voigt, Riess, and Goldstein already cited, see Benjamin G. Rader, *Baseball: A History of America's Game*, 2d ed. (Urbana: University of Illinois Press, 2002); Jules Tygiel, *Past Time: Baseball as History* (Oxford: Oxford University Press, 2000); Steven M. Gelber, "Working at Playing: The Culture of the Workplace and the Rise of Baseball," *Journal of Social History* 16 (Summer 1983): 3–22. Seymour's *Baseball: The People's Game* serves as the main exception to the emphasis on the professional game, but it too largely ignores farmers and other rural people; see Steven A. Reiss, "The Lead-off Batter who Slugged Home Runs: Harold Seymour and the Making of the History of Baseball," *Journal of Sport History* 29 (Spring 2002): 135–44; and Charles C. Alexander, "Baseball for Everybody," *Reviews in American History* 19 (March 1991): 104–108.

40. Barth, *City People*, 160; Wes D. Gehring, *Mr. Deeds Goes to Yankee Stadium: Baseball Films in the Capra Tradition* (Jefferson, N.C.: McFarland and Co., 2004); Will Irwin, "Baseball: Before the Professionals Came," *Collier's*, May 8, 1909, 12–13; Robert L. Henderson, *Ball, Bat, and Bishop: The Origin of Ball Games* (1947; reprint, Urbana: University of Illinois Press, 2001); Block, *Baseball before We Knew It;* Zoss and Bowman, *Diamonds in the Rough*, 39–76; Gelber, "Working at Playing," 6 (quote).

41. Barron, "Old Wine in New Bottles," 49 (quote); Hahn and Prude, *The Countryside in the Age of Capitalist Transformation;* Danbom, *Born in the Country*, 95–96, 165–66, 193–94; Danbom, *The Resisted Revolution: Urban America and the Industrialization of Agriculture, 1900–1930* (Ames: Iowa State University Press, 1979), 61; Mary Neth, *Preserving the Family Farm: Women, Community, and the Foundations of Agribusiness in the Midwest, 1900–1940* (Baltimore, Johns Hopkins University Press, 1995), 4 (quote); Hal S. Barron, *Mixed Harvest: The Second Great Transformation of the Rural North, 1870–1930* (Chapel Hill: University of North Carolina Press, 1997); Ronald R. Kline, *Consumers in the Country: Technology and Social Change in Rural America* (Baltimore: Johns Hopkins University Press, 2000).

SAMUEL O. REGALADO

"INVISIBLE BASEBALL" JAPANESE AMERICANS AND THEIR GAME IN THE 1930S

"I am invisible, understand, simply because people refuse to see me." So said novelist Ralph Ellison in *Invisible Man*—his statement on the lack of black presence in the American mainstream.[1] Indeed, while the perceptive Ellison spoke well and accurately of the plight that black Americans confronted in their quest for balanced and equal treatment, Japanese Americans of the second generation (Nisei), too, faced similar circumstances in the 1930s, in their attempts to win recognition as viable members of a larger U.S. community that, in reality, knew so very little about them.

Since the 1890s, the Japanese had forged a path across the Pacific Ocean and established small settlements across the West. Though their numbers, relative to the general population, were exceedingly small, racial alarmists—many of whom less than a decade earlier used their fierce opposition of the Chinese to successfully lobby for a federal "exclusion" act—trumpeted another fear campaign with a resurrection of the "yellow peril" mantra.[2] The tenacious Issei, or first-generation Japanese, weathered that and other nativist storms in their effort to build the type of futures in the United States that they could not then hope for in Japan. With the advent of the "picture bride" era, the largely bachelor Issei residents, having by the end of the second decade of the twentieth century built small enclaves, abandoned their earlier dreams of returning to Japan, committed themselves to life as U.S. residents, and started families. Nevertheless, challenges to their presence remained. In a xenophobic era, as they had done decades earlier with the Chinese, western lobbyists fiercely pushed through a provision in the Immigration Act of 1924 that prevented Issei from attaining U.S. citizenship. Denied any opportunity for citizenship and basically shunned by western power brokers, the Issei turned to their offspring to help bring about an acceptable identity and presence among mainstream Americans—a visibility of respect that had long been denied to them.

Born largely between 1918 and 1922, many of the Nisei came of age during the Depression years. Though their experiences varied based on their urban or rural upbringing, as a result of their parents' prodding, the drive to excel was a commonality known to all. As such, they targeted educational goals. Academic achievement, so they and their parents believed, was essential to reach acceptance in the mainstream. Many immigrants, however, failed to grasp that U.S. principles of merit as the sole criteria for success stopped short of including people of color; and the Nisei generation was no exception.

"Fully credentialed Nisei education majors, . . . were virtually unemployable as teachers in the very schools in which they [as students] had excelled," observed historian Roger Daniels.[3] In fact, even beyond teaching careers, their invisibility was such that by 1940, for example, sociologist John Modell noted that in Los Angeles, a city with the largest concentration of Nisei residents, "only 5 percent of [Los Angeles] Nisei worked for white Americans." Moreover, that 5 percent worked almost entirely in agriculture—a vocation most whites associated with being distinctly "Japanese."[4] One of the most telling statements came from the often-told sentiments of a young Nisei who, as a fruit stand worker in 1937, wrote of his discouraged dreams to someday be a doctor or a lawyer: "I am only what I am," he said, "a professional carrot washer."[5]

Frustration aside, the Nisei looked for venues by which they might bridge the gap between mainstream whites and themselves. Material success, however, did not solely motivate them. Their Issei elders had bequeathed upon the Nisei the symbolic responsibility of serving as a metaphoric and international "bridge" between cultures. As with their educational endeavors, they sought to exhibit their bicultural identity as U.S. patriots in other areas, such as athletics. Although few, if any, envisioned sport in terms of a career, the enthusiasm in which they embraced athletic competition catapulted that activity to among their most valued interests. In many cases, they became completely absorbed in those sports that both drew upon their ancestral roots and pacified their symbolic obligations to serve as a cultural bridge. Moreover, athletics, the origins of which stemmed from American roots, drew even greater significance in the eyes of the Nisei. "Putting on a baseball uniform was like wearing the American flag," remembered Takeo Suo.[6]

If education was a means to earn respect, sport was a means to gain notice. Competition had long been valued in Japanese heritage. On those grounds, Japanese and Americans had that much in common. Indeed, for many Nisei who were children or adolescents in the 1920s, the names of Babe Ruth, Red Grange, and others were as familiar to them as they were to their white counterparts. So popular were these athletic icons that often they appeared in many of the ethnic newspapers in the Japanese communities. To be sure, the least observant among the Nikkei (all resident Japanese) could probably have surmised that American love for sport had been a continuum whose origins even predated the American Revolution.

Even in the dark days of the Great Depression, Americans thirsted for sport. Thanks to the New Deal's Works Progress Administration (WPA) and Public Works Administration (PWA), for instance, thousands of public recreational parks were built throughout the nation, many with lighting units for evening sports. This in turn spawned the advancement of a softball craze in several regions. In the major leagues, while the depressed economy impacted the gate, it hardly crippled the game to the point of extinction. In 1932, the bleak era also did little to undermine American enthusiasm for the summer Olympics, held that year in Los Angeles, which was home to the largest concentration of Japanese Americans. Indeed, a one-million-dollar referendum approved by California voters in support of the Olympics seemed proof positive of the resilience of sport in American life. Thus, platforms such as athletics, even at the local level, seemed to be entirely reasonable forums wherein Japanese Americans could visibly display their competitive virtues to the public at large.

Unfortunately, as war loomed on the horizon, mainstream Americans, with so little working knowledge of the Nikkei, drew from decades of stereotypes to construct their impressions. In a span of nearly a half century, from the 1890s to 1941, the cultural and, in some cases, even geographical gaps between the ethnic Japanese and Caucasians had grown too large for any type of bridge, symbolic or otherwise, to be built between the two communities. Thus, the Nisei, whose attempts to assimilate their enclave seemed monumental from the outset, at the news of the Pearl Harbor raid, had virtually no redeeming profile in the eyes of the larger society for whom they hoped to establish a patriotic visibility. Interned in 1942 primarily as a result of their ethnicity, many Japanese Americans rested upon the hope that lawyers in their defense could make the case that the government's actions that led to their incarceration by virtue of Executive Order 9066 had been a violation of the constitution under the mandate of the Fourteenth Amendment.

June 21, 1943, represented a critical date for the one hundred twenty thousand Japanese Americans. On that day, the U.S. Supreme Court rendered its decision in a case in which Gordon Hirabayashi, a University of Washington student and Seattle Nisei, had challenged Lt. Gen. John L. DeWitt's 1942 military curfew that applied only to those who were ethnically Japanese. "Why in the hell am I running back?" Hirabayashi then thought to himself, as he recalled his initial efforts to honor the curfew. "Am I American or not? Why am I running back and nobody else is?"[7]

The day did not end well for Hirabayashi or the thousands of Japanese Americans who had hoped that this case might help bring a quick end to their incarceration. A unanimous court ruled that "military necessity" justified the ethnically focused curfew and that, in the eyes of the justices, the Japanese in America posed a "danger of espionage and sabotage."[8] Chief Justice Harlan Stone, in reading the majority opinion, went even further: Based on the government's brief, on the question of the Japanese and assimilation, he added that the Japanese residents in the United States had "relatively little social intercourse between them and the white population."[9] The Court's decision ultimately doomed Japanese Americans into a then indefinite period of internment—a plight that, during a time of crisis, was generally reserved for those who were deemed well outside of the mainstream.

Indeed, a major portion of the federal government's case had rested upon the notion that the Japanese had remained geographically and culturally isolated from the larger community. This argument, of course, was both a convenient and an oversimplified conclusion to satisfy the proponents of internment. Had thoughtful introspection of Japanese American life in America been considered, another story would have emerged. The saga of the Japanese presence in the United States was, in fact, a dual sense of patriotism and cultural conundrum. Their albatross was in the question of where they might effectively draw the line between honoring ethnic heritage and adopting assimilated nationality. This continued conflict ultimately doomed them at a most critical time in their existence in the United States.

Japanese American baseball in this period personified this dilemma and served as a microcosm of this struggle. The game carried important elements of old folkways, but it also harbored the characteristics of New World values. Although it symbolized this desired bridge into the American mainstream, the entire structure of the Nisei baseball institutions existed in virtual isolation from the very group with whom they hoped to fuse someday. Ironically, in the Issei era, it did not begin that way.

Following their exposure to baseball's beginnings in Japan and Hawaii, and once in the United States, the Issei quickly formed athletic clubs—entities created to satisfy both their recreational appetites and social agendas. From these clubs, the baseball proponents recruited players and formed teams. Records at the National Japanese American Historical Society credit San Francisco's Fuji Athletic Club, formed in 1903, as the first known mainland baseball team of Japanese background.[10] Others quickly followed suit. Between 1903 and 1915, in a region that spanned from San Jose, in the southern periphery of the Bay Area, to Florin, outside of Sacramento, Issei teams blossomed. From this generation came the founding fathers of Japanese American baseball: Frank Fukuda in the Pacific Northwest, Kenichi Zenimura of Fresno, and Chiura Obata, a San Francisco resident. They were the ones who stimulated, organized, and promoted baseball interests in their respective regions. Eventually, of course, Japanese in more inland regions formulated clubs in a similar manner.

Zoruku "Chiura" Obata entered San Francisco during these formative years of the Japanese presence in the United States. The future sojourner was born in 1885 in Sendai, a seaport in northwestern Honshu. At age fourteen, the self-proclaimed "rough-neck" ran away from home to find his destiny in Tokyo.[11] There, his interest and propensity in freehand art earned him an apprenticeship. Having adopted the trade name Chiura ("a thousand bays"), Obata gained notoriety as a painter, but the restless artist was dissatisfied with life in the Japanese capital and yearned for other adventures. "The greater the view, the greater the art, the wider the travel, the broader the knowledge," he told his father as young Obata prepared, in 1903, to venture eastward to the United States.

Arriving that same year, the talented painter wandered into, what was for the Japanese, a traumatic climate. "Far from the rapturous accounts of earthly paradise reported in Japan, California offered the most inhospitable environment imaginable for the Japanese immigrant," recounted writer Susan Landauer.[12] At times spat on and assaulted by whites, Obata, most likely, was "clearly disappointed with the San Francisco he encountered" shortly after his appearance there.[13] Yet San Francisco, for most young adventurers, was teeming with excitement and carried the potential for economic opportunities. To that end, Obata opted to endure the discomforts of the discrimination he encountered.

As the publisher Abiko had done after his arrival, the then eighteen-year-old Obata worked as a domestic and studied English. To earn extra money, he utilized his skills and drew illustrations for various Japanese-language publications. As he developed friendships in Japantown, Obata also exhibited another passion he had apparently acquired in Japan: a love for baseball.

Young and full of energetic optimism after only one year in San Francisco, in 1903, Obata brought other like-minded Issei together and formed a baseball team called the Fuji Athletic Club. As noted, this organization represented the first U.S. mainland baseball team made up of entirely Japanese players. Though Obata's own playing skills are not entirely clear, his ability to draw athletically minded Issei together was pioneering. Moreover, his application of artistic skills in designing the team uniforms and logos served as yet another example of his passion for the game, a passion which ignited others of his generation in settlements in and around the San Francisco region.

Only a year after the Fuji Club formed, a rival outfit, the KDC, came into existence. The team, whose name symbolized the land of their origins, like other early Issei clubs, competed against teams of varied ethnic groups. In an era of outright hostility, however, contests against mainstream whites were played with caution. "A lot of these white teams didn't take losing very well. As the game got closer to the end and we were winning, we would start gathering up our equipment and as soon as the game ended, we would grab our gear and run," recounted a Nisei of having seen his father's ball playing career.[14]

In 1906, San Francisco experienced a devastating earthquake, which, in addition to a large toll on lives, rendered thousands of people homeless and unemployed. Though some Japanese had already migrated to other locales, the disaster drove still more to Sacramento, San Jose, and various spots in the Bay Area. Not surprisingly, the Issei baseball habit survived these moves and clubs emerged in new locales. San Jose saw its first Issei team in 1910. Further, in the Sacramento community of Florin, Issei settlers founded their baseball activities in 1912, and in Oakland, the game appeared in the Japanese enclave as early as 1915.

Like Obata, Frank Tokichi Fukuda sought adventure in the United States. Born in Shimonoseki, Japan, in 1889, at age seventeen and adventurous, he made the trek across the Pacific and landed in Seattle in 1906.[15] Fukuda's own baseball roots stemmed from his days at Shimonoseki Commercial School, where he completed his formal education. Upon his arrival in Seattle, Fukuda advanced his education in a local business school, learned the rudiments of the English language, and started a laundry service. In 1908, having become more settled, he joined the Mikados, a club formed only a year earlier.[16]

Baseball had actually taken hold of the tiny Japanese community in Seattle prior to Fukuda's appearance. As early as 1904, first-generation immigrants formed the Nippon, a team that initially played games against mediocre white teams. Baseball interest in the area, however, greatly increased when a Japanese team from Waseda University in Japan initiated a U.S. tour in the Puget Sound area. This trip signified two important factors for the Japanese community and baseball: First, it greatly stimulated baseball interest in the Pacific Northwest; second, it led to several more trips. Fukuda played an important role in such trips, which were imperative for those Issei who wanted to maintain strong ties with the homeland.

Fukuda expanded his baseball ties while playing second base for the Mikado, one of the most popular teams in the area. "The Mikado team dominated the Japanese baseball league the next few years and Fukuda became a premier second baseman in the league," claimed Ryoichi Shibazaki.[17] In fact, so good were the Mikados that the *Seattle Post-Intelligencer* posted a picture of the club, with the caption "Japanese Baseball Champions of the Northwest," after a 1910 victory over the Columbias of Tacoma, another Issei team.[18] In an assessment of the club's parity with white teams, the daily was gracious but cautious: "The Japanese team is not the best amateur aggregation in the city, but it can give any of [its opponents] a battle," the paper announced. ". . . [they] have shown that they rank well with the American players. While a little weak in batting, the little fellows are wonderful fielders, fast, and good base runners."[19]

Fukuda's significance as a player was secondary to his eventual role as a motivator for the expansion of Japanese American baseball in the Pacific Northwest. An important step in that direction took place in 1909, when Fukuda founded a young Nisei team (similar to the contemporary Little League level), which he called the "Cherry" team. Fukuda's devotion to the community's youth—the enclave's future, respect for heritage, and personal love for the game—fueled his drive to see their baseball activities blossom within and beyond the Puget Sound area. In 1912, Fukuda christened the Cherry team the "Asahi Club," and promoted it as a social organization for young men.

Social, or athletic, clubs like the Asahi were common in Issei communities. Though the names carried recreational connotations, these institutions had a much broader appeal. Most included Issei who saw themselves as "refined." "The Asahi club," Ryoichi Shibazaki points out, "was not a baseball team in the strict sense. It was an organization consisting of Japanese students and the main purpose was to produce the future leaders of Japanese society in Seattle through various activities like baseball."[20] The clubs also served as an important bridge between the first and second generations. Kenji Kawaguchi, a Seattle Nisei, passionately recalled his early desire for inclusion in one of the clubs: "We wanted to belong. Everybody wanted to be part of the Taiyo Athletic Club. We wanted to be affiliated with the older boys so as to get their support."[21]

Strong on initiative, Fukuda, then a clerk and eventually vice president with a Japanese bank in Seattle, took the Asahi Club and expanded its largely social functions to include recreation. Given Fukuda's upbringing in competitive-minded Meiji, Japan, it is not surprising that he and others like him saw sport as a key factor in assimilating into their new surroundings. As had been the case in the San Francisco region, Seattle's Issei, between 1905 and 1910, "were moving toward genuine immigrant status rather than simply transient workers from Japan."[22] Therefore, it seems reasonable to assume that most, if not all, of Fukuda and the Asahi Club's goals were designed for long-range results. To that end, he was the major influence behind several baseball teams that emerged from that club.

In 1927, the bank where Fukuda worked went out of business. Soon thereafter, Fukuda left Seattle for a position as principal in a Portland, Oregon, Japanese-language school. During the next few years, he ended up teaching Japanese at various schools in the Portland region. As he had done in Seattle, Fukuda nurtured the baseball interests of the Nikkei in northern Oregon.

In this early era, first-generation Japanese Americans competed in several racially mixed, city and semiprofessional leagues. Teams such as the Mikados of Seattle, Fuji Club of San Francisco, and Asahi of San Jose played in their initial years against clubs outside of their neighborhoods. Since the number of Issei baseball clubs was then relatively sparse, in order to compete for the better part of any given summer, they had to participate in racially mixed leagues. Furthermore, intuitive Issei leaders, perhaps driven by their ideals, also recognized that athletics, such as baseball, provided an opportunity to find common ground with the larger mainstream. Though their early designs did not include a vision of permanent residency in North America, by the first decade of the twentieth century, many came to adopt the view that remaining in the United States was in their best interest. "Stay in America and make it your country," came to be the new slogan trumpeted in the Issei neighborhoods.[23]

Their commitment to make things work in their adopted country, of course, carried with it the consequences of reconstructing their identity. It hardly helped matters that this struggle came under a shadow of mainstream discrimination toward their enclave. The aforementioned conundrum, of course, proved to be an even more debilitating millstone around the necks of the second-generation Nisei.

As the Nisei came of age, the dilemma of cultural duality persisted like a shadow. "It's a wonder we weren't all schizos," recalled one Nisei woman. "Our parents were always telling us to be 'good Japanese.' Then they'd turn right around and tell us to be 'good Americans.'"[24] To address the former, the Issei established Gakuens—Japanese-language schools—to help maintain the Japanese culture among their children. Other community activities, such as theater and literature readings, provided yet another method to keep the Japanese elders and their offspring close to one another.[25] But athletic competition was the neighborhood's most popular activity. To serve that end, Buddhist and Christian churches, language schools, and Japanese YMCA and YWCAs sponsored leagues and teams, and the ever-expanding Japanese dailies touted the games.[26] During the late spring and summer months, baseball was a major focus of attention.

As in other regions in the West, by 1935, the baseball euphoria took hold of Nisei in the San Francisco Bay Area and beyond. In Monterey to the south, the Minatos of that fishing village spearheaded the eight-team California Coast Counties Athletic Association. In the San Joaquin and Stanislaus regions, the Livingston Dodgers and Stockton Yamatos led a cast of several clubs in the Central California League, while, to their north, the Florin Athletic Club, near Sacramento, dominated their Nisei counterparts in the Rural League. In the immediate Bay Area, the Asahi of San Jose, Oakland Merritts, and Alameda Kono routinely competed for honors in the Northern California Japanese Baseball League (NCJBL).

The game resonated with Japanese Americans for various reasons, its links to American heritage and patriotism being among those foremost in that attraction. By exhibiting these virtues in a public setting, many hoped to provide further evidence of their strong desire to be fully assimilated. Educational achievement, of course, was their primary path. Historian David K. Yoo points out that, even at the Japanese-language schools, "Textbooks and teachers encouraged the Nisei to be good Americans and become fully conversant with life in the United States."[27] Good citizenship was routinely stressed in civic activities. The Japanese American Citizen's League (JACL), claimed James Sakamoto, its co-founder as well as the editor of Seattle's *The Japanese American Courier,* fully concurred that the Nisei destiny was to become "an integral part of national life."[28] The methods to reach that acceptance ultimately, they believed, were numerous.

Because baseball was key in that quest, U.S. themes and messages often laced Nisei baseball events. Fourth of July tournaments provided one forum for patriotic activity. In 1936, the northern California Nisei "A" clubs, for instance, initiated the first such event in their state. Though only four teams participated, *The New World-Sun Daily*, a San Jose Japanese American paper that sponsored the tournament, naturally referred to it as "an epoch in the history of Japanese sportsdom in America." The opening ceremony even featured an airplane flight in which the pilot dropped onto the field a baseball tied to a combined American and Japanese flag.[29] The report went on to claim an attendance of some six thousand patrons at the games.[30]

Ironically, the Nisei campaign was in part driven to display their sense of American nationhood to the public by the mid-thirties, but their "public" was only others like themselves. In their baseball world, for instance, as opposed to that of their elders, the Nisei retreated into their own leagues and competed exclusively against others like themselves. They did so, to some degree, simply because there were, by 1930, more of them. For instance, in San Francisco, there were approximately forty-four hundred more people of Japanese heritage in 1930 than in 1900; in Alameda County, forty-five hundred more Japanese; in San Joaquin County, four thousand; in the San Jose region, four thousand; and in Sacramento, a whopping sixty-nine hundred more than had been the case thirty years earlier.[31] Consequently, each area fielded several Nisei teams in different levels of competition. In the Sacramento vicinity alone, ten teams were routinely active.

Apart from simply demographic changes, other factors contributed to the rise of the self-proclaimed "golden age" of Nisei baseball. First, transportation had modernized. Between 1933 and 1940, New Deal policy makers allocated $1.8 billion for the construction and improvement of roads.[32] To be sure, northern California's Nisei residents were among the benefactors; better roads made it easier for the ball clubs to travel. The Issei had not had this advantage and, as such, apart from the occasional trip to Japan, rarely ventured beyond the proximity of their communities. The Nisei, on the other hand, often strayed well beyond their home areas. In fact, apart from the metropolitan locales, Nisei teams routinely participated in leagues in which hundred-mile round trips were not uncommon. Their ability to travel also afforded them the opportunity to compete solely against other Nisei.

All-Nisei leagues became the norm in the 1930s. By then, baseball's importance had transcended well beyond weekend entertainment. Issei elders saw value in a sport that many of them had adopted years earlier. To them, the game, one writer speculated, "nourished traditional virtues of loyalty, honor, and courage."[33] Alongside sumo and kendo, baseball was one of the few remaining umbilical cords that they had with the homeland. For many of the Issei, vestiges of their homeland, in part symbolically recreated in the Americanized game, carried weight during their own days as players. That their sons continued the tradition was entirely acceptable. To observers of that era, the game's symbolic connection between generations was no surprise. "Baseball," writer Wayne Maeda remembered, "allowed each generation to interpret the meaning of the sport and yet the excitement of the game crossed generations."[34] Thus, with Issei support, the Nisei leagues flourished. George Yoshio Matsumoto, a player on the Sebastopol team, recalled Issei financial support at fundraisers for the club. At games, his father and others of his generation routinely "passed the hat around" to pay for umpires.[35] In Sacramento, Issei acted in a similar fashion. "They may have been poor farmers," Maeda points out, "but when it came time to donate money for uniforms and equipment, they reached down into their pockets and always came up with something to help the team out."[36]

All-Japanese athletic sites also appeared in some locales. At a time when the New Deal's WPA program included the construction of thousands of recreational parks across the country, many Japanese Americans built their own baseball facilities. For instance, of the eight ball clubs in the NCJBL, four of those—Oakland, San Jose, Sebastopol, and Florin—played in their own ballparks. Additionally, beyond the scope of the NCJBL, several other Japanese communities in the central Californian agrarian regions such as Cortez, Walnut Grove, and Livingston had built their own sports facilities.

Though many of these so-called stadiums were, in fact, stitched-together ball fields laced with wooden stands and improvised chicken-wire backstops, which were set behind their churches or on a community member's farm, these humble sanctuaries drew the enclave together on game days. Contests also could be easily scheduled, particularly after the morning church services. More importantly, the little ballparks provided a sense of comfort for the Nikkei. There, they could conduct their affairs and play their beloved game free from the discrimination that, most decidedly, lay beyond the outfield fence. To a large degree, the parks themselves were microcosms of the communities themselves. Unfortunately, these games and the all-Nisei structure kept Japanese Americans at a distance from the mainstream at a time when suspicion as to their loyalty reached its greatest height.

Long before the December 7, 1941, bombing of Pearl Harbor, western nativists, it is well known, disdained the Japanese in their respective states. The Pearl Harbor attack simply granted them a carte blanche to lobby for the evacuation of all Nikkei. Whether it was fear of a "yellow peril" or concern that the Japanese in the United States had in play "a sinister 'invisible government,' [as] part of the Japanese plan to take over America," Pearl Harbor elevated the hatred of the Japanese to a new level, but the prewar social gap between mainstream communities and the Japanese contributed massively to the animosity.

The Nisei golden age of baseball, due to voluntary or involuntary reasons, was primarily an age of segregated baseball. Rarely did the Nisei compete beyond the boundaries of their race. To a degree, their invisibility characterized the description given by a late-nineteenth-century Slavic immigrant: "My people do not live in America. They live underneath America. America goes on over their heads."[37] Few people in the U.S. mainstream knew of Nisei baseball.

For example, between 1935 and 1941, the *San Francisco Chronicle*, which routinely had listed box scores of approximately fifty to sixty semiprofessional and amateur teams each Sunday, reported the results of only three Nisei games within that six-year period. Much of the same also held true with the *San Jose Mercury-News* and the *Stockton Record*.[38] Barred from social acceptance by U.S. society, the organizers of Nisei baseball made little or no effort to connect with mainstream baseball institutions. Indeed, they played the game as Americans "underneath" America.

Of course, U.S. immigrant and ethnic history finds itself filled with examples of isolated communities. To a certain extent all incoming groups, as a result of resistance from the outside, voluntarily turned inward for solace and growth. Having done so, Irish, Italian, and Germans, among others, eventually "melted" into the mainstream and, in many cases, became power brokers in their respective regions. Yet not all groups assimilated in the same manner and with similar results. The Mexican community in the United States, like the Japanese, struggled to get a foothold within the mainstream. Through the 1920s, civic activism grew in Texas, and in 1929, Mexican American proponents of assimilation formed the League of United Latin American Citizens (LULAC). Still, for all of their efforts through the 1930s and into the war years of the 1940s, leaders from the Mexican enclaves continued to operate well outside the mainstream. The distance was so great that it prodded Carey McWilliams to pronounce that Mexicans in the United States were "a forgotten people."[39]

Life for the Nisei was clearly analogous to that of their Mexican counterparts. By sheer coincidence, Nisei leaders, too, formed in 1930 the JACL, a year after LULAC came into existence. To be sure, the Nisei era knew a torn community. As opposed to Mexicans in the United States, whose divisions existed largely as a result of nationalist and cultural sentiments, Nikkei leaders argued not over the desire or need to assimilate, but to what degree they should abandon the principles of their heritage. The Issei understandably sought a larger degree of ancestral values, but their offspring leaned heavier toward U.S. nationalism. To their own ends, members from both generations employed various means to appease their concerns. Sport, theoretically, fulfilled both these components. In reality, however, both approaches came to insulate their community.

Some Issei also found the isolated leagues disturbing. In a 1936 reunion of the older Seattle Asahi baseball club, one veteran chided the second generation for not reaching further out into the mainstream. Calling for the creation of an all-star squad, he wrote that a squad of the most talented players should "enter a strong American league. This, of course, will mean sacrifice on the part of various teams to give up their best players, but it will be good for the community."[40] The players, however, often balked at the notion of competing against whites and other non-Japanese athletes. Most believed that they were at a disadvantage because of their smaller stature. Still others, such as Kenji Kawaguchi, who grew up in the Seattle area, recalled that "whites weren't friendly with you. So I realized that [playing ball with them] was not the kind of situation I'd give my efforts to. I'd rather play Sunday ball with my [Nisei] friends."[41]

In the broader context, the Nisei isolation was rather unique. Other immigrant communities actively sought competition beyond their neighborhoods. Sammy Kaplan testified of his New York City Jewish neighborhood that the local activities clubs "were trying to get the immigrant children and their parents into the American mainstream."[42] One popular and successful basketball club, the Dux, "played throughout New York's five boroughs" and throughout the region, claimed historian Peter Levine.[43] Things were much the same for Italians in St. Louis. Joe Correnti, a former soccer player from that area, claimed that his ethnic neighborhood was "almost a closed community. Sports was an outlet for us."[44] "Athletic competition forced Hill [Italian Americans] players outside the sheltered neighborhood," Gary Mormino pointed out in his study of Italians there.[45]

Activities in most Japanese communities, on the other hand, were entirely internal. As such, their "invisibility" undermined the larger goal of assimilation. The Japanese elders, from the very outset of their existence in America, viewed the second generation as the *kusabi* or *kakehashi*—the bridge of understanding between the United States and Japan. Abiko Kyutaro, a prominent Issei who founded San Francisco's *Nichibei Shimbun*, popularized this concept and declared "repeatedly that the future of the Japanese in the United States lay with the Nisei."[46] By the 1930s, Nisei leaders, such as Seattle publisher James Sakamoto, advanced this position. He concluded that, with the emergence of Japan as an equal global power broker with the United States, the Nisei position as *kusabi* was imperative. "You are expected to be the most effective of the connecting links between Japan and the United States," he often reminded his Nisei readers.[47] Despite Sakamoto's chidings, however, in reality even the Seattle publisher's own peers operated in a non-mainstream world.

By the 1930s, the Japanese American press wore a different face than it had in an earlier era. Issei publishers like Kyutaro Abiko of the San Francisco-based *Nichibei Shimbun,* Michiharu Maruyama of the *Shin Sekai,* another Bay Area daily, and Masahuru Yamaguchi, Seijiro Shibuya, and Eitaro Iijima, three students who started the Los Angeles *Rafu Shimpo,* founded their newspapers to provide first-generation subscribers with community news and to keep readers informed of activities in Japan. Accordingly, they printed their papers entirely in Japanese. These journals were not unlike those found in other ethnic communities in the west, such as the Los Angeles-based *La Opinion,* which reached out to the homesick Mexican immigrants with inspirational stories about their country and its heroes. As early as 1922, writer Robert E. Park recognized, "The immigrant press serves at once to preserve the foreign languages from disintegrating into mere immigrant dialects, hyphenated English, and to maintain contact and understanding between the home countries and their scattered members in every past of the United States and America."[48]

As the Nisei generation increased its presence, many of the papers began to offer to their readership English-language sections. Practical reasoning, undoubtedly, lay at the heart of the transformation. In a four-year span between 1926 and 1930, the population of Nisei jumped from 26.7 percent to 49.2 percent of all Japanese in the United States.[49] Other factors also contributed to the change. Toyosaku "Henry" Komai, one of two publishers who conceived the idea of the English-language portion for the *Rafu Shimpo,* "hoped that the new section would serve as a public forum for Nisei, awakening their social, economic, and political consciousness."[50] The arrival of English-language sections also came as a result of the 1924 National Immigration Law that brought the migration of Issei from Japan to an end. The *Nichei Bei,* for example, adopted a bilingual daily in 1924. The *Rafu Shimpo* did the same two years later. A final factor, the Issei newspaper echelons fully understood the long-term implications behind this change. "The support of the Issei," argued historian David Yoo, "represented an investment in the next generation and the future of Japanese America. Making space for the Nisei reinforced generational ties, even if little collaboration took place between the two staffs."[51]As the Nisei matured, their Issei elders echoed their sentiments on values and principles through the Japanese American press. "The newspapers, by making constant suggestions of proper behavior, showed that they held positions of prestige among their audiences," wrote Dorothy Ann Stroup in her 1960 thesis on the Japanese American press.[52]

Consider also that the Japanese American press was more than simply a tool for Issei ideology. Beyond being a forum for values, the press grew in importance for two reasons: an increase in the population of Japanese Americans, and the continuing racial policies aimed at their community. By 1928, in the two largest California cities, Los Angeles and San Francisco, the *Rafu Shimpo* of the south had 8,013 subscribers and the Bay Area's *Nichei Bei* 16,258 readers.[53] Moreover, of the forty-four papers that began in the Issei era, only the *Rafu Shimpo* and *Nichei Bei* survived into the Nisei generation.[54] Since they provided the only news for a larger number of California Japanese Americans, they serviced not only the cities where they were based but also the central coast and inland regions of that state.

The papers also found themselves on the front lines of racial discrimination toward their enclave. "Children of European [immigrants] were able to merge into the mainstream and became the readers of American newspapers," claimed writer Katie Kaori Hayashi. "However, children of Japanese immigrants were isolated from the mainstream because of their color and therefore needed media that would lead the fight against racism, as blacks needed their own newspapers."[55] Having the advantage of U.S. citizenship did little good for Nisei when it came to racial discrimination.

Faced with a rigid barrier of prejudice against them, the Nisei press took on the mantel of setting an agenda for "racial responsibility." Much akin to Booker T. Washington's late-nineteenth-century call for accommodation as a formula to eliminate racial barriers in his era, Japanese American journalists called upon the Nisei "to respond to racism by embracing life in America as loyal, hard-working citizens who would 'prove' their worth."[56]

As with their counterparts in sports, Nisei journalists remained invisible to mainstream readers. Apart from the occasional human-interest story during the 1930s, Nisei journalists rarely saw articles that they had penned in papers outside of their enclave. Nor were they employed by any of the same news services used by the *San Francisco Chronicle, Los Angeles Times,* or *Sacramento Bee,* even though the communities of those papers held the largest number of Japanese Americans in the western region. Though many Nisei reporters had earned degrees in journalism, employment avenues, by far, were confined to those papers that were based in Nisei communities. Like James Sakamoto, writers such as Harry Honda and Togo Tanaka, among others, were capable journalists who carried the burden of being the "voice" of all Japanese Americans while laboring with the knowledge that their presence and that of their subscribers disappeared at the water's edge of the Nikkei world.

Baseball activities also were confined to their sphere in a manner not unlike what the Nisei would encounter during the internment. Game summaries were virtually nonexistent to the "outside" world, contests were played, when possible, on their own properties, and, even at the high school level, few of the Nisei's most talented players landed on varsity rosters. Indeed, to the general public, one might easily have gotten the impression that notable activities among Japanese Americans rested solely in the classroom and not beyond. Perhaps not surprisingly in 1942, as the War Relocation Authority (WRA) designed camp-activity "Americanization" programs, several memos sent back to headquarters from shocked field analysts pointed to the fact that the Nisei were well versed in the national pastime and other "American" activities.

Inside the Nisei world, the game was anything but invisible and it was quite American. Whereas several team names reflected Japanese heritage, others, such as "Dodgers," "Giants," and "Yankees," spoke to their enthusiasm for major league baseball—an institution that, in the 1930s, lay some two thousand miles or more to the east of their own locale. Moreover, as in the mainstream press, through the creativity of Nisei sportswriters, blue-chip players often found themselves dubbed "Babe," "Yogi," and had other such notable titles attached to their names. Readers of the *Nichei Bei, Japanese American Courier, Rafu Shimpo,* and others were transfixed by a seemingly avalanche of "championship" contests, "gargantuan" battles, and embellished adjectives for what, in reality, often were games at the sandlot level on real sandlots. Rivalries were constantly touted and players' statistics routinely listed in each issue. Even though Sunday afternoon attendance rarely reached the high numbers sportswriters described in their reports, the number of Issei and Nisei baseball aficionados who attended games clearly rivaled that of their counterparts found in the Mexican American, Italian, and black leagues at the amateur level. Nisei games, moreover, were often spectacles that, like the JACL, often started with patriotic symbols. Games also were social magnets for those who saw them as a display of prospective suitors. Teams criss-crossed regions and, in some cases, state lines, and found welcome mats that included food, drinks, and other means by which to make visiting players feel comfortable. In all respects, Nisei baseball as played in southern and northern California, Oregon, and Washington State was every bit as vibrant and "American" as any other league at the same level. Nisei reporters wrote as passionately about their contests as did Wendell Smith, Sam Lacy, and other black journalists of the fabled Negro Leagues. Japanese American baseball players and organizers displayed a fervent sense of patriotism unsurpassed by the counterparts of their day, and yet they remained invisible.

To be sure, as vibrant as were the Nisei leagues, they produced nothing in the way of celebrated ballplayers who had emerged from other ethnic communities. From the Nisei circles came no Hank Greenberg, Joe DiMaggio, or Lou Gehrig. In the meantime, Italian neighborhoods, such as those found in St. Louis, produced such highly touted stars as Yogi Berra and Tony Lazerri. Even in the segregated black leagues notoriety visited upon such players as Josh Gibson, Cool Papa Bell, and the talented and cleverly self-promoted and legendary right-handed pitcher, Satchel Paige. Indeed, for the Nisei, who were often written off because, in part, of their generally small stature, thoughts of mobilizing themselves through baseball were not realistic at that time. Furthermore, even at the amateur level, their exploits on the diamond rarely, if ever, made it onto the pages of any large mainstream papers. Beyond the diamond, Japanese Americans of that era had no political or social clout. Thus, with no Nisei voice existing among the power brokers, white Americans and, indeed, Americans of other ethnicities had virtually no contact with their Japanese American neighbors. Not until after December 7, 1941, did the Nisei community receive any real attention, and that, of course, did anything but put a respected and positive face on the community.

Even during its golden era, Nisei baseball was invisible baseball. Nisei enthusiasm and passion for the national pastime never fully resonated with the world outside of their enclave. Fourth of July tournaments, a plethora of "championship" contests, games against highly touted teams from Japan, and even a 1927 visit to Fresno, California, by Babe Ruth and Lou Gehrig, who played in a contest with and against Japanese American players, failed to win proper merit. Thus, the national pastime, as played by the Nisei, only existed in the hearts and vision of their immediate community. What was clearly visible to them was also abundantly invisible to the public at large.

NOTES

1. Ralph Ellison, *Invisible Man* (New York: The Modern Library, 1994), 3.

2. Roger Daniels, *Concentration Camps: North America: Japanese in the United States and Canada during World War II* (Malabar, Fla.: Robert E. Krieger Publishing Com-

pany, 1989), 6. Demographic data compiled in this book indicate that by 1890, there were 24,326 Issei residing across the United States, largely in the West, compared to a 76 million overall U.S. population. Daniels further reveals that in 1890, of the 1.5 million California, only 10,151 were Issei.

3. Daniels, *Concentration Camps,* 23.

4. David K. Yoo, *Growing Up Nisei: Race, Generation, and Culture among Japanese Americans of California, 1924–49* (Urbana, Ill.: University of Illinois Press, 2000), 33.

5. Daniels, *Concentration Camps,* 23.

6. Kerry Yo Nakagawa, *Through a Diamond: 100 Years of Japanese American Baseball* (San Francisco: Rudi Publishing, Inc., 2001), 27.

7. Peter Irons, *The Courage of Their Convictions: Sixteen Americans Who Fought Their Way to the Supreme Court* (New York: Penguin Books, 1990), 53.

8. Peter Irons, *A People's History of the Supreme Court: The Men and Women Whose Cases and Decisions Have Shaped Our Constitution* (New York: Penguin Books, 2000), 357.

9. Ibid.

10. Japanese American National Museum, "Diamonds in the Rough: Japanese Americans in Baseball," *Museum Magazine* (Spring 2000): 1, 8.

11. Chiura Obata, *Topaz Moon: Art of the Internment* (Berkeley, Calif.: University of California Press, 2000), 3.

12. Susan Landauer's comments appear in *Obata's Yosemite: The Art and Letters of Chiura Obata from His Trip to the High Sierra in 1927* (Yosemite National Park, Calif: Yosemite Association, 1993), 21.

13. Ibid.

14. Nakagawa, *Through a Diamond,* 32.

15. Frank Fukuda Collection, box 1, accession no. 128, Special Collections Archives, Allen Library, University of Washington, Seattle.

16. Ryoichi Shibazaki, "Seattle and the Japanese-United States Baseball Connection, 1905–1926" (MA thesis, University of Washington, 1981), 74.

17. Ibid., 79.

18. *Seattle Post-Intelligencer,* May 23, 1910. Clipping found in Frank Fukuda Collection.

19. *Seattle Post-Intelligencer,* no date. Clipping found in Frank Fukuda Collection.

20. Ibid.

21. Kenji Kawaguchi interview with author, June 15, 1993, Seattle, Wash.

22. Robert A. Wilson and Bill Hosokawa, *East to America: A History of the Japanese in the United States* (New York: William Morrow and Company, Inc., 1980), 45.

23. Ronald Takaki, *Strangers from a Different Shore: A History of Asian Americans* (New York: Penguin Books, 1989), 52–53.

24. Paul R. Spickard, *Japanese Americans, The Formation and Transformations of an Ethnic Group* (New York: Twayne Publishers, 1996), 80.

25. Ibid., 73–75.

26. Ibid., 83; Samuel O. Regalado, "Sport and Community in California's Japanese American 'Yamato Colony,' 1930–1945," in *Journal of Sport History* 19, no. 2 (Summer 1992): 130–43; Kesa Noda, *Yamato Colony: 1906–1960 Livingston, California* (Livingston, Calif.: Livingston-Merced JACL Chapter, 1981), 99.

27. Yoo, *Growing Up Nisei,* 29.

28. Regalado, "'Play Ball!' Baseball and Seattle's Japanese-American Courier League, 1928–1941," *Pacific Northwest Quarterly* 87, no. 1 (Winter 1995/96): 29.

29. Harvey Kenji Tahara, "A Historical Study of the California Nisei 'A' Baseball Championship Tournaments from 1962 to 1973" (MA thesis, Sacramento State College, 1967), 20–21. Beyond the scope of this paper, it should be noted that in Seattle, *The Japanese American Courier* sponsored a similar and much larger tournament. See Regalado, "Play Ball!" 34.

30. Ibid., 21.

31. Spickard, *Japanese Americans,* 48.

32. Tom Lewis, *Divided Highways: Building the Interstate Highways, Transforming American Life* (New York: Penguin Books, 1997), 23; John B. Rae, *The Road and the Car in American Life* (Cambridge, Mass.: The MIT Press, 1971), 74.

33. Donald Roden, "Baseball and the Quest for National Dignity in Meiji, Japan," *American Historical Review* 85 (1980): 520.

34. Wayne Maeda, *Changing Dreams and Treasured Memories: A Story of Japanese Americans in the Sacramento Region* (Sacramento, Calif.: Japanese American Citizen's League, 2000), 150.

35. George Yoshio Matsumoto interview, Oral History Project, California State University, Sacramento.

36. Maeda, *Changing Dreams and Treasured Memories,* 150. For another example of baseball's connection between the Issei and Nisei, see Gail M. Nomura, "Beyond the Playing Field: The Significance of Pre-World War II Japanese American Baseball in the Yakima Valley," in *Bearing Dreams, Shaping Visions: Asian Pacific American Perspectives,* ed. Linda A. Revilla (Pullman, Wash.: Washington State University Press, 1993); and Regalado, "Sport and Community," 135–36.

37. John D. Buenker, "Mainstream America and the Immigrant Experience," in *The Development of an American Culture,* 2d ed., ed. Stanley Coben and Lorman Ratner, (New York: St. Martin's Press, 1983), 330.

38. At the California State Library in Sacramento, I examined each Monday, when Sunday box scores were printed, of each June and July between 1935 and 1941 to reach my conclusions. As a comparison, I found that Mexican American and Italian American clubs were listed from time to time. Even a club from the California State Prison at San Quentin made the box scores on occasion. Additionally, a reading of the *Los Angeles Times* was comparable to that found in the *San Francisco Chronicle.*

39. Carey McWilliams, *Brothers under the Skin* (Boston: Little, Brown, 1951), 113.

40. Frank Fukuda Collection, Special Collections Archives, University of Washington, Seattle.

41. Regalado, "Play Ball!" 33.

42. Peter Levine, *From Ellis Island to Ebbets Field: Sport and the American Jewish Experience* (New York: Oxford University Press, 1992), 32.

43. Ibid., 33.

44. David K. Wiggins, ed., *Sport in America: From Wicked Amusement to National Obsession* (Champaign, Ill.: Human Kinetics, 1995), 236.

45. Ibid.

46. Yuji Ichioka, "A Study in Dualism: James Yoshinori Sakamoto and the *Japanese American Courier,* 1928–1942," *Amerasia Journal* 13, no. 2 (1986–1987): 57–59.

47. Ibid., 59.

48. Robert E. Park, *The Immigrant Press and Its Control* (Westport, Conn.: Greenwood Press Publishers, 1922), 55.

49. David Yoo, "'Read All about It': Race, Generation and the Japanese American Ethnic Press, 1925–41," *Amerasia Journal* 19, no. 1 (1993): 72–73.

50. Katie Kaori Hayashi, *A History of the Rafu Shimpo: Japanese and Their Newspaper in Los Angeles* (Chuo-ku, Osaka: Union Press, 1997), 73.

51. Yoo, "Read All about It," 73–74.

52. Dorothy Ann Stroup, "The Role of the Japanese-American Press in Its Community" (MA thesis, University of California, Berkeley, 1960).

53. Hayashi, *A History of the Rafu Shimpo,* 69.

54. Stroup, "The Role of the Japanese-American Press in Its Community," 52.

55. Hayashi, *A History of the Rafu Shimpo,* 72.

56. Yoo, "Read All about It," 75.

DANIEL A. NATHAN

CHASING SHADOWS THE BALTIMORE BLACK SOX AND THE PERILS OF HISTORY

When knowledgeable baseball fans hear the phrase "Black Sox," they usually think of the eight members of the Chicago White Sox, most famously outfielder "Shoeless" Joe Jackson, who were implicated in the infamous 1919 World Series game-fixing scandal.[1] This is certainly appropriate, because the Black Sox scandal, as the event soon became known, was an extremely influential moment in baseball history. It contributed to the hiring of baseball's first commissioner, Judge Kenesaw Mountain Landis, and it established a zero-tolerance policy for gambling. Moreover, for many people the scandal was a significant moment of betrayal, disillusionment, and crisis. As the Chicago writer Nelson Algren put it, the Black Sox were "Benedict Arnolds! Betrayers of American Boyhood, not to mention American Girlhood and American Womanhood and American Hoodhood."[2] Due to folklore, scores of articles and books, several films, and the ongoing controversies about whether Joe Jackson and Pete Rose should be in the Baseball Hall of Fame, the Black Sox scandal has retained its resonance, its ability to stoke debates and fire imaginations.[3]

The banished Chicago game-fixers, however, are not the only Black Sox worth remembering and contemplating. For different reasons, the Baltimore Black Sox, a long-defunct Negro League team, also deserves our attention, especially the extraordinarily talented 1929 squad, which earned a fleeting and now forgotten moment of glory by winning the first and only American Negro League pennant, taking both halves of the closely contested split season. Winning that pennant may have been a bittersweet achievement for some of the Black Sox, simultaneously heroic and hollow, exciting and dispiriting, a validation of their talent and competence, and yet a painful reminder of their second-class status as citizens and ballplayers. Denied the opportunity to play in the major leagues due to racism, the Black Sox were also denied the opportunity to play in the Negro League version of the World Series because the Negro National League champion Kansas City Monarchs would not play them, owing to an ongoing feud between the rival leagues.[4] The 1929 Black Sox, nevertheless, further distinguished themselves by soundly beating a team of white major and minor leaguers in an exhibition series. Soon thereafter, the American Negro League collapsed and the team was relegated to barnstorming. The Black Sox struggled to survive, joined the short-lived East-West League, changed ownership, folded in 1933, and eventually faded from most memories.[5]

Today, most baseball fans have never heard of the Baltimore Black Sox and, even though scholarly attention to the Negro Leagues has flourished for more than a generation, most historians do not give them much consideration. Thirty-five years ago, former Black Sox outfielder Crush Holloway insisted: "Those were great players back then. But nobody knows about us any more. If you put all these stories in the sporting pages, they could read all about it and understand how it was. But that's lost history, see? Nobody's going to dig it up, it's just past now, that's all."[6] In many ways, Holloway's lament still rings true.

The Black Sox's fate was and is unsurprising. Invisible to most white Americans, Negro baseball leagues were popular and socially significant institutions for many African Americans in the years between the two world wars and into the early 1950s. Yet, because they were frequently undercapitalized and hindered by social conditions that did not allow them to flourish, Negro League teams often failed, even in the heyday of black baseball, a phenomenon that intensified with the coming of the Depression. So, despite their on-field success, the Black Sox's failure as a business was predictable, perhaps even inevitable.

Being forgotten is more common than not. In the long run, most of us will not be remembered. Regardless of our best efforts, doing something truly memorable and lasting is difficult, in part because of the vagaries of memory and history. Further, being forgotten, although unfortunate and sometimes sad, is not necessarily tragic, even if one has accomplished something exceptional, something that is usually celebrated and commemorated. In my view, forgetting baseball players does not rise to the level of tragedy.

Yet any form of glory is rare, and usually hard earned. This was especially true for African Americans in the late 1920s, when the United States was undeniably divided into separate and unequal societies, with a rigid color line. In Baltimore, commonly regarded as the most southern of northern cities (or vice versa), with a black population of approximately one hundred

The 1929 Baltimore Black Sox, winners of the American Negro League Pennant. Courtesy National Baseball Hall of Fame Library, Cooperstown, N.Y.

and forty thousand people, segregation was a fact of life.[7] Because the Baltimore Black Sox can provide us with a portal to that specific time and place—a romanticized, poorly understood era and a city in transition—remembering and thinking about it has some historical utility. Doing so can help us to understand something about a certain African American experience, about local race relations, about a time when and place where institutional racism limited what some men could do and who they could become. Recalling the ballplayers' deeds may also have virtue if one believes that achieving glory should be honored, or at the very least acknowledged.

Arguably just as important, the 1929 Baltimore Black Sox help exemplify a larger point. Because the particulars of the Black Sox's pennant-winning season are now rife with uncertainty, and the available documentary sources are laden with indeterminacy, this chapter highlights the limits of historical knowledge—how difficult it is to know and convey the past—and the frailty of collective memory. These may seem like obvious matters, but they need to be articulated and demonstrated, repeatedly, not taken for granted. For some people who do not practice or think critically about the craft, history appears to be a relatively simple matter: Unearth the "facts" and let them speak for themselves. Yet even if the facts can be determined and are undisputed (and this does not always happen), that is not how history and historians work. Rather, as Simon Schama eloquently argues in *Dead Certainties (Unwarranted Speculations)*:

> [H]istorians are left forever chasing shadows, painfully aware of their inability ever to reconstruct a dead world in its completeness, however thorough or revealing their documentation. Of course, they make do with other work: the business of formulating problems, of supplying explanations about cause and effect. But the certainty of such answers always remains contingent on their unavoidable remoteness from their subjects.[8]

Schama is right about the contingent nature of the endeavor (more so than he suggests in this passage), and about the self-consciousness many of us experience when trying to reconstruct the past. Who is more keenly aware of a historical narrative's flaws, inadequacies, and lacunae than its author? Still, there are good reasons for chasing shadows, for a poorly understood or forgotten past is a diminished one, which often impoverishes the present. Another reason to chase shadows, not to be underestimated, is the sheer pleasure of knowing, and the intrinsic thrill of the chase, the quest for historical knowledge, usable or not.

◆ Like baseball itself, black baseball and the Negro Leagues have long, rich histories. It is important to remember, though, that professional leagues comprised exclusively of teams with African American players were not always "necessary," for professional baseball in this country was not always segregated.[9] In the nineteenth century there were several all-black baseball teams—the Philadelphia Orions, Cuban Giants, and Lord Baltimores—yet nearly one hundred black men competed with and against white professional ballplayers.[10]

This is not to suggest that baseball in the nineteenth century was egalitarian, any more so than the United States itself was at the time. Although some teams and leagues were integrated, baseball was never a democratic meritocracy as its promoters claimed. Nineteenth-century African American baseball players experienced discrimination on a daily basis in the form of racial taunts and, less frequently, physical abuse, such as being deliberately thrown at and being spiked on the base paths.[11] One of the earliest acts of institutional racism associated with professional baseball occurred in 1867 when the National Association of Base Ball Players voted to bar "any club which may be composed of one or more colored persons," thus establishing baseball's first color line.[12] The National League was organized nine years later and its team owners tacitly agreed to the same prohibition.[13]

Despite these developments, during the last quarter of the nineteenth century a few African Americans played on integrated teams. Most notably, in 1884, Moses Fleetwood Walker, the Oberlin-educated son of a minister and physician, and his younger brother Welday Walker played for Toledo of the American Association, which then had major league status.[14] It was a short-lived experience, as the Toledo franchise dropped out of the league the following season. Fleet Walker, who played for five more years in the high minor leagues, never again played for a major league team.[15] Three years later, in 1887, Adrian "Cap" Anson, the talented and popular first baseman and manager of the Chicago White Stockings, threatened not to field a team as long as a black ballplayer, George Stovey, remained on the opposing team. "No one could afford to lose money on forfeited games," explains historian Leslie A. Heaphy, "and so Anson's actions helped push African Americans out of professional baseball."[16] Gradually, due to racism, intolerance, and (perceived) economic imperatives, African American players were systematically excluded from the white professional game, just as other African Americans were barred from virtually all white-controlled social institutions at the time.[17] By the beginning of the twentieth century, there were no African American ballplayers in the major leagues.

Living under apartheid conditions, African Americans interested in baseball responded to segregation the same way that other people responded to other forms of racial exclusion: They created and promoted their own institutions, in this case baseball teams and leagues.[18] The first successful all-black league, the Negro National League, was founded by Andrew "Rube" Foster in 1920, "very nearly at the start of the Harlem Renaissance," notes cultural critic Gerald Early:

> This means that black baseball, no matter how poorly arranged and managed, tried to become an institutional presence in African American life at the time when the concept of the New Negro—a reconstituted, reconstructed, if you will, image of the Negro, no longer as the folk "darky" of the 1890s but as an assertive, self-reliant, enterprising urban dweller—was being bandied about among intellectuals, writers, and journalists.[19]

In many ways, Foster fit the description of the New Negro. A brilliant pitcher in the early twentieth century, Foster was intelligent and articulate, had exceptional leadership and organizational skills, and believed that a black-owned and operated league would keep black baseball from being controlled and exploited by white entrepreneurs.[20] The Negro National League, which usually fielded eight teams from the Midwest and played approximately eighty regular season games, was initially popular and profitable. Indeed, historian Donn Rogosin contends that "the Negro Leagues were among the largest black businesses in the United States before the breakdown of segregation; in their prime they were a multi-million-dollar operation."[21]

Negro League baseball was also an important cultural institution in many African American communities, especially in burgeoning northern cities. Professional (and in some cases semipro and sandlot) baseball teams "contributed a sense of cohesion to black communities after the disruptive impact of the World War I-era northward migrations," argues historian Rob Ruck. "They helped define the consciousness of a people and offered a bridge to white America at a time when the major leagues and much else in society were still off-limits."[22] In several instances, such as Pittsburgh and Kansas City, Negro League teams were integral components of African American communities, providing people with a common allegiance and experience, which could be intensified amid the diversity and anonymity of urban life.[23]More than simply baseball, the Negro Leagues were a valuable source of entertainment and racial pride for many, not just a source of economic opportunity for the extremely talented few.

Athletically, there was nothing inferior about the best black ballplayers when compared to white major leaguers, as superstars like Honus Wagner and Babe Ruth acknowledged.[24] Many of the men who played in the Negro Leagues were of major league caliber. After all, when black teams competed against white ones in exhibition games during the off-season, the black ballplayers won most of the time, according to Negro League historian John Holway, who has closely examined more than four hundred interracial ballgames.[25] But financially the Negro Leagues were "precarious, undercapitalized" endeavors, often poorly administered and supported, especially compared to the major leagues.[26]

For those good enough to play in the black leagues, and they were more exceptional than W. E. B. Du Bois's "talented tenth," the experience was mixed.[27] In some respects, it could be exciting, glamorous, and relatively remunerative. "Throughout the 1920s the average black player earned from $135 to $175 a month during the six-month season," explains historian Janet Bruce. "In comparison, workers in meat-packing plants made about $80 a month. Club owners bragged that even their lowest salary was comparable to that made by a post-office clerk, a schoolteacher, or the sportswriter who reported their games."[28] In 1929, Negro League superstars like Oscar Charleston and Martin Dihigo earned $375 and $400 a month, respectively.[29] For a population that suffered relentless oppression and intense poverty with few opportunities for advancement or travel, playing professional baseball was attractive work, if you could get and keep it. On the other hand, Negro Leaguers were poorly paid compared to "their white counterparts," Janet Bruce continues. "Players in the black major leagues made about as much as a white Class B minor-league player."[30] The travel was often difficult and exhausting, as one would expect of long road trips in ramshackle buses or overloaded cars. Once they arrived at their destinations, comfortable accommodations were often unavailable. In 1962, Laymon Yokely of the Baltimore Black Sox remembered: "When we went to cities, we stayed at hotels; but we had long jumps between hotels. We had to sleep in the buses. We used to get out of those buses hardly able to walk. I have dressed in a horse stable many a day."[31] At times Negro Leaguers literally played hungry. At times they lacked locker room privileges at stadiums. They often encountered racism. Negro League third baseman Judy Johnson succinctly encapsulated the duality of the Negro League experience: "We used to have a lot of fun, and there were some sad days, too, but there was always sun shining some place."[32] A preferred memory, to be sure.

As a result of the Negro National League's financial and cultural success, in December 1922, a group of businessmen, several of whom were white, met in Philadelphia and formed the six-team Mutual Association of Eastern Colored Baseball Clubs, better known as the Eastern Colored League. The league was comprised of the Atlantic City Bacharach Giants, Baltimore Black Sox, Brooklyn Royal Giants, Hilldale Daisies (Philadelphia), Lincoln Giants (New York), and Cuban Stars.[33] A baseball "war" ensued, "as the Easterners raided [Rube] Foster's West for talent," writes John Holway. "Although the West had long been doing the same thing to the East, bad blood flowed."[34] Despite the newfound competition for talent and fans, the Negro National League operated successfully for almost a decade before experiencing fatal financial problems. It folded in 1931, largely due to the Depression and Rube Foster's death. When the Eastern Colored League collapsed halfway through the 1928 season, a replacement, the American Negro League, was organized for 1929, consisting of essentially the same teams as its predecessor, including the Baltimore Black Sox.[35]

By 1929, the Baltimore Black Sox was a well-established local institution. Neither the city's first nor only all-black baseball team, it was nevertheless the most accomplished and professional. Robert V. Leffler Jr. maintains in his valuable 1974 thesis that the Black Sox "advertised regularly in the black press, engaged in organized promotions, played in its own ballpark, and had a consistent schedule."[36] Founded in 1913 by Howard E. Young and John R. Williams (both presumably black, as it was the convention of the *Baltimore Afro-American Ledger* to indicate otherwise), the Baltimore Black Sox was "composed of most of the best ballplayers of the old Weldon Club," one of many such athletic clubs in the city.[37] For several years the self-proclaimed "baseball champions of the South" played games at Oriole Park, Union Park, and on the road. As an independent club, the Black Sox scheduled a variety of opponents: local and regional semipro, service, and industrial league teams such as the Famous Cuban Giants, the Camp Meade Colored Troops, the Bartlett-Hayward South Plant team, and the Baltimore Yanigans, the latter two being white ballclubs.[38] It seems the Black Sox and white teams competed against each other without incident and that interracial competition was popular with fans.[39]

After Charles P. Spedden—sometimes identified as a clerk with the Baltimore & Ohio Railroad or a "railroad man," sometimes as a barkeep and a traveling salesman—took control of the team in 1918, the Black Sox finally established a home field, Westport Park (later renovated and renamed Maryland

Park) in southwest Baltimore.[40] Thanks to the play of such men as Frank "Doc" Sykes, a control pitcher and a college-educated dentist with a local practice,[41] and to Spedden's leadership, the franchise built a reputation as a solid, competitive team, and "developed marketing ideas to attract fans," writes historian Leslie Heaphy. "Ads encouraged women's attendance, special deals appealed to people's patriotic fervor during the First World War, and an official scorer helped at all ball games, giving a professional finish to contests."[42]

Several important developments occurred soon thereafter. In 1921, the team was incorporated, officially becoming The Black Sox Baseball and Exhibition Club. According to the *Baltimore Afro-American,* "stock amounting to $20,000 was authorized and will be sold at 100 per share."[43] How well it sold cannot be determined. At some point, George Rossiter, a white Hanover Street restaurateur and former semipro ballplayer, "bought the controlling interest of the Black Sox," but retained Spedden as the team's "manager and financial agent."[44] That is, until 1927, when Rossiter fired Spedden at the urging of the Eastern League Commission, which claimed that he had not turned over its share of the recent World Series receipts.[45] Prior to this falling out, Rossiter and Spedden seemed to work well together. They found and signed talented ballplayers, such as Oscar "Heavy" Johnson, Jud "Babe Ruth" Wilson, and Crush Holloway. They hired Pete Hill, "the first great outfielder in black baseball history," and then the widely respected Ben Taylor as the team's manager.[46] They attempted (or at least consistently promised) to improve the playing conditions at the team's home ballpark.[47] They purchased "motor trucks," including a "special touring sedan" that could seat thirty passengers, so the team could travel comfortably and economically.[48] According to Richard Powell, who had been a Black Sox fan in his youth and became the business manager for the Baltimore Elite Giants (a later Negro League team), they "brought in the best major-league all-star teams to play the Black Sox."[49] Arguably most importantly, they decided to have the Black Sox become a charter member of the Eastern Colored League, a move that further legitimized the team as a professional, respectable operation and, as Rossiter and Spedden undoubtedly hoped, would provide it with more stability and profits.[50] During the league's five full seasons, from 1923 to 1927, the Black Sox did reasonably well on the field, but did not distinguish itself, never winning a pennant and finishing with an overall winning percentage of .502 (133–132).[51] Although the team apparently did not fare well financially, given the many difficulties associated with sustaining a Negro League team, one would have to conclude that the Baltimore Black Sox's fifteen-year history prior to 1929 was a success.

Comparatively, however, the team's hometown was more successful during these years. Like many American cities in the first decades of the twentieth century, Baltimore, long a prominent port, had become increasingly industrial, with the creation of numerous small factories.[52] As a result, it was becoming "an integral part of the national economy."[53] Hand in hand with business, local political leaders engaged in active civic planning. In the process, businessmen and politicians contributed to what historian Sherry H. Olson calls the "redefinition of race spaces."[54] This happened just as the city's black population grew almost 50 percent, compared with 25 percent for whites.[55] Baltimore's growth was also physical. Writer Burt Solomon points out that the city grew by annexing "enough sparsely settled land to triple its size," and that "skyscrapers modeled after New York's" were in the process of reshaping the landscape.[56] Simultaneously, some of the city's iconic rowhouses were built.[57] Clearly Baltimore in the 1920s was a bustling place of significant changes and relative though unevenly distributed prosperity. It was the Baltimore of jazz composer and pianist Eubie Blake and the thriving Pennsylvania Avenue show district, as well as the cantankerous journalist and critic H. L. Mencken, who "suffered fools so ungladly," quips historian Robert J. Brugger, "that strangers kept their distance."[58]

It was also the Baltimore in which my paternal grandparents were raised, a fact that explains some of my interest in the Black Sox. Unlike my grandmother, who immigrated to the United States as an infant, my grandfather was born in Baltimore, in a tiny rowhouse, the first of three generations of Nathans to call the city his birthplace. He never lived anywhere else, and thus had a somewhat parochial, Balmer-centric view of the world. A feisty youngster growing up on the streets and in the parks of Baltimore in the 1920s and early 1930s, my grandfather became a lifelong baseball fan, and later an armchair manager who helped explain the game to me and contributed to my affection and appreciation for it. My grandfather and I talked baseball for almost thirty years, but he was not responsible for teaching me about the Negro Leagues, a subject he did not know well. When he was eighty-two years old, I asked him, "Did you ever see the Negro League teams in Baltimore when you were a kid?" He said no, even though he had heard that "they were great. All-Stars, most of 'em." When I pressed him why not, he responded matter of factly, "You weren't supposed to be down there." Because the boy who became my grandfather, and many others like him, followed that social convention, one that buttressed the racial status quo of a segregated city, they missed an opportunity to see great baseball and perhaps to have some of their assumptions about racial superiority challenged. In retrospect, their absence has also had a profound effect on our ability to access and understand that past.

Several years before that conversation with my grandfather, in 1994, while doing research on the Chicago Black Sox scandal, I first learned about the Baltimore Black Sox. Thanks to a keyword search in a history database, I came across Robert Leffler's essay "Boom and Bust: The Elite Giants and Black Baseball in Baltimore, 1936–1951." By way of providing context for the Elite Giants (pronounced "EE-light"), Leffler briefly mentions the "ill-fated Black Sox," a phrase I found intriguing.[59] It made me wonder: Were all the Black Sox ill-fated? Coincidently, that fall Ken Burns aired his nine-episode, eighteen-and-a-half-hour documentary about baseball, which devotes a great deal of attention to the Negro Leagues. I was interested in the shadow world that he rendered, and soon thereafter read the following sentence in Robert Peterson's pioneering *Only the Ball Was White: A History of Legendary Black Players and All-Black Professional Teams:* "The eastern circuit was reorganized in 1929 as the American Negro League but it lasted only that season, with the Baltimore Black Sox winning the pennant."[60]

On the basis of that sentence, which seemed so full of possibilities—with its untold stories and perhaps cultural significance, set in a time and place that already interested me—I created a Baltimore Black Sox folder, filed it away, and turned my attention back to my work on the World Series game-fixing scandal. Occasionally, I would see a citation or a reference to the Baltimore Black Sox and the Negro Leagues and would add it to the file. Five years later, I finally had the chance to think seriously about the Negro Leagues. At the time, I was most interested in why the Negro Leagues have enjoyed a steady historical revival over the last thirty-plus years; and what it means that more white people may be aware of, knowledgeable about, and interested in the Negro Leagues today than when the leagues actually existed.[61] It was only later, after doing some primary research on the Baltimore Black Sox, that I began to see the possibilities of telling a small, allegorical story, set in a specific historical moment, to explore larger issues about memory and forgetting. I mention all of this because we need to be mindful that history does not write itself, that historians have histories, and, "like most people, operate within a web of vested interests."[62] Some of us may seem or in fact be dispassionate, but no matter how fair minded and critically alert, we are all undeniably "subject to the limitations of time and place."[63] We all see and understand the past and the present via our own subjectivities.

Talking with my grandparents and other Baltimoreans about the city's past has taught me that there are at least three Baltimores: as it was, as it is, and as it is imagined—all of which are multifarious and subject to debate. What is not debatable, however, is that the Baltimore of the 1920s was not the Baltimore of the Inner Harbor, the popular waterfront area with dozens of retail stores and restaurants, or Oriole Park at Camden Yards, the downtown baseball stadium that one critic describes as "a simulacrum of the historic as a front for increased revenues."[64] A postmodern, publicly financed ballpark, Camden Yards has been a huge success. It has drawn millions of people every season since it opened in 1992 (despite the Orioles consistent mediocrity on the field), and has inspired a generation of multimillion-dollar retro stadiums.[65]

Unknown to most of the fans at Orioles games, just south of Camden Yards—near the intersection of Russell and Bush streets, at the foot of Ridgely Street—is the site of the now demolished Maryland Park, where the Baltimore Black Sox played their home games. There is no trace of it today. Where there was once a ballpark, there are now warehouses. Built in 1921, Maryland Park had covered grandstands, first- and third-baseline bleachers, and "was on a main streetcar line," a fact often emphasized in advertisements.[66] It seated anywhere from thirty-five hundred to nine thousand people.[67] Nevertheless, even by the standards of the day, Maryland Park left much to be desired: "The seats were said to be dirty, the roof full of holes, the grandstand unpainted and foul smelling, the infield rough, and the outfield full of weeds with uncut grass," writes historian Neil Lanctot.[68] Disgruntled fans and journalists sometimes complained. A former ballplayer who became a writer for the *Philadelphia Tribune,* Otto Briggs, suggested in May 1929 that the fans "stay away from the park" until conditions have been improved. He noted: "Fans wearing nice clothes take a chance on getting them ruined unless they spread something down to sit on. It is reported that the bleachers in right field that are now missing, were torn down after being condemned. Why the rest of the stands were not condemned is not known because the roofs are full of holes. When it rains there is no way to keep from getting wet."[69] Maryland Park was, in short, a third-rate ballpark, even less than second-class citizens and ballplayers deserved. In 1934, it became a junkyard.[70]

Although the loss of a landmark is unfortunate, it is not a tragedy. Buildings are razed every day; many would argue that progress demands it. The preservation (and usually the celebration) of built environments, however, is one way memories are maintained. "People visit historic sites in large measure to 'get in touch with history,'" sociologist Diane Barthel explains. "Like research scientists who demand to see experimental results with their own eyes before they will believe them, visitors to historic sites want to see history with their own eyes."[71] This is all but impossible with regard to the Black Sox home field. Not only is there nothing at Russell and Bush streets to signify the former ballpark site, but also curators at the recently opened Sports Legends Museum in Baltimore have been unable even to locate a photograph of Maryland Park.[72]

Considering the place brings us to the men who played there. Obviously talented, the team George Rossiter assembled in 1929 was also experienced. Everywhere one looked there were veterans, many of whom had played together before, either with the Black Sox or with other Negro League teams. In his eighth year with the team, Jud "Babe Ruth" Wilson was at first base. A pugnacious, barrel-chested man, Wilson was a great hitter, an adequate fielder, and violently temperamental, especially prone to assaulting umpires.[73] At second base was the newly acquired Frank Warfield, who doubled as the team's manager, the same dual post he previously held with Hilldale, where he won two pennants in a row (1924 and 1925) and the Negro World Series in 1925. Aggressive and intelligent, Warfield was entering his thirteenth year as a professional ballplayer and, like Wilson, "was tough with a streak of meanness and [was] always ready to fight."[74] Also new to the team was veteran switch-hitting shortstop Dick Lundy, the former player-manager of the Atlantic City Bacharach Giants, which he also led to two consecutive pennants (1926 and 1927). An acrobatic fielder who hit .409 in 1928, Lundy was "one of the greatest gate attractions of his day," writes Negro League historian James A. Riley, and was widely considered to be the best black shortstop of the 1920s.[75] Louisiana native and third baseman Oliver "Ghost" Marcelle was likewise new to the team.[76] Lundy's former teammate with the Bacharachs, Marcelle (whose name was spelled inconsistently by the press, sometimes Marcel, sometimes Marcell) was "scrappy and aggressive," and generally "recognized as the most accomplished third baseman in black baseball."[77] These four men comprised the so-called "million dollar infield" because that is what they reportedly would have earned collectively had they been allowed to play in the major leagues. Behind the plate was Robert "Eggie" Clarke, a smart, sure-handed, light-hitting catcher who had been with the Black Sox since 1923. In June 1929, the *Baltimore Afro-American* claimed that Clarke "is regarded as one of the best backstoppers in race baseball."[78] The team's star pitcher was Laymon Yokely, a tall, lanky, hard-throwing righthander who came to Baltimore in 1926 from North Carolina, where he played for Livingstone College.[79] "Since his stay with the Black Sox," the *Afro-American* gushed, "he has developed into one of the best pitchers in race baseball.

Yokely has pitched against some of the best of the big league stars and has turned them back with ease."[80] The team also featured outfielder Herbert "Rap" Dixon, who may have been the most complete hitter on the club and was "among the best defensive outfielders" of his era.[81] Formerly with the Harrisburg Giants, Dixon joined the Black Sox in 1928 and was lauded for his throwing arm, although apparently he too could be temperamental.[82]

I need to emphasize two points here. First, there were other talented ballplayers on the Black Sox in 1929, too many to describe here. Second, and more important, historian Larry R. Gerlach is probably correct when he argues that "the biographical sketches of career Negro league players are invariably hagiographic and rest heavily on the subject's personal reminiscences."[83] Given the paucity of records and reliable written sources about these men, the vagaries of individual memories, and the romantic, nostalgic impulse that many people bring to the subject, this is hard to avoid.

Even so, we should resist hagiography. If nothing else is clear, these ballplayers were not saints. They were, instead, athletically gifted African American men from all over the country, mostly the South (Florida, Louisiana, North Carolina, Texas, Virginia), mostly in their early thirties, mostly from working-class or impoverished backgrounds, and with dramatically different educations and personalities. The most striking things about many of them (and other Negro Leaguers, *and* white major leaguers) were their tenacity and their combative, combustible personalities, which probably contributed to their on-field success. Professional baseball, white or black, has never been a tea party. Robert Peterson puts it well: "Negro baseball was baseball for keeps. It was tough on the field as well as off."[84] In 2005, when I mentioned that some Negro Leaguers were surly and even violent, an eighty-year-old African American Baltimorean and lifelong baseball fan, Eugene Myles, who has lived in the same rowhouse for sixty years, said somewhat caustically but not unreasonably, "They had bad tempers because it was bad times back then."[85]

Those "bad times" were caused by intense segregation and discrimination, underemployment and poor housing, and of course racially motivated violence—actual and, more commonly, threatened. The *Baltimore Afro-American* provides a revealing index of these realities, as its articles "and editorials fought a continual battle against segregated education and recreation, as well as discrimination in employment, housing, and justice."[86] Unwittingly, these inequitable social conditions led to the rise of Pennsylvania Avenue, "a bustling shopping center for Old West Baltimore residents by day" that turned into a vibrant "entertainment mecca" at night.[87] More than just local establishments, the restaurants, bars, pool halls, and theaters along Pennsylvania Avenue collectively became an important social refuge for many African American Baltimoreans.[88] For some, this was also presumably true of Maryland Park.[89]

Before the 1929 season began there were, understandably, concerns about the American Negro League's viability, given the Eastern Colored League's recent collapse. Many of the same problems persisted. Most of the teams were underfinanced, two lacked regular home fields (the Stars and the Grays), and there was a widespread lack of institutional authority, discipline, and stability.[90] In March, *Pittsburgh Courier* columnist W. Rollo Wilson, who was also the league's secretary, expressed his apprehensions: "Until all clubs have parks and until economic conditions make it possible for teams to play league games each day in the week, it will be IMPOSSIBLE for any league to lay out an equitable schedule."[91] Still, Wilson was sure that the "moguls" had done their best, and in April he wrote: "On the eve of battle all of the owners and managers are confident of a successful season."[92] A week before that pronouncement, Bill Gibson of the *Baltimore Afro-American*, surveying all the league entrants, thought that "the teams are more evenly matched than some dopesters would have you believe."[93] Gibson added: "Twill be no cinch, whatever team wins the rag in the first half of the American Baseball League pennant race, take it from this maniac."

◆ The space allotted here does not allow for a detailed chronicle of the 1929 Black Sox season; and the fragmented, sometimes incomplete and confusing evidence does not help matters. The following sketch will have to (and should) suffice.

After playing several exhibition games, the Baltimore Black Sox opened the 1929 season on April 27 by beating the Cuban Stars, 10–2; for some undetermined reason, the game was played in Norfolk, Virginia.[94] Rain bedeviled the Black Sox throughout April and May, forcing the cancellation of games against the Hilldale Daisies and Homestead Grays. When the Black Sox played, the team did well, finishing the month in first place with a 7–2 record.[95] The season gained momentum in June, when the Black Sox played all five league clubs, taking advantage of weak teams like the Bacharachs and the Cubans (collectively, the Black Sox went 7–0 against these two in June), and split a June 2 doubleheader with Hilldale. Then again, the Black Sox lost a doubleheader against the Lincoln Giants in New York, and immediately thereafter dropped four consecutive games to the Homestead Grays in Pittsburgh. From then on, however, the Black Sox won ten of its last eleven games. It should be noted that the Black Sox caught a fortuitous break. On June 25, while en route to Atlantic City, the bus in which the Homestead Grays was traveling ran off the road and crashed, injuring seven ballplayers, three seriously.[96] When the shaken, bruised, and shorthanded Grays came to Baltimore less than a week later, the Black Sox swept their four-game series.[97] In the process the Black Sox won the first half of the American Negro League's split season, finishing with an official record of 24–11.[98] The league's final first-half standings were as follows:

Baltimore Black Sox	24	11	.686
New York Lincoln Giants	22	11	.667
Homestead Grays	15	13	.536
Hilldale	15	20	.429
Atlantic City Bacharach Giants	11	20	.355
Cuban Stars	6	16	.273

Bill Gibson of the *Baltimore Afro-American* was ecstatic. "There is rejoicing, yes there is the sound of the lute and the trumpet in Baltimoreland," Gibson cheered, "and rightly so, for Frank Warfield and his cohorts have brought to the Monumental City the gonfalon for the first half of the American League baseball pennant race." Surely others were similarly excited, such as George Rossiter and his ballplayers. At the same time, it is extremely difficult (if not impossible) to gauge the public response to the Black Sox accomplishment, to hear echoes of the rejoicing Gibson described. What is clear, though, as Gibson noted:

> The winning of the flag was no cinch for the local tossers, for they met some reverses that almost knocked them off their feet. Fighting gamely until the end, however, they overcame their handicaps to cop the bunting. Fortune, in the guise of misfortune, aided the locals, for it was evident that the injuries sustained by the Homestead Grays in their auto smash took some of the pep out of the Pittsburgh entry in their series here.

Homestead manager Cum Posey was understandably frustrated by the situation, and "swore by the god baseball that if he had had all of his men here that there would have been a different ending to the Sox-Grays series."[99] Perhaps, but it is impossible to know. Still, reading Gibson's column one can sense some of the excitement and pride that the Black Sox first-half championship engendered for black baseball fans in Baltimore. When Gibson asked, "Say, fans, how about having a Warfield Day during the second half to show our appreciation for what the chunky little second baseman has done for baseball in Baltimore?" some Black Sox enthusiasts heeded his call.[100]

The day after Gibson trumpeted the Black Sox first-half glory, the team began the second half of the season in New York by splitting a doubleheader with the Lincoln Giants "before a crowd of 6,000 fans."[101] After beating Atlantic City and splitting games with Hilldale the following week, the Black Sox returned to Pittsburgh to face the Grays, this time taking three of four, the lone loss coming on July 20 at Forbes Field in front of four thousand spectators, a contest that went thirteen innings and ended 7–6.[102] The next day, Baltimore hosted Homestead at Maryland Park, their doubleheader marking the sixth time in four days that the two teams played each other; almost certainly exhausted, they split the pair.[103] The Black Sox concluded July by going 4–0 against the Bacharachs and the "re-vamped" Hilldale club,[104] thereby securing first place in the standings. They also played several exhibition games in Philadelphia, no doubt because they were profitable affairs.[105] The Black Sox began August with a brief slump, losing three of its first four league games; but Baltimore turned the second half of the season around by winning sixteen of its final eighteen league games, the two losses coming against Hilldale, after the Sox had clinched the pennant. The league's final second-half standings were as follows:

Baltimore Black Sox	25	10	.714
Hilldale	24	15	.615
New York Lincoln Giants	18	15	.545
Homestead Grays	19	16	.543
Cuban Stars	9	23	.281
Atlantic City Bacharach Giants	8	25	.242

It was certainly a hard-earned championship, as four of the league's top clubs were very competitive. Offensively, the Black Sox leaders were Rap Dixon (with a .432 batting average, and sixteen home runs, both third-best in the league) and Jud Wilson (.405, eleven home runs). Defensively, the stars were Dick Lundy, Oliver Marcelle, Eggie Clarke, Pete Washington, Dixon, and pitchers Laymon Yokely (15–6) and Pud Flournoy (9–8), the latter going 6–1 in the season's second half.[106] There were, of course, many other less heralded contributors to the Black Sox success. Clearly Rossiter had assembled, Warfield had managed, and Baltimore fans had witnessed an exceptional ball club. So, "Was there euphoria up and down Pennsylvania Avenue?" wonders journalist James H. Bready, the author of *Baseball in Baltimore: The First 100 Years*. "Hard at this distance to gauge Baltimore's rejoicing."[107]

We do know, however, that the team was respected by some of the men who covered the games in 1929. W. Rollo Wilson of the *Pittsburgh Courier* was direct: "The Baltimore Black Sox deserved to win the pennant. They had the best club in the league and a highly efficient leader in Frank Warfield." After praising George Rossiter for his many off-season personnel moves, Wilson acknowledged that Warfield "proved his leadership by making a half dozen temperamental stars give him sound teamwork. These men were so many barrels of gunpowder but Warfield trod lightly and blithely over them with never an explosion of consequence." Using a common sports cliché, then and now, Wilson added: "Every man on the team played his part for each was a functioning cog in a great machine."[108] Randy Dixon of the *Philadelphia Tribune* was similarly effusive, praising the Black Sox for "showing little of the looseness and leniency that has characterized the play of their quintet of opponents throughout the season." By winning both halves of the American Negro League season, Dixon wrote, the Black Sox "have asserted themselves as the outstanding diamond aggregation in Eastern domains." He characterized their play as "brilliant and consistent" and, like Wilson, concluded that "the Sox won because they deserved to win. They were the sole American Negro League aggregation playing real baseball."[109]

By most accounts, the American Negro League was a success, at least compared to the Eastern Colored League. "Not only were statistics and standings issued on a regular basis, but teams made a genuine attempt to complete the schedule, and five of the six clubs played at least sixty of the eighty games originally planned," contends historian Lawrence D. Hogan, adding that it "was arguably the most successful league ever developed in the East."[110] The American Negro League had problems, though, one of which was with umpires, who were often disrespected and sometimes threatened with violence. There was, moreover, a racial dimension to the issue. In Baltimore, several fans and Bill Gibson persistently criticized the Black Sox management for failing to hire "race umpires" at Maryland Park.[111] In August, Gibson maintained, "For years race baseball has prospered in Baltimore, but under the eyes of white arbiters. The time has come, we believe, when the race umpire, if he exists, should be given a break. Race umpires should be at the Black Sox park."[112] A week later his newspaper went further, declaring that it "stands for Negro umpires or no umpires. The League officials can take their choice."[113] The league and Black Sox management ignored the ultimatum and continued to use white umpires, exclusively. There were other problems, too, some of which proved to be fatal.

In September 1929, though, of more immediate concern to some interested participants and observers was whether there would be a Negro World Series. Well before the Black Sox won the pennant, rumors and press reports indicated that the American Negro League and Negro National League would not stage a World Series, as the latter and the Eastern Colored League had for four consecutive years beginning in 1924.[114] Responding to rumors about the doubtfulness of a postseason series, Bill Gibson used his *Afro-American* column to argue for it. He admitted that all the ballplayers got out of the last World Series, in 1927, was "a lot of exercise and carfare to and from the park as their share of the gate." He also acknowledged "there are many things to be considered in staging a world series. Transportation and accommodation and the uncertainty of the weather are the principal bugaboos." At the same time, he was convinced that there was money to be made hosting a Negro World Series.

> Here in Baltimore, we wager that a properly advertised series would draw at least 15,000 people to four games, played as doubleheaders on Saturday and Sunday afternoons. Games could be played possibly in Philadelphia or New York as well. In the West, from what we hear, the Black Sox would prove a big drawing card. The fans want to see Yokely, Wilson, Dixon, Lundy, Warfield, and the other satellites. We believe they'd turn out to see the boys.

Finally, he argued that a sanctioned postseason series would be salutary for the rival leagues, that it "would no doubt go a long way toward pouring oil on the troubled waters that wash the shores of the two territories. The hostility that has grown up over player stealing and other unethical practices might be lessened and possibly destroyed as a consequence of such a contact."[115] A week later, in late August, a news story cited a "well-known baseball fan, of Kansas City," Dr. Howard Smith, who claimed that the "failure of the American League of the East to keep its contract agreement with the National League of the West is declared to be the cause of [the] broken relations."[116] There was some truth to some of Smith's claims. Then again, owners in both leagues "stole" players, and players in both leagues jumped contracts.

No matter, the rumors and news stories were correct. The Monarchs, owned by J. L. Wilkinson, a white businessman, decided not to play the Black Sox.[117] Led on the field by player-manager "Bullet" Joe Rogan (a 1998 Hall of Fame inductee), the 1929 Kansas City Monarchs won both halves of the Negro National League split season. They dominated the second half with a 34–6 record, more than .100 percentage points better than the second-place Chicago American Giants. Success was the Monarch's tradition. As a charter member of the Negro National League, Kansas City had won three pennants (1923 through 1925) and one of the two Negro World Series in which it played.[118] But in 1925, the last time the team competed in the World Series, it "was a financial failure," Janet Bruce notes in *The Kansas City Monarchs: Champions of Black Baseball:* "Only twenty thousand supporters turned out for the [six] games, half of the previous year's total, and the receipts before expenses were only $21,000. By the time the commissioners had paid the bills, they had less than $6,000 to distribute. Kansas City's share was again divided 50/50; each of the fourteen players took home $57.64 for twelve days work."[119] Considering the time and effort involved in putting on a World Series, the acrimony between the leagues, and the financial risk, it is unsurprising that Wilkinson decided not to play the Black Sox. Instead, the Monarchs played against (and beat) the Houston Black Buffalos, champions of the Texas-Oklahoma-Louisiana League.[120]

While some ballplayers and fans must have been disappointed that the Black Sox did not compete against the pennant-winning Monarchs, Baltimore did play postseason games against a talented Negro National League team from Missouri: the St. Louis Stars.[121] The league's second best team in 1929, the Stars won the pennant the previous year.[122] Led by player-manager "Candy" Jim Taylor, one of the famous baseball-playing Taylor brothers, the Stars featured slugger George "Mule" Suttles, shortstop Willie "Devil" Wells (a 1997 Hall of Fame inductee), and outfielder James "Cool Papa" Bell (a 1974 Hall of Fame inductee), the latter often said to be "the fastest man ever to play baseball."[123] The Black Sox and Stars competed against each other four times in five days in late September. Trying to draw the biggest crowds possible, they played at three different venues, in three different states: Wilmington, Delaware; Baltimore, Maryland; and Norfolk, Virginia. Although the teams were evenly matched, splitting the four games, only the first game was close, with the Stars winning 2–0.[124] The other three games were all won by margins of at least seven runs.[125] Were the games well attended? Profitable? Meaningful? It is difficult to know, but the limited sources we have suggest that the answer to the last question is probably no, the games were not terribly significant. Maybe they would have been had they been sanctioned by the Negro National League.

Yet as a warm-up for the Black Sox's annual postseason series against local white professional "All-Stars," perhaps the games with the St. Louis Stars were useful. Usually competitive and well attended, the interracial series in Baltimore was one of many such exhibitions nationwide, which often featured famous white ballplayers. The year before, the All-Stars fielded two prominent Marylanders and members of the Philadelphia Athletics: first baseman Jimmie Foxx, an emerging star, and All-Star pitcher "Lefty" Grove.[126] In 1929, the All-Stars were led by manager Fritz Maisel of the International League's Baltimore Orioles and included pitcher Jack Ogden of the St. Louis Browns and outfielder Dick Porter of the Cleveland Indians, among other major and minor leaguers.[127]After the World Series between the Philadelphia Athletics and the Chicago Cubs concluded, several members of the champion A's, such as pitchers Eddie Rommel and Howard Ehmke, second baseman Max Bishop, and outfielder Mule Haas, joined the All-Stars. To gain some perspective on the Athletics, a few generations later journalist William Nack favorably compared Connie Mack's 1929 to 1931 pennant winners to the virtually mythical 1927 New York Yankees of Babe Ruth and Lou Gehrig.[128]

Playing Sunday doubleheaders at Maryland Park—because the more convenient and potentially profitable Oriole Park "shuts its gates in the face of dark-skinned players," said columnist Bill Gibson—the Black Sox and the white All-Stars split the first four games.[129] After the first doubleheader, it is worth noting, Black Sox management added two superb ballplayers to its roster: outfielder Charlie Smith of the Lincoln Giants, the American Negro League's leading hitter (with a .464 batting average and twenty-three home runs), and the versatile "Jawn" Beckwith, a former member of the Black Sox and "one of the hardest sluggers in the American League."[130] Perhaps taking the games more seriously than their white counterparts, the Black Sox won the next four, sweeping two doubleheaders. In the final game of the year, on October 27, the Black Sox faced pitcher Howard Ehmke, and were without Dick Lundy, Jud Wilson, Pete Washington, and Charlie Smith, "Lundy having gone to Atlantic City to join the police force and the others having gone to prepare for winter baseball or other work."[131] Ehmke had just had a great World Series against the Cubs, setting a World Series record for most strikeouts in a game, with thirteen.[132] The Black Sox were neither intimidated nor impressed. To the "Negro champions," observed the *Baltimore Sun,* Ehmke "was just another pitcher," a hittable one at that, as the Black Sox collected sixteen hits against him.[133] "When the Black Sox sharp shooters ceased firing at Howard Ehmke," declared the *Afro-American,* "their victory banner was floating over the Westport citadel with a 14–7 verdict showing in the breeze."[134] It must have been a satisfying moment for the Black Sox, and perhaps later a cherished memory.

◆ At least I think that is what happened; it is hard to know. Telling the story of the 1929 Baltimore Black Sox is obviously fraught with many challenges. "Anyone who has ever tried to carry out research on the history of sports in the United States will no doubt have confronted significant problems of evidence," observes historian Andrew M. Fearnley. "Rarely do sportsmen and women leave archives documenting their achievements, either on or off the field of play."[135] This is certainly the case with the Baltimore Black Sox, for which there are no known business records, and no surviving ballplayers.[136] Additionally, the ballplayers' descendents are very difficult to locate; so far, I have only found a few, but have not been able to realize every historian's fantasy of stumbling upon a forgotten scrapbook full of clippings and photographs, a dusty diary, or bundle of letters. Fortunately, a few Black Sox, like Laymon Yokely and Jesse Hubbard, did give interviews to the enterprising, seemingly tireless historian John Holway, and a few others.[137] In general, however, the information provided in interviews is sometimes factually suspect, especially regarding particulars from long ago. On the other hand, various folklorists and historians have persuasively argued that the principal value of oral histories is in establishing "a record of consciousness," that is, "how people felt about their experience, how they understand their world and their place in it."[138] In these ways, the handful of interviews we have are valuable. The same is true of the relatively few Black Sox photographs, despite how shadowy their subjects often appear. Yet even photographs, historian Lawrence W. Levine reminds us, need "to be interpreted and supplemented by other evidence. They are incomplete, as historical sources always are. They have been collected and filtered through other hands, as historical sources always have been."[139]

As one would expect, the most useful source of information about the Baltimore Black Sox is the black press, particularly the *Baltimore Afro-American*, at the time one of the most widely circulated black newspapers in the country.[140] But even under the best of circumstances, newspaper reportage is necessarily selective and incomplete, offering readers not much more than "tissue-thin slices of reality."[141] A weekly, rather than a daily, the *Baltimore Afro-American* in 1929 was published on Saturday, and therefore, explains James Bready, "it was more interested in tomorrow's games than in the previous Sunday's." Bready adds, "No newspaperman was along on [Black Sox] road trips, and the coverage of Baltimore's away games was skimpy, sometimes non-existent."[142] Even the box scores published in the *Baltimore Afro-American* are problematic, as they usually fail to denote the number of times a hitter batted, thus making the computation of batting averages impossible. (Some black newspapers followed this practice, such as the *Pittsburgh Courier,* whereas others, such as the *New York Amsterdam News,* did not, most of the time.) Unfortunately, using this scanty, sometimes flawed, fragmented evidence is our only option; and by flawed and fragmented, I mean that literally. Consider the fact that the microfilm version of the July 6, 1929, *Baltimore Afro-American* is missing the headline and first two paragraphs (someone apparently cut them out of the newspaper before it was photographed) of the story about the Black Sox's first-half championship clinching series with the Homestead Grays. Or even more disconcerting, and challenging for a historian, the microfilm version of the *Baltimore Afro-American* does not include the September 7 and 14, 1929, newspapers *at all.*[143] This brings home the commonsensical yet germane observation proffered by historian James Wilkinson: "Not everything in the past has left traces, and not all traces have survived. In the absence of remains, there can be no evidence, and in the absence of evidence, there can be no history."[144]

When faced with this situation, between the desire to know and a paucity of sources, between a historian's ambition and the discipline's strictures, what is one to do? My first response is write historical fiction instead of history. Too bad I am not a novelist. My second response is dig deeper, try to find and use forms of evidence that can articulate the historical experience of people whose lives are not usually preserved in traditional sources. In this respect, I have taken inspiration from the work of people who have told hard-to-document stories.[145] One of these writers is journalist Laura Hillenbrand, the author of the best-selling *Seabiscuit: An American Legend.* Certainly Seabiscuit, an unlikely champion and American icon in the late 1930s and early 1940s, did not perform in cultural shadows like the Baltimore Black Sox and other Negro Leaguers. But to tell the generally well-documented story with depth and nuance, Hillenbrand had to be remarkably persistent. She explains that writing *Seabiscuit* was

> a four-year lesson in how history hides in curious places. I obtained the narrative's basic framework from the usual suspects—newspapers in the Library of Congress and other archives, official track chart books, racing histories, magazines. But the narrative they offered, though intriguing, was incomplete. The textures of my subjects' personalities, their complex relationships, motives, fears, thoughts, and secrets, all remained elusive,

> as did the small but telling details that give historic figures immediacy and resonance in the imagination. My subjects had long since died, but I was convinced that they must have left behind some detritus. I began prowling Internet search engines, memorabilia auctions, and obscure bookstores, writing letters and placing "information wanted" ads, and making hundreds of calls to strangers in hopes that someone or something could illuminate what seemed to be a lost past.[146]

In the process Hillenbrand learned that the Seabiscuit "story wasn't lost. It was scattered all over North America, tucked in back pockets and bottom drawers," and that her "greatest source was living memory."[147] If only the same was true of the Baltimore Black Sox. My research thus far suggests otherwise. There is virtually no living memory and only a modest archival record of the men who played at Maryland Park and won the American Negro League pennant.

Following Hillenbrand's example, I have closely read more than a year's worth of the *Baltimore Afro-American,* and supplemented that by selectively reading the *New York Age, New York Amsterdam News, Philadelphia Tribune,* and *Pittsburgh Courier,* in addition to the *Baltimore Sun, Philadelphia Inquirer,* and *Pittsburgh Post-Gazette.* I have scoured libraries and archives (including the National Baseball Hall of Fame Library, the Maryland Historical Society, the Negro League Oral History Collection at the University of Baltimore, and the Schomburg Center for Research in Black Culture), history databases, and census rolls. I have networked with local public historians, archivists, museum curators, baseball historians, and members of the Society for American Baseball Research. I have telephoned and emailed journalists, talked with strangers in diners and on front stoops. I have put an "Information Wanted" advertisement in the classified sections of the *Baltimore Afro-American* and the *Baltimore Sun,* and posted it on Internet message boards. To date, my work suggests that there is almost no Baltimore Black Sox detritus. This goes a long way toward explaining why its story has been neglected, and may be irretrievable.

◆ In the grand scheme of things, what the 1929 Baltimore Black Sox accomplished was not important to most people, just as in the grand scheme of things the importance of the fixed 1919 World Series is often exaggerated.[148] Given what happened to America and the world in late October 1929, when the stock market crash toppled the economy and served as the symbolic beginning of the Depression, it would be foolish to overstate the social importance of any baseball team. Rather, the Baltimore Black Sox matters because the team provides us with an opportunity to consider a specific time and place, and complicated relationships that helped define the cultural moment.

To appreciate these things we need to remember what baseball meant to many Americans during the 1920s. Simply put, it was the undisputed national pastime, for many reasons, including the widespread belief that the game's origins were American, that it developed character, and that it simultaneously promoted rugged individualism and democracy. As historian Richard Crepeau puts it, those who administered and reported on the major league version of the game consistently argued "that American cultural values and baseball were intertwined."[149] If they were, they were for many African Americans as well. This is why Gerald Early asserts that Negro League baseball "symbolized the power of non-protest organizing, of teamwork, of saving yourself through your own effort. Baseball was about black people coming into the modern age as an organized, industrial, urban people."[150] Unwittingly, the white-owned 1929 Baltimore Black Sox was in the thick of that process. Its moments of glory, however fleeting, enabled ballplayers such as Rap Dixon, Frank Warfield, Jud Wilson, and Laymon Yokely to personify competence and achievement for some black people. "Because they provided joy and excitement in their often dramatic quest for victories and Negro league pennants," argues Donn Rogosin, "they enriched life in black America. When their baseball victories came against white opponents, they undermined segregation itself."[151]

The 1929 Baltimore Black Sox also help us consider the processes of remembering and forgetting, of storytelling and the limits of historical knowledge. Most of us know from personal experience that memory is fragile and selective. Given the sheer number and complexity of our experiences, we do not remember much because we constantly filter, prioritize, and conflate. The process demands that we forget more than we remember. It is an exaggeration to suggest that "there is no remembrance of former things," but obviously memory is fragmentary and provisional.[152] Nevertheless, we not only rely on memory, we have no choice in the matter. Memory permeates our lives; it is as important to our survival as the air we breathe.

So why remember some things and not others? Why remember the 1929 Philadelphia Athletics (as William Nack's 1996 *Sports Illustrated* article implored readers to do), but not the 1929 Baltimore Black Sox? On one level, most people do not remember or know about the Baltimore Black Sox because they were socially marginalized men, invisible to most white people

Jud Wilson, member of the 1929 Baltimore Black Sox, "looked more like a wrestler than one of the finest batters who ever lived," writes Negro League historian John Holway. "At least Satchel Paige thought he was. Paige faced Ted Williams, Stan Musial and Joe DeMaggio, but he always thought Wilson and Josh Gibson were better." In 2006, Wilson finally received widespread recognition for his ball playing accomplishments when he was inducted into the National Baseball Hall of Fame. Courtesy National Baseball Hall of Fame Library, Cooperstown, N.Y.

at the time. One cannot remember what one has never known. But even African American memories of the Baltimore Black Sox are hard to locate. This forces us to consider how ordinary, or even extraordinary, people win and keep a place in memory and history. The short answer, explains historian Alfred F. Young: "It has a lot to do with the political values of the keepers of the past—who decides whose heroes and heroines school children learn about, what statues and monuments are erected, what historic buildings are saved, and what events are commemorated."[153]

In the "Monumental City," as Baltimore is sometimes still called, there are no monuments to the Baltimore Black Sox. They are not commemorated. Their ballpark is long gone, as are the ballplayers themselves and the fans who watched and cheered them. Because the ballplayers' lives and accomplishments were poorly documented, at this remove it is extremely hard to know the Baltimore Black Sox with the precision that I would like. It is difficult to know what they did on and off the field and what they meant to others, and it is certainly challenging, even perilous, to represent those things in words, with nuance and complexity.

This brings me back to the Black Sox scandal of 1919, an event that, for all the words written about it, resists definitive historical treatment. Looking back across the years, I think that the Chicago Black Sox are in some ways the mirror image of the Baltimore Black Sox. The ballplayers' racial identities are the most obvious way this is true, but there are others. On the one hand, few events in American sport history have been as closely examined and repeatedly discussed as the 1919 World Series scandal. Conversely, the 1929 pennant-winning Baltimore Black Sox have long been overlooked, if not completely forgotten by most people. It is true, of course, that the Chicago Black Sox were involved in a national controversy that had far-reaching implications. In contrast, the Baltimore Black Sox won the inaugural pennant in a fledgling, undercapitalized league that most people did not know or care about and was an event of indeterminate local meaning. Still, it is a fascinating juxtaposition. Some ethically challenged ballplayers intentionally lost a celebrated institution, causing widespread disappointment. In the process they have become entrenched in American collective memories, and in a few instances have become folk heroes. Another group of ballplayers, suffering discrimination because of something over which they had no control, played extremely hard, with integrity, intelligence, and passion, and in the process won a championship, only to be ignored by most people and subsequently relegated to surviving, barely, in historical shadows.

I am pleased to acknowledge and thank Bob Fairbanks, Don Kyle, Irvin Nathan, Greg Pfitzer, and Joanna Zangrando for their constructive criticism of this chapter. A fellowship from the National Endowment for the Humanities supported some of this work.

NOTES

1. This chapter is a précis for a larger work-in-progress and an inquiry into the perils of writing history, the challenges that confront those who wish to know and describe the past. As is true of some of my previous work, I do not affect (at least all of the time) the authoritative, "objective" voice of a traditional historian. Trying to craft a narrative from incomplete evidence and imperfect memories is best done self-consciously. For more on the importance of being reflexive, see Douglas Booth, *The Field: Truth and Fiction in Sport History* (New York: Routledge, 2005), 211–20.

2. Nelson Algren, *Chicago: City on the Make* (New York: McGraw-Hill Book Company, [1951] 1983), 36.

3. For those unfamiliar with the Black Sox scandal, in a nutshell, several prominent White Sox ballplayers conspired with gamblers to lose the World Series to the Cincinnati Reds. Their deceit became public almost a year later in September 1920, which led team owner Charles Comiskey to suspend the accused ballplayers. Eventually, the ballplayers were indicted on a variety of conspiracy charges, but in August 1921 they were acquitted. The next day, newly appointed baseball commissioner Judge Kenesaw Mountain Landis expelled the accused men from the game. Despite several attempts by some of the ballplayers to be reinstated and to have their names cleared, Landis's ruling has never been reversed. See Eliot Asinof, *Eight Men Out: The Black Sox and the 1919 World Series* (New York: Henry Holt and Comp., [1963] 1987), and Daniel A. Nathan, *Saying It's So: A Cultural History of the Black Sox Scandal* (Urbana: University of Illinois Press, 2003).

4. "No East-West World Series This Year," *Baltimore Afro-American,* August 24, 1929, 14.

5. Robert V. Leffler Jr., "The History of Black Baseball in Baltimore from 1913 to 1951" (MA thesis, Morgan State College, 1974), 55–73; John Holway, "Baltimore's Great Black Ball Team," *Baltimore Sun,* August 28, 1977, K3; James H. Bready, *Baseball in Baltimore: The First 100 Years* (Baltimore: Johns Hopkins University Press, 1998), 164–71; James A. Riley, *The Biographical Encyclopedia of the Negro Baseball Leagues* (New York: Carroll & Graf Publishers, Inc., [1994] 2002), 49. Riley notes that a different iteration of the Black Sox existed in 1934, owned by Jack Farrell, "a black sportsman from Chester, Pennsylvania," who "appropriated the team name for his franchise and entered the Negro National League for the second half of the season."

6. Crush Holloway (with John Holway), "I Remember . . . Baseball with Baltimore's Black Sox," *The* (Baltimore) *Sun Magazine,* July 11, 1971, 2.

7. U.S. Census 1930, 22–27; Francis F. Beirne, *The Amiable Baltimoreans* (Baltimore: Johns Hopkins University Press, [1951] 1984), 271.

8. Simon Schama, *Dead Certainties (Unwarranted Speculations)* (New York: Alfred A. Knopf, 1991), 320.

9. Steven A. Riess and Donn Rogosin, "Baseball," in *Encyclopedia of African-American Culture and History,* vol. 1, ed. Jack Salzman, David Lionel Smith, and Cornel West (New York: Simon & Schuster Macmillan, 1996), 272.

10. Riess and Rogosin, "Baseball," 270.

11. Jules Tygiel, *Baseball's Great Experiment: Jackie Robinson and His Legacy* (New York: Oxford University Press, 1983), 11.

12. Quoted in Robert Peterson, *Only the Ball Was White: A History of Legendary Black Players and All-Black Professional Teams* (New York: Oxford University Press, [1970] 1992), 16–17.

13. Tygiel, *Baseball's Great Experiment,* 13.

14. David W. Zang, *Fleet Walker's Divided Heart: The Life of Baseball's First Black Major Leaguer* (Lincoln: University of Nebraska Press, 1995).

15. Lawrence D. Hogan, *Shades of Glory: The Negro Leagues and the Story of African-American Baseball* (Washington, DC: National Geographic Society, 2006), 55.

16. Leslie A. Heaphy, *The Negro Leagues, 1869–1960* (Jefferson, NC: McFarland & Company, Inc., Publishers, 2003), 14.

17. John Hope Franklin and Alfred Moss, *From Slavery to Freedom: A History of African Americans,* 8th ed. (New York: McGraw Hill, [1947] 2000), 272–91.

18. Negro Leagues had been organized in the past; the first was established in 1886 in Jacksonville, Florida, but only lasted a few games. Riess and Rogosin, "Baseball," 270–71.

19. Gerald Early, "Baseball and African American Life," in *Baseball: An Illustrated History,* ed. Geoffrey C. Ward and Ken Burns (New York: Alfred A. Knopf, 1994), 414.

20. Robert Charles Cottrell, *The Best Pitcher in Baseball: The Life of Rube Foster, Negro League Giant* (New York: New York University Press, 2001).

21. Donn Rogosin, *Invisible Men: Life in Baseball's Negro Leagues* (New York: Athenaeum, 1983), 6.

22. Rob Ruck, *Sandlot Seasons: Sport in Black Pittsburgh* (Urbana: University of Illinois Press, [1987] 1993), x–xi.

23. Janet Bruce, *The Kansas City Monarchs: Champions of Black Baseball* (Lawrence: University Press of Kansas, 1985); Ruck, *Sandlot Seasons.* On the other hand, Michael E. Lomax asserts: "While the scholarly works have agreed that black baseball served as an unifying element within the black community, the claim is more asserted than demonstrated." Lomax, "Black Baseball, Black Entrepreneurs, Black Community" (Ph.D. dissertation, Ohio State University, 1996), 10.

24. John B. Holway, *Blackball Stars: Negro League Pioneers* (New York: Carroll & Graf Publishers, Inc., [1988] 1992), 36, 47.

25. John Holway, "Blacks 268, Whites 168," *Los Angeles Times,* August 16, 1975, C1. For a useful dissenting view of the meaning of interracial exhibition baseball games, see Mark Ribowsky, *A Complete History of the Negro Leagues, 1884 to 1950* (New York: A Birch Lane Press Book, 1994), xii.

26. Gerald Early, "Why Baseball *Was* the Black National Pastime," in *Basketball Jones: America above the Rim,* ed. Todd Boyd and Kenneth L. Shropshire (New York: New York University Press, 2000), 40–41.

27. W. E. B. Du Bois, "The Talented Tenth," in *The Negro Problem: A Series of Articles by Representative Negroes of To-day* (Miami, FL: Mnemosyne Pub., [1903] 1969), 31–75.

28. Bruce, *The Kansas City Monarchs,* 32.

29. Neil Lanctot, *Negro League Baseball: The Rise and Ruin of a Black Institution* (Philadelphia: University of Pennsylvania Press, 2004), 162.

30. Bruce, *The Kansas City Monarchs,* 32.

31. Quoted in Walter R. Dean Jr., "Baseball Just Isn't the Same as Before," *Baltimore Afro-American,* August 25, 1962, feature page, 15.

32. Quoted in Ward and Burns, *Baseball: An Illustrated History,* 222.

33. Neil Lanctot, *Fair Dealing and Clean Playing: The Hilldale Club and the Development of Black Professional Baseball, 1910–1932* (Jefferson: McFarland & Company, Inc., Publishers, 1994), 93.

34. Holway, *Blackball Stars,* 31.

35. For the rest of the Negro League story—that is, the rise of new, vibrant leagues in the early 1930s, and arguably concluding with Jackie Robinson's reintegration of the major leagues in 1947—see Lanctot, *Negro League Baseball,* and Hogan, *Shades of Glory.*

36. Leffler, "The History of Black Baseball in Baltimore," ii.

37. "Fans to Have Plenty of Good Baseball," *Baltimore Afro-American Ledger,* May 3, 1913, 8.

38. *Baltimore Afro-American Ledger,* May 3, 1913, 5; July 12, 1919, 2; June 28, 1918, 2; April 25, 1919, 5.

39. Janet Bruce explains that the Kansas City Monarchs rarely experienced discrimination from white players in interracial contests "because prejudiced players usually just refused to take the field." Bruce, *The Kansas City Monarchs,* 60.

40. Leffler, "The History of Black Baseball in Baltimore," 16, 28; Bready, *Baseball in Baltimore,* 160; "Spedden No Longer Black Sox Boss," *Baltimore Afro-American,* February 12, 1927, 14. It is worth noting that there is some uncertainty about Spedden's racial identity. Several historians (Leffler, Holway, Riley, Bready, among others), list him as white; at least one (Heaphy) claims he was African American. For a time, the more I dug the more I suspected that Spedden was African American. To begin with, in the 1920s, and for many years thereafter, newspapers tended to identify people who were racially "other" than their intended readers. White papers would

write, "Joe Smith, colored, hit a home run." Black papers would do the same: "Bob Jones, white, died yesterday." But the *Baltimore Afro-American* never identifies Spedden as white, as they do George Rossiter, who later bought the team. Then I found the following entry in the 1930 U.S. Census: SPEDDEN, CHARLES P., MARYLAND, BALTIMORE, 28-WD BALTIMORE; Age: 55, Male, Race: WHITE, Born: MD; Series: T626 Roll: 871 Page: 41. This may seem dispositive; but the same census erroneously lists my grandfather's name as Solomon (it was Sol), my grandmother's place of birth as Russia (it was Poland), and my great-grandfather's occupation as a tailor (he was a carpenter).

41. For more on Sykes, see Riley, *Biographical Encyclopedia*, 757; Hogan, *Shades of Glory*, 174.

42. Lanctot, *Fair Dealing and Clean Playing*, 99; Leffler, "The History of Black Baseball in Baltimore," 16; Bready, *Baseball in Baltimore*, 160; Heaphy, *The Negro Leagues*, 34.

43. "Black Sox Incorporate," *Baltimore Afro-American*, July 29, 1921, 2.

44. Bready, *Baseball in Baltimore*, 160; Leffler, "The History of Black Baseball in Baltimore," 22; "Spedden No Longer Black Sox Boss," *Baltimore Afro-American*, February 12, 1927, 14. Leffler claims that Rossiter took over the team in the spring of 1920. However, prior to July 1921, there does not seem to have been any "controlling interest" to purchase. Additionally, in July 1921 the *Baltimore Afro-American* does not list Rossiter as one of the team's "incorporators."

45. "Spedden No Longer Black Sox Boss," *Baltimore Afro-American*, 14.

46. Hogan, *Shades of Glory*, 108.

47. "Black Sox Are Getting Ready," *Baltimore Afro-American*, March 9, 1923, 14.

48. "Baseball on Wheels," *Baltimore Afro-American*, February 29, 1924, 14; "Sox New Pullman Bus," *Baltimore Afro-American*, July 25, 1925, 7.

49. Quoted in Bill Glauber, "Powell's Records, Memory Are Key to Historic Past," *Baltimore Sun*, April 29, 1990, 13C.

50. Lanctot, *Fair Dealing and Clean Playing*, 98.

51. Peterson, *Only the Ball Was White*, 258–65.

52. Sherry H. Olson, *Baltimore: The Building of an American City*, rev. and expanded bicentennial ed. (Baltimore: Johns Hopkins University Press, [1980] 1997), 304–305.

53. Burt Solomon, *Where They Ain't: The Fabled Life and Untimely Death of the Original Baltimore Orioles, The Team That Gave Birth to Modern Baseball* (New York: The Free Press, 1999), 262.

54. Olson, *Baltimore: The Building of an American City*, 325.

55. Ibid.

56. Solomon, *Where They Ain't*, 262.

57. Mary Ellen Hayward and Charles Belfoure, *The Baltimore Rowhouse* (New York: Princeton Architectural Press, 2001), 140–59.

58. Robert J. Brugger (with the assistance of Cynthia Horsburgh Requardt, Robert I. Cottom Jr., and Mary Ellen Hayward), *Maryland, A Middle Temperament, 1634–1980* (Baltimore: Johns Hopkins University Press in association with the Maryland Historical Society, 1988), 472–75, 487.

59. Robert V. Leffler Jr., "Boom and Bust: The Elite Giants and Black Baseball in Baltimore, 1936–1951," *Maryland Historical Magazine* 87 (Summer 1992): 183.

60. Peterson, *Only the Ball Was White,* 90.

61. Daniel A. Nathan, "Bearing Witness to Blackball: Buck O'Neil, the Negro Leagues, and the Politics of the Past," *Journal of American Studies* 35 (December 2001): 453–69.

62. John H. Arnold, *History: A Very Short Introduction* (New York: Oxford University Press, 2000), 55.

63. Carl Becker, "Everyman His Own Historian," *American Historical Review* XXXVII (January 1932): 230.

64. David McGimpsey, *Imagining Baseball: America's Pastime and Popular Culture* (Bloomington: Indiana University Press, 2000), 63.

65. Daniel Rosensweig, *Retro Ball Parks: Instant History, Baseball, and the New American City* (Knoxville: University of Tennessee Press, 2005).

66. Bready, *Baseball in Baltimore,* 160.

67. Leffler, "The History of Black Baseball in Baltimore," 38.

68. Lanctot, *Fair Dealing and Clean Playing,* 100.

69. Otto Briggs, "Comments on Baseball," *Philadelphia Tribune,* April 25, 1929, 10.

70. Leffler, "The History of Black Baseball in Baltimore," 74.

71. Diane Barthel, *Historic Preservation: Collective Memory and Historical Identity* (New Brunswick, NJ: Rutgers University Press, 1996), 2–3.

72. On the lower level of the Sports Legends Museum, which is associated with the Babe Ruth Birthplace and Museum and is next to Oriole Park at Camden Yards, there is a photographic display of most of Baltimore's prominent ballparks. There is a label for Maryland Park, but no photograph.

73. Holway, "Baltimore's Great Black Ball Team," K3.

74. Riley, *Biographical Encyclopedia,* 815.

75. Ibid., 497.

76. "Marcelle and Cason Traded to Black Sox," *Philadelphia Tribune,* March 28, 1929, 11.

77. "Guards Hot Corner," *Baltimore Afro-American,* June 15, 1929, 16; Peterson, *Only the Ball Was White,* 239.

78. "They Stop'em and How," *Baltimore Afro-American,* June 1, 1929, 20.

79. Laymon Yokely (with John Holway), "I Remember Pitching Six No-hitters for the Black Sox," *The* (Baltimore) *Sun Magazine,* July 19, 1970, 2.

80. "Sox Big Gun," *Baltimore Afro-American,* May 25, 1929, 1.

81. Riley, *Biographical Encyclopedia,* 239.

82. "Boy, What an Arm," *Baltimore Afro-American,* June 29, 1929, 15.

83. Larry R. Gerlach, "Not Quite Ready for Prime Time: Baseball History, 1983–1993," *Journal of Sport History* 21 (Summer 1994): 122.

84. Peterson, *Only the Ball Was White,* 116.

85. Personal interview, Eugene Myles, June 27, 2005.

86. Karen Olson, "Old West Baltimore: Segregation, African-American Culture, and the Struggle for Equality," in *The Baltimore Book: New Visions of Local History,* ed. Elizabeth Fee, Linda Shopes, and Linda Zeidman (Philadelphia: Temple University Press, 1991), 68.

87. Olson, "Old West Baltimore," 65.

88. Philip J. Merrill and Uluaipou-O-Malo Aiono, *Baltimore* (Charleston, SC: Arcadia Publishing, 1999), 7–26.

89. Robert Leffler contends: "For blacks the Elites (and Black Sox before them) of course offered much more than entertainment, for places like Bugle Park brought pleasant escape from the embarrassments of Jim Crow. Fans could sit where they wanted to, bring food into the park, and be relieved of the name-calling that was part of a trip to an Orioles game." Leffler, "Boom and Bust," 185.

90. Peterson, *Only the Ball Was White,* 80.

91. W. Rollo Wilson, "Sport Shots," *Pittsburgh Courier,* March 9, 1929, sec. 3, 4. Also see Bill Gibson, "The Passing Review," *Baltimore Afro-American,* April 6, 1929, 13.

92. Ibid., April 27, 1929, sec. 2, 5.

93. Bill Gibson, "The Passing Review," *Baltimore Afro-American,* April 20, 1929, 17.

94. W. A. Johnson, "Heavy Artillery of Sox Nets 10–2 Win," *Baltimore Afro-American,* May 4, 1929, 14.

95. *Baltimore Afro-American,* May 18, 1929, 16; "Sox Break Even in Jousts with Lincoln Giants," *Baltimore Afro-American,* June 1, 1929, 16; "Sox Win and Lose," *Baltimore Afro-American,* June 1, 1929, 16.

96. "Grays in Auto Crash," *Baltimore Afro-American,* June 29, 1929, 14.

97. Wilson, "Sport Shots," July 6, 1929, sec. 2, 5.

98. I use the qualifier "official" because I can only document twenty-seven Black Sox games, in which they went 19–8. Compared to the *Baltimore Afro-American* and other newspapers, I am missing eight games (5–3). What happened? Why did they not make the newspapers? Where are they, and can they be located? Does it matter?

99. Gibson, "The Passing Review," July 6, 1929, 14.

100. Ibid.; July 13, 1929, 14.

101. "Red Ryan Blows up as Sox Lose First," *Baltimore Afro-American,* July 13, 1929, 14.

102. "Baltimore Wins Four; Drops Two," *Pittsburgh Courier,* July 27, 1929, sec. 2, 4.

103. S. B. Wilkins, "Sox Snare Four of Six from Poseymen," *Baltimore Afro-American,* July 27, 1929, 14.

104. "Hilldale Bent on Trouncing Locals," *Baltimore Afro-American,* July 27, 1929, 14.

105. "Local Sports," *Baltimore Afro-American,* August 3, 1929, 14.

106. *New York Amsterdam News,* September 25, 1929, 12.

107. Bready, *Baseball in Baltimore,* 164.

108. Wilson, "New American League Completes Schedule; All Loop Teams Impress," *Pittsburgh Courier,* September 28, 1929, sec. 2, 4.

109. Randy Dixon, "Sport Sidelights," *Philadelphia Tribune,* September 19, 1929, 11.

110. Hogan, *Shades of Glory,* 232.

111. Bill Gibson, "The Passing Review," *Baltimore Afro-American,* July 20, 1929, 15.

112. Ibid., August 10, 1929, 15.

113. "Race Umpires or No Baseball," *Baltimore Afro-American,* August 17, 1929, 14.

114. Larry Lester, *Baseball's First Colored World Series* (Jefferson, NC: McFarland & Company, Inc., Publishers, 2006).

115. Gibson, "The Passing Review," *Baltimore Afro-American,* August 17, 1929, 15.

116. "No East-West World Series This Year," *Baltimore Afro-American,* August 24, 1929, 14.

117. The *Kansas City Call* did not explain precisely why, and neither does Janet Bruce in *The Kansas City Monarchs.*

118. Riley, *Biographical Encyclopedia,* 843.

119. Bruce, *The Kansas City Monarchs,* 58. Interestingly, Bruce makes no specific mention of Wilkinson's decision not to play the Baltimore Black Sox in 1929.

120. *Baltimore Afro-American,* October 12, 1929, 14; "Beat Down Bisons in Fourth and Deciding Game of Series," *Kansas City Call,* October 4, 1929, np.

121. For more on black baseball in St. Louis, see Joel Walsh, "Shining Stars: The Negro Leagues in St. Louis," *Gateway: The Quarterly Magazine of the Missouri Historical Society* (Winter 2004–2005): 10–21.

122. Peterson, *Only the Ball Was White,* 267.

123. Riley, *Biographical Encyclopedia,* 765, 753, 826, 872.

124. "St. Louis Stars Blank Baltimore in Opener," *St. Louis Argus,* September 20, 1929, 7.

125. "Black Sox Win, Lose with St. Louis Nine," *Baltimore Afro-American,* September 28, 1929, 14; "Sox Win at Norfolk," *Baltimore Afro-American,* September 28, 1929, 14.

126. *Baltimore Sun,* October 15, 1928, 24; "Dixon, Charleston Shine in Victory," *Baltimore Afro-American,* October 20, 1929, 15; "Warfield Big Noise in Sox 2–1 Victory," *Baltimore Afro-American,* October 27, 1929, 14; Bill James, *The Bill James Historical Baseball Abstract* (New York: Villard Books, [1985] 1987), 657.

127. *Baltimore Afro-American,* October 12, 1929, 14.

128. William Nack, "Lost in History," *Sports Illustrated* (August 19, 1996): 74–85.

129. Bill Gibson, "Hear Me Talkin' to Ya," *Baltimore Afro-American,* September 28, 1929, 14.

130. "Charlie Smith Tops East in Hitting," *Baltimore Afro-American*, September 28, 1929, 14; "Beckwith Traded to Lincolns for Scales," *Baltimore Afro-American*, September 7, 1929, 14.

131. "Black Sox Rap Ehmke to Win 14–7 Verdict," *Baltimore Afro-American*, November 2, 1929, 15.

132. Grantland Rice, "Ehmke Hurls Mackmen to 3–1 Victory," *Baltimore Sun*, October 9, 1929, 1.

133. "Black Sox Pound Ehmke for 16 Hits to Win, 14–7," *Baltimore Sun*, October 28, 1929, 9.

134. "Black Sox Rap Ehmke to Win 14–7 Verdict," *Baltimore Afro-American*, November 2, 1929, 15.

135. Andrew M. Fearnley, "Telling Truth from Tales," *Reviews in American History* 33 (2005): 404.

136. Neither was true of the Baltimore's other prominent Negro League baseball team, the Elite Giants. In 1990, journalist Bill Glauber reported that Dick Powell, then seventy-eight years and the traveling secretary-business manager of the Giants, had scattered about his apartment all sorts of documents: "statistics, minutes of league meetings, old contracts, ticket stubs, and three tattered score books." Powell died in 2004; his daughter, Barbara Golden, is in possession of his papers. Glauber, "Powell's Records," April 29, 1990, 13C; telephone interview with Barbara Golden, March 3, 2006.

137. Yokely, "I Remember;" John Holway, "Historically Speaking Jesse Hubbard," *Black Sports* (February 1974): 18–20; Dean, "Baseball Just Isn't the Same as Before."

138. Linda Shopes, quoted in *Unlocking the Secrets of Time: Maryland's Hidden Heritage* (Baltimore: The Maryland Historical Society, 1991), 51.

139. Lawrence W. Levine, *The Unpredictable Past: Explorations in American Cultural History* (New York: Oxford University Press, 1993), 270; also see Robert M. Levine, *Insights into American History: Photographs as Documents* (Upper Saddle River, NJ: Pearson Education, 2004).

140. Hayward Farrar, *The Baltimore Afro-American, 1892–1950* (Westport, CT: Greenwood Press, 1998), 8–11.

141. James W. Carey, quoted in *Reading the News*, ed. Robert Karl Manoff and Michael Schudson (New York: Pantheon Books, 1986), 6.

142. Bready, *Baseball in Baltimore*, 166–67. Bready notes that Baltimore's white newspapers, the *Evening Sun*, the *News*, and the *Sun* sometimes "printed pregame publicity releases" for the Black Sox, but "failed to report game outcomes."

143. The *Afro-American* itself, located at 2519 North Charles Street in Baltimore, does have a hard copy of these dates, but its archives are not open to the public, and thus I was fortunate that the archivist allowed me to look at the issues in question.

144. James Wilkinson, "A Choice of Fictions: Historians, Memory, and Evidence," *Publications of the Modern Language Association* 111 (January 1996): 80.

145. These disparate authors include historian Natalie Zemon Davis and journalist Sebastian Junger. See Natalie Zemon Davis, *The Return of Martin Guerre* (Cambridge, MA: Harvard University Press, 1983); Sebastian Junger, *The Perfect Storm: A True Story of Men against the Sea* (New York: Harpertorch, [1997] 2000).

146. Laura Hillenbrand, *Seabiscuit: An American Legend* (New York: Random House, [2001] 2002), 342.

147. Ibid.

148. Nathan, *Saying It's So*, 5.

149. Crepeau, *Baseball: America's Diamond Mind*, ix.

150. Early, "Why Baseball *Was* the Black National Pastime," 39–40.

151. Rogosin, *Invisible Men*, 4.

152. Ecclesiastes 1:11, *The Oxford Annotated Bible*, ed. Herbert G. May and Bruce M. Metzger (New York: Oxford University Press), 805.

153. Alfred F. Young, *The Shoemaker and the Tea Party: Memory and the American Revolution* (Boston: Beacon Press, 1999), vii.

STEVEN A. RIESS

THE PROFITS OF MAJOR LEAGUE BASEBALL, 1900 TO 1956

The National League was formed in 1876 with the intention of putting baseball on a solid business basis. It achieved that goal in less than a decade.[1] At the turn of the century, when baseball was the unchallenged national pastime, entrepreneurs considered the future so bright that a new high-level organization was established, which called itself the American League. It proclaimed itself a major league in 1901, and merged with the NL two years later.[2] The team owners then, and for some years to come, were mainly middle-class entrepreneurs trying to make money, typically men with important political connections. Few owners were fabulously rich men for whom baseball was a pastime through which to gain social status.

This essay examines the profitability of Major League Baseball (MLB) in the period from 1900 to 1956, just before the Giants and Dodgers abandoned the lucrative New York City market for the West Coast. It will analyze the factors that went into building profits, including the size of the home city, a given team's quality, the ambiance at the ballpark and its accessibility, as well as sources of revenues and expenditures.

THE EARLY YEARS: 1900–1920

In the early twentieth century, the owners, mostly men from modest origins, made a lot of money. Major league franchises were excellent investments in the early 1900s, especially for men with influential political ties. A 1913 article in the prestigious *Independent* magazine noted, "The profits of baseball investment have proven so dazzling in the last ten years that many prominent businessmen, politicians, and capitalists have gone into the business with every promise of success."[3] This was certainly true in Chicago, which had franchises in both major leagues. The White Sox (AL) were founded and owned by Charles Comiskey, a former major league star player and manager, possibly the only magnate then who owned all his team's stock. The team benefited from a large metropolitan population and accessibility, as well as a high-quality team, second best in the AL in the 1900s, and World Champions in 1906, which produced the highest attendance in the league. He reportedly made about $850,000 by 1912.[4] The Cubs, then located on the West Side of town, were owned in the early 1900s by Albert Spalding, a former star player who had made a fortune as a sporting goods manufacturer. He sold the team in 1905 to Charles W. Murphy, a former journalist, and the club's press agent, for $105,000, although Spalding kept the ownership of West Side Ball Park. Murphy was financed by millionaire publisher Charles P. Taft, his former editor with the Cincinnati *Times-Star.* The Cubs won pennants in 1906 to 1908, including two consecutive Series titles, and made big profits, $1,260,000 between 1906 and 1915. Dividends issued from 1907 to 1913 amounted to 810 percent on the original investment; but thereafter, mismanagement and competition from the Federal League resulted in small profits. Murphy sold the team prior to the 1916 season for half a million dollars.[5]

Another big moneymaker was the New York Giants. The team was purchased in 1902 by John T. Brush, former owner of the Cincinnati Reds, for $125,000 from Tammanyite Andrew Freedman, a well-connected realtor, when they were among the worst teams in the National League. Two years later, the club won the NL pennant, set a league record with six hundred and ten thousand spectators, and made an estimated one hundred grand. The Giants followed that up with a World Championship in 1905, and became one of the best teams in baseball. This enabled them to draw one-fifth of NL attendance in the 1900s. The Giants shared New York City with the Highlanders (Yankees) and Dodgers, but they fielded weak teams and drew less than 12.5 percent of their respective league's attendance in an eight-team league. In 1920, Brush's heirs sold the team for one million dollars to Tammanyite Charles Stoneham, who operated a bucket shop, a store unaffiliated with any stock market where people dabbled in stocks and other forms of gambling.[6] One of the most important teams in this era was the Philadelphia Athletics, founded in 1901 for $30,000. Ben Shibe, a partner in A. J. Reach & Co., a sporting goods manufacturer, owned half the stock; manager Connie Mack had one-fourth, and the rest belonged to Philadelphia sportswriters, who sold their shares to Mack in 1913. According to the *Sporting News,* Mack became wealthy through baseball. He had a base salary of $15,000 by 1906, and dividends that varied from $6,000 to $37,000 as the team made $350,000 from 1902 to 1913.[7]

The A's won the World Series in 1910 and 1911, 1913, and a pennant in 1914. Historian Bruce Kuklick points out that during this span Mack learned the importance of the bottom line. He discovered that having a competitive team was essential for making money, but that a championship team might hurt profits by boring fans and raising demands for higher salaries. After the 1914 season, Mack broke up his team to help pay off his $113,000 loan to Shibe, which had enabled Connie to buy another 25 percent of the team. Historians have pointed to other reasons: the threats of several stars to jump to the rival Federal League, concerns about declining attendance, the ramifications of war in Europe, and the possibility that some players might be laying down on the team.[8]

Several popular middle brow magazines examined in depth the business of baseball in the early 1910s. Journalist Edward Mott Woolley, reporting in *McClure's,* the noted muckraking periodical, found that in 1908 the St. Louis Browns earned $168,000 on a capital investment of $80,000, while the Cardinals and Pirates of the NL were said to net $100,000 annually, and the Detroit Tigers, led by Ty Cobb, earned $343,000 from 1907 through 1911. The Tigers were soon reputedly worth $650,000 after they built their fire-resistant stadium in 1912, and made $48,000 a year from 1914 to 1918. The Cleveland Indians, who played in a city whose NL team in the late 1890s had been the worst draw in the league, with an average attendance of 145 in 1899, earned about $500,000 between 1904 and 1912. The Dodgers under Charley Ebbets had profits in the early 1910s of about $100,000, reaching $250,000 in the pennant-winning 1916 season. These profits enabled most teams between 1909 and 1915 to build $500,000 fireproof ballparks. This in turn helped them make even more money with increased capacities (averaging twenty-five thousand seats), higher ticket prices, and finer accommodations. Six teams were sold in the 1910s for an average price of $585,000, a quick and significant appreciation in value.[9]

The bulk of profits in the first decades of the century came from ticket sales and products sold to spectators. In 1910, 55.5 percent of that income came from home game ticket sales, 2.6 percent from the sale of concession privileges, and 41.9 percent from the team's share of road games. In addition, teams also made money from renting their ballpark and playing exhibition games (which, for accounting purposes, included the World Series). The biggest expenses were players' salaries (41.2 percent) and the president's salary, estimated very generously at $25,000, which became a good tax gambit, because that expense was really profit and not an expense, as the president was usually the principal stockholder. Other major expenses were ballpark maintenance, $20,000 to rent the park site, $12,000 for travel, and $24,000 for losses incurred by postponed games.[10]

Teams in this era encountered a few bumps in the road. In 1914, only half of the teams made money because of competition from the rival Federal League, which significantly hurt business. Profits were also affected by World War I, which resulted in an abbreviated 1918 season; however, prosperity returned after the war, especially in New York, where Sunday baseball was initiated in 1919.[11]

Team performance in the period 1900 to 1919 was statistically related to attendance, which is logical, because fans wanted to see winning teams. In the early 1900s, there was a significant correlation (Rs = correlation coefficient) in the American League between quality of team and attendance (Rs = 0.7619), and attendance and population (0.7381), and the strong correlation between performance on the field and attendance continued into the 1910s (0.7381). The NL also had a strong correlation between team performance and attendance in the 1900s (0.7143). In the 1910s, its big-city market teams (New York, Chicago, and Philadelphia) were first, second, and third in attendance, with significant correlations (0.7306) between performance and attendance, and population and attendance (0.7143).[12]

THE BUSINESS OF MAJOR LEAGUE BASEBALL IN THE JAZZ AGE

In baseball lore, Babe Ruth (or maybe it was Judge Landis) saved baseball from the ravages of the Black Sox scandal. Despite the ignominy of the affair, the business of baseball thrived in the 1920s. Major League Baseball's net income was at a record high until 1947, with a yearly average profit of $115,000. The profit margin (net income divided by gross operating income) was the highest ever for any decade through 1950, averaging 18.3 percent on annual gross incomes in excess of $10 million, and only slipping to 10 percent in 1928. In 1920, the net income was $2.271 million with a 23.7 percent profit margin, and the profit margin exceeded 20 percent through 1926 (except for 1924). Yet, curiously, there was a wide discrepancy between the leagues. The AL dominated profits at first, with 57 percent of all MLB revenue in 1920. Its best year was 1925 (when the Yankees came in seventh) with a record $1,459,352, not even approached until 1946, when the AL tallied $3,048,591 in profits. However, the AL fell behind the NL in 1927, when it earned only 36 percent of total ML revenue, and then just 11 percent in 1928. In 1929, the NL made $750,590 and the AL made $595,152, a 500 percent improvement over 1928.[13]

These teams were highly valuable enterprises. According to economist Michael Haupert, the average team in 1920 was worth $794,000 ($7.12 million in 2002 dollars). Team values annually rose by 5.7 percent (but lagged behind the surging Dow Downs Index of 14.8 percent). Nine teams were sold in the 1920s for an average purchase price of $1.2 million. There was a lot of owner stability as the typical magnate kept his team twelve years in the period 1923 to 1932.[14]

THE NATIONAL LEAGUE

In the 1920s, the biggest overall factor in profits was attendance, and that in turn was heavily tied to size of city and then team quality. The teams in the largest cities, New York, Brooklyn and Chicago, but not Philadelphia, had the highest box office sales. Brooklyn was a good draw in the late nineteenth century, but, since the turn of the century, did not draw its proportionate share of attendance until 1916, when it won the pennant. Then beginning in 1919 (except for 1928 and 1937), it always achieved its expected share, even when it had some pretty awful teams. The Giants from 1910 through 1942 always drew at least one-eighth of the entire NL attendance, which reflected New York's large potential fan base, and the quality of John J. McGraw's outstanding teams, which for years dominated the NL. The team's popularity continued even after McGraw retired from the team in 1933, since from 1935 through 1938 the Giants drew over 20 percent of NL attendance. The Cubs were also an excellent attraction, bringing in its proportionate share of the NL audiences from 1923 through 1939. From 1928 through 1933, the Cubs drew over 20 percent of NL crowds, topping off with 30.15 percent in 1930.[15]

Baseball was Stoneham's primary business, and he made out very well. In the 1920s, the Giants earned $1,831,431 for Stoneham and his partners, second to the small-market Pittsburgh Pirates (see Table 1). Giants benefited royally from the coming of Sunday baseball in 1919, enabling them a year later to set an NL record with 929,609 customers and make $296,803, a league high and team best until 1936. Management distributed $1.25 million in dividends in the 1920s, including $625,000 in 1926. Overall, the Giants made a 400 percent profit and were worth three million dollars at the end of 1929 (see Table 2).[16]

The Cubs were the number-one draw in the 1920s, even though they were mainly a middle of the road team until the end of the decade, and surpassed $1.4 million in profits. No other NL team drew over a million fans in a single year, which the Cubs exceeded every year between 1927 and 1932. In 1925, the Cubs became the first team to regularly broadcast home games, and at no charge to local stations, which apparently did not hurt them at the box office. This reflected owner Philip Wrigley's sense of responsibility to the community. He admitted youth free to the bleachers every Monday through Thursday, and women got in free on Friday, Ladies Day, which helped build

ABLE 1. NATIONAL LEAGUE CLUBS CONSOLIDATED PROFIT AND LOSS, 1920–1956

'ear	Boston/Milw	Brooklyn	Chicago	Cincinnati	New York	Philadelphia	Pittsburgh	St. Louis
920	($593)	$189,785	$87,969	$121,056	$296,803	$84,295	$156,052	$37,388
921	90,393	151,604	4,959	75,450	262,950	20,977	248,807	200,151
922	79,399	146,372	181,337	76,278	(13,540)	(7,420)	173,933	136,770
923	(88,844)	93,092	43,970	104,176	185,754	(18,424)	143,084	(13,919)
924	(34,111)	264,070	69,924	47,029	256,786	35,852	254,203	(48,680)
925	62,440	4,166	(20,049)	(1,000)	169,657	7,648	341,365	79,372
926	(38,966)	135,668	134,425	136,560	218,219	15,470	286,246	359,223
927	(60,756)	148,296	227,186	(7,806)	183,038	1,118	467,046	235,455
928	(24,042)	61,985	304,949	(23,299)	111,681	(32,358)	90,030	444,737
929	19,587	124,060	426,874	(203,091)	160,583	24,611	147,382	50,584
930	22,401	426,976	523,651	(17,027)	151,063	23,563	95,443	230,918
931	(16,247)	(5,308)	179,455	(161,331)	(19,630)	38,482)	89,401	345,263
932	14,094	(160,170)	56,799	(116,133)	(214,812)	100,176	(86,960)	(73,895)
933	(120,597)	(48,682)	(247,667)	(56,473)	59,416	3,184	(96,275)	(80,198)
34	(10,974)	(137,868)	(169,994)	(62,625)	101,920	13,670	(56,972)	109,229
35	(48,625)	(148,692)	135,736	47,293	199,258	1,468	45,165	61,718
36	(20,222)	(42,453)	60,953	105,545	301,870	21,256	37,087	68,025
37	(13,608)	(129,140)	99,627	29,781	331,186	(16,932)	58,838	53,074
38	(14,828)	(3,751)	32,540	157,324	28,526	(44,411)	167,100	(14,823)
39	22,400	143,637	(21,528)	335,210	94,914	(69,250)	(40,316)	89,466
40	7,309	125,221	(182,019)	270,240	(69,437)	(40,325)	(14,954)	68,190
41	(61,075)	146,794	(157,846)	123,025	45,969	(60,797)	19,615	154,557
42	(57,941)	155,451	(7,188)	4,916	54,151	(56,251)	(33,735)	63,553
43	(41,166)	(62,719)	33,009	16,503	(248,973)	6,076	56,160	105,791
44	(133,022)	3,923	69,660	30,611	53,489	(136,669)	111,112	146,417
45	(137,142)	252,721	45,554	(33,224)	339,079	(202,923)	43,942	94,826
46	39,565	412,314	510,053	192,499	(211,546)	124,563	71,799	699,093
47	229,153	519,143	278,918	207,685	529,827	64,163	39,497	630,978
48	238,104	543,201	141,128	163,632	(114,286)	(197,886)	66,071	608,663
49	147,934	642,614	211,523	73,162	(88,103)	46,757	194,899	857,553
50	(316,510)	(8,587)	(133,124)	(64,873)	(264,114)	309,579	138,220	263,202
52	(459,099)	446,102	154,793	(68,368)	(222,344)	(118,029)	(677,263)	(89,152)
53	637,718	290,006	(418,363)	15,518	(63,307)	(10,688)	(421,422)	(702,193)
54	457,110	209,979	(72,014)	24,198	395,725	(256,306)	(198,920)	(589,382)
55	807,395	427,195	68,684	53,145	151,113	(270,671)	(601,846)	(43,142)
6	414,398	487,462	(159,712)	301,216	81,415	(78,063)	(47,852)	329,495

te: No data available for 1951.

oklyn Dodgers and Pittsburgh Pirates profits include associated real estate companies.

ston moved to Milwaukee in 1953.

entheses indicate net loss.

ırce: U.S. Congress, House Judiciary Committee, *Organized Baseball, Hearings before the Subcommittee on Study of nopoly Power,* 82nd Cong., 1st Sess., 1951, serial 1, part 6 (Washington, DC: Government Printing Office, 1952), 1600.

up future fandom. The chewing gum king spent generously on his team, investing some $400,000 for new talent before the 1929 season, which paid off with the Cubs first pennant since 1918. The team set a major league attendance record of 1,485,166, and made $426,874, with a profit margin of 11.3 percent. The team that year was valued at $4 million.[17]

The Dodgers, who put a poor product on the field, coming in seventh overall in the 1920s, even with a pennant in 1920 and a second place in 1924, was the third biggest draw in the NL (14.98 percent). The Dodgers in the championship season drew 808,722, earning $189,785, second only to the Giants, and in 1924 earned a league leading $264,070. The following season, Ebbets claimed the team was worth $3 million. Overall, the Dodgers averaged $131,909 annually in profits and paid out over $700,000 in dividends in the 1920s (see table 2).[18]

Yet attendance was not everything when it came to making money. Pittsburgh, the second smallest city in the NL, was actually the most profitable, earning $2,308,148 in the 1920s and declared $708,700 in dividends. The Pirates had a 14 percent share of NL attendance with a solid club that never finished out of the first division. In 1925, the pennant-winning squad set a record season-high attendance of 804,254 and a profit mark of $341,365, with dividends of $166,445. In 1927, the Pirates clinched the pennant on the next to the last day of the season, compiling a 94–60 record, and the excitement helped generate a new attendance record of 869,720. The club made $467,046, an NL record, and distributed $171,000 in dividends. The good times were short lived, though, because the club made over $100,000 only five times through 1956, and never even reached $200,000.[19]

The Cardinals found a way to make money even though they were the fifth best draw in the NL in the 1920s; they only drew their proportionate share of attendance six times from 1916 through 1941. St. Louis was the sixth largest city in the United States with a population of 772,897, but had to share the local market with the Browns (AL), who were the fan favorites in the early 1920s, outdrawing the Cards in five of the first six years of the 1920s. The principal owner was wealthy car dealer Sam Breadon who slowly bought up the team's stock, and by 1923, owned 78 percent of the shares at below market value because the franchise was heavily in debt. He had demoted the prior team president Branch Rickey to vice president, but also made him general manager, and together they dominated the team's board of directors. The hundreds of minor stockholders did not press for dividends, which made it easier for Breadon and Rickey to reinvest any profits and build up their newly created minor league system. The reinvigorated franchise quickly paid off

TABLE 2. NATIONAL LEAGUE DIVIDENDS, 1920–1956

Year	*Boston/Milw*	*Brooklyn*	*Chicago*	*Cincinnati*	*New York*	*Philadelphia*	*Pittsburgh*	*St. Louis*	*Total*
1920	(1)	(1)	0	(1)	0	0	$17,000	0	$17,000
1921	(1)	(1)	$69,965	(1)	$25,000	$30,000	17,000	0	141,965
1922	0	(1)	23,988	(1)	25,000	30,000	27,200	0	106,188
1923	0	$40,000	47,976	(1)	0	0	52,000	$28,317.5	168,294
1924	0	80,000	0	(1)	125,000	0	30,000	0	245,000
1925	0	50,000	0	(1)	125,000	20,000	167,000	0	362,000
1926	0	100,000	100,000	(1)	625,000	20,000	112,000	0	957,000
1927	0	225,000	100,000	(1)	125,000	0	171,000	28,317.5	549,318
1928	0	125,000	0	0	100,000	0	95,.500	50,800	429,000
1929	0	184,000	100,000	0	125,000	0	20,000	0	471,300
1930	0	175,000	100,000	0	312,500	0	20,000	50,800	718,300
1931	0	75,000	160,000	0	0	0	20,000	101,600	366,600
1932	0	50,000	170,000	$1,122.5	100,000	0	20,000	0	341,123
1933	0	0	170,000	830	0	0	20,000	0	130,830
934	0	0	110,000	0	100,000	0	20,000	101,520	221,520
935	0	0	0	0	124,500	0	20,000	101,520	276,020
936	0	0	30,000	0	305,693	0	27,550	121,824	495,067
937	0	0	40.000	0	258,522	0	46,425	81,216	446,163
938	0	0	60,000	0	82,257	0	114,375	0	196,632
939	0	0	0	108,620	23,502	0	27,550	101,520	261,192
940	0	0	0	84,770	0	0	20,000	71,064	175,834
941	0	0	0	42,770	11,751	0	20,000	101,520	176,041
942	0	0	0	18,770	47,004	0	20,000	20,304	106,078
943	0	21,000	0	24,770	0	0	20,000	30,456	96,226
944	0	0	0	30,770	0	0	52,850	30,456	114,076
945	0	0	0	12,770	94,008	0	42,650	0	149,428
946	0	0	0	39,770	23,502	0	10,000	71,064	194,336
947	0	0	50,000	42,770	23,502	0	0	670,032	816,304
948	0	49,000	80,000	36,770	70,506	0	0	0	236,276
949	0	24,500	0	21,770	23,502	0	0	0	69,772
950	0	99,750	0	14,270	23,502	0	16,000	0	153,522
952	0	0	0	14,270	0	0	0	0	14,270
953	0	0	0	14,270	0	0	0	0	14,270
954	0	0	0	24,270	70,506	0	0	0	94,776
955	0	0	0	30,770	47,004	0	0	0	77,774
956	0	0	0	60,770	0	0	0	0	60,770
otal	0	1,308,250	1,391,929	624,953	3,016,761	100,000	1,246,100	1,762,331	9,450,324

ote: No data available for 1951.

). No data available.

ource: U.S. Congress, House Judiciary Committee, *Organized Baseball, Hearings before the Subcommittee on Study of onopoly Power,* 82nd Cong., 1st Sess., 1951, serial 1, part 6 (Washington, DC: Government Printing Office, 1952), 1601; U.S. ongress, House Judiciary Committee, Subcommittee on Study of Monopoly Power, *Organized Professional Team Sports, earings before the Antitrust Subcommittee,* 85th Cong., 1st Sess., June 17–August 8, 1957, serial 8, part 1 (Washington, DC: overnment Printing Office, 1957), 352.

its debts and became quite profitable, mainly from the $600,000 pulled in from four World Series (1926, 1928, 1930, 1931). The team made nearly $360,000 in the world championship 1926 season, and peaked at $444,737 in the pennant-winning 1928 season. Overall, the Cards in the 1920s made $1,430,487, nearly double their cross-town rivals, the Browns, whose park they had used since 1920. Rickey got a lot of credit for their success. He was a great evaluator of talent, who built up his club even before the farm system, which in 1929 had only five teams, really got going.[20]

The teams at the bottom of the heap were the Boston Braves, Philadelphia Phillies, and the Cincinnati Reds. The Reds were in the smallest major league market, and finished sixth in attendance, although tied with the Cubs for fourth place in the pennant races. They were a going concern in the early 1920s, but lost money each year from 1927 through 1929, including $203,091 in 1929, the only team in the NL to finish in the red that season. The Reds ended the decade up $325,353.[21]

The Phils were the biggest underachiever, operating in the nation's third largest city with a population of 1.8 million. From 1918, they did not attain their fair share of attendance until 1950 when they won the pennant. They did not even get 9 percent of the NL attendance until 1943. The Phillies were the second team in Philadelphia, but more importantly, suffered from terrible ownership and awful teams, with an average finish of 7.35 in the 1920s. The Phillies were the worst draw in the league, with an average attendance of 266,000, but paid their bills and brought in $131,769.[22]

As poor as the Phillies were, they did better than the Braves, who earned all of $4,507 in the 1920s, which included six years in the red. The team's on-field performance reached its all-time low from 1922 to 1924 when the club annually dropped over one hundred games. Besides the poor play, the Braves had to compete with the Red Sox in the smallest city that had two teams, both of which were poorly supported. Attendance was dreadful, bottoming at 4.03 percent of NL audiences in 1920. Between 1916 and 1946, the Braves achieved a proportionate share of attendance only in 1932 and 1933. The team broke even because of revenue from concessions and the rental of Braves Field for football games. During all these years the Braves never once issued dividends.[23]

AMERICAN LEAGUE

In the AL, the Yankees, a franchise that struggled on the field and at the cash register in the early 1900s, turned the corner in 1919 and went on to become the dominant financial force in the game. This reflected their huge population base, outstanding play, and, in 1923, the biggest ballpark in MLB. The Yankees led the league in attendance every year in the decade, and had at least 20 percent of all AL attendance from 1920 through 1933, except for 1925 when Babe Ruth was injured. Owners beer baron Jacob Ruppert and businessman Col. Tillinghast Huston bought the team in 1915 for $460,000 from Bill Devery, the former police chief, and Frank Farrell, the city's gambling kingpin, who had done a terrible job running the squad. When they sold the team it was over $300,000 in debt and had nearly no liquid resources. The new owners struggled at first, losing $30,000 in their first five years, and did not even take a salary until 1919, when the Yankees made nearly $107,000. Ruppert and Huston introduced a new management style to baseball, leaving their general manager and field manager to run the franchise, while the independently wealthy owners invested heavily in the team, putting all profits in the 1920s back into the team to build a winner, which was more important to them than profits. They used their funds wisely to bring in such great players as Babe Ruth and Lou Gehrig. They hired Miller Huggins as manager, and he led the club to six pennants (1921 to 1923, 1926 to 1928), and three world championships (1923, 1927, 1928).[24]

The presence of great teams and the accessibility of the Polo Grounds, and then Yankee Stadium in the nation's biggest city, brought in huge crowds. The Yankees drew 18.27 percent of AL attendance from 1921 to 1930, followed by Chicago (16.6 percent) and Detroit (16.19 percent). The Yankees big upward bump actually began in war-shortened 1918, when the team drew 16.51 percent, solidified the following year when attendance reached 619,164, with the coming of Sunday baseball and a third-place finish. Then in 1920, the team set a MLB record 1,289,422 (and a team record that lasted until 1946), drawing one-fourth of the AL's attendance. The gate was $860,000. The big new attraction was right fielder, Babe Ruth, who hit an astounding fifty-four home runs. The Yankees earned a MLB record profit of $373,862 (see table 3). Economic historian Robert Burk has estimated Ruth's presence as worth at least $200,000 a year to the Bronx Bombers.[25]

In the 1920s, the Yankees drew over one million fans eight times and Detroit was the only AL team to reach that mark even once. The Yankees made $3,272,214 in the 1920s, a return that exceeded the stock market returns. In 1923, Yankee Stadium was opened with the largest seating capacity in baseball, and it was an important factor in the team's profit margin. The stadium brought in an average of $129,101 a year outside of Yankee games, mainly from its rental for college football and boxing. Intercollegiate matches in 1927 to 1930 produced an average return of $109,969, peaking in 1928

TABLE 3. AMERICAN LEAGUE CLUBS CONSOLIDATED PROFIT AND LOSS, 1920–1956

Year	*Boston*	*Chicago*	*Cleveland*	*Detroit*	*New York*	*Philadelphia/KC*	*St. Louis/Baltimore*	*Washington*
1920	(1)	$155,671	$314,836	$111,762	$373,862	$63,291	$125,541	$153,608
1921	(1)	93,642	289,080	120,529	226,237	42,512	63,687	133,410
1922	(1)	111,829	65,712	239,854	294,387	64,327	260,498	75,134
1923	($37,258)	90,465	126,006	214,106	451,116	46,169	79,818	33,167
1924	(15,867)	102,216	66,188	297,369	288,616	18,994	162,850	231,037
1925	2,573	200,057	68,564	204,529	69,332	313,036	192,515	408,746
1926	(56,327)	139,613	88,091	193,703	472,123	138,646	49,954	95,573
1927	(41,321)	20,351	(73,302)	151,237	531,586	(7,710)	(709)	90,222
1928	(59,096)	100,898	(126,726)	(85,150)	293,927	88,842	(126,606)	33,106
1929	(35,053)	10,750	(22,556)	123,184	271,028	276,483	5,251	(43,935)
1930	7,674	15,473	27,952	75,348	244,734	162,542	(87,152)	56,808
1931	(71,717)	(135)	(38,482)	(42,228)	25,457	109,123	(103,084)	(28,343)
1932	(83,754)	(244,319)	(120,754)	(61,553)	(31,527)	10,023	(109,872)	(76,634)
1933	(537,004)	(156,288)	(132,427)	(84,566)	(98,126)	(21,047)	(33,559)	(501)
1934	(113,819)	(208,163)	33,978	378,562	36,810	(139,174)	(54,937)	20,382
1935	(204,877)	8,802	35,708	521,202	(103,610)	(4,059)	572	18,247
1936	(229,708)	(5,323)	71,465	204,709	328,322	(41,694)	(159,202)	30,019
1937	(251,894)	8,707	104,996	181,595	285,246	(1,922)	(107,998)	(85,513)
1938	(165,249)	(88,967)	147,522	115,361	365,232	(50,595)	(119,712)	94,803
1939	(106,858)	16,739	95,910	57,101	382,501	(42,940)	(124,792)	1,759
1940	(84,297)	40,790	169,292	194,320	136,548	(55,862)	27,963	56,189
1941	57,342	63,866	60,639	(6,568)	237,621	4,898	(141,842)	(11,358)
1942	28,343	(55,251)	35,775	1,966	136,567	(44,198)	80,855	42,526
1943	(312,417)	24,423	27,873	132,046	(88,521)	(28,255)	45,375	46,631
1944	(43,131)	61,295	86,803	207,043	151,043	(6,133)	285,034	90,429
1945	(30,287)	102,237	108,737	191,755	200,959	(17,026)	30,452	222,473
1946	405,133	291,262	375,679	467,283	808,866	82,709	260,225	357,414
1947	(95,109)	209,264	318,801	196,750	846,737	129,809	303,170	457,195
1948	(202,875)	69,106	499,819	255,146	516,476	233,258	156,783	261,020
1949	21,257	102,554	506,218	33,229	346,806	90,306	83,482	(18,323)
1950	(100,992)	65,363	458,694	112,638	497,000	(315,921)	42,957	5,117
1952	(342,014)	65,052	204,088	(26,265)	223,943	(51,437)	(329,637)	58,471
1953	(421,276)	204,720	157,288	43,639	622,185	(102,461)	(706,998)	26,607
1954	3,086	202,897	583,283	86,465	174,876	(217,936)	643,407	48,800
1955	242,901	201,631	89,756	257,191	121,852	28,214	(86,715)	4,222
1956	122,032	141,089	(167,110)	81,591	301,483	1,657	69,307	23,218

Note: No data available for 1951.

St. Louis Browns profits include associated real estate companies. St. Louis Browns became the Baltimore Orioles in 1954 and Philadelphia Athletics became the Kansas City Athletics in 1955.

Parentheses indicate net loss.

Source: U.S. Congress, House Judiciary Committee, *Organized Baseball, Hearings before the Subcommittee on Study of Monopoly Power,* 82nd Cong., 1st Sess., 1951, serial 1, part 6 (Washington, DC: Government Printing Office, 1952), 1601; U.S. Congress, House Judiciary Committee, Subcommittee on Study of Monopoly Power, *Organized Professional Team Sports, Hearings before the Antitrust Subcommittee,* 85th Cong., 1st Sess., June 17–August 8, 1957, serial 8, part 1 (Washington, DC: Government Printing Office, 1957), 353.

at $140,612. Boxing brought in $70,629 a year, with a high of $124,451 in 1927.[26]

The second most profitable American League team was the Tigers, whose booming city was the fourth in population in 1920. The team was second in attendance in the league, which helped the team make $1,571,123 in the 1920s, with $750,000 in dividends (see table 4). The team generally finished in the middle of the pack, but the Tigers had a big and growing fan base that rooted for superstar Ty Cobb and outfielder Harry Heilmann, who won four batting championships in the decade.

The Washington Senators in the 1920s were owned by Clark Griffith, a former star ballplayer. He managed the team from 1912, when he bought a 10 percent share in the team for $27,500, making him the largest single stockholder, until 1920. He secured a majority share after the 1919 season with the help of exporter William Richardson and a $100,000 bank loan. The team historically had the lowest attendance in the AL, but turned things around in the 1920s, which was their finest era. The Senators had the second best team in the AL in these years, and their share of AL attendance rose to 10.63 percent. Under kid skipper Bucky Harris and superstar hurler Walter Johnson, they took the World Series in 1924 and the pennant the following year. In 1924, the team made $231,037 with a team record attendance of 584,310. These profits enabled Griffith to move into a large home near Washington's Embassy Row. In 1925, the excited fans set a team attendance record of 817,199 that lasted until 1946. Overall in the 1920s, the team made $1,210,068, and paid an average of $58,750 a year in dividends, including $317,000 in 1925 when the club made $408,746. The Senators of the 1920s were not the Senators later memorialized in the quip: "First in War, First in Peace, and Last in the American League."[27]

The Philadelphia Athletics, who had come in last from 1915, when Mack broke up his team, through 1921, rebuilt in the early 1920s. They finally broke out of the second division in 1925 by coming in second, the team's first winning season since 1914. The fans poured out to see the revived team, and the A's led the AL in attendance with 869,703, a team record until 1947, and earned a franchise record $313,036. The roster included future Hall of Famers Al Simmons, Mickey Cochrane, and Lefty Grove. From 1925 through 1933, the team never finished worse than third, with four second-place finishes, and three pennants, and at least ninety victories through 1932. The fans loved their Athletics, and made them second in attendance five times from 1926 through 1931. In 1928, the A's went 98–55 (.641), and were the second best team in MLB after the Yankees. They then dominated the majors

TABLE 4. AMERICAN LEAGUE DIVIDENDS, 1920–1956

Year	*Boston*	*Chicago*	*Cleveland*	*Detroit*	*New York*	*Philadelphia/KC*	*St. Louis/Balt.*	*Washington*	*Total*
1920	(2)	0	$186,350	$100,000	0	0	0	$20,000	$306,350
1921	(2)	0	124,225	50,000	0	0	0	10,000	184,225
1922	0	0	0	50,000	0	$100,000	$240,000	20,000	410,000
1923	0	0	99,400	50,000	0	50,000	40,000	0	239,400
1924	0	0	59,640	50,000	0	50,000	40,000	80,000	279,640
1925	0	0	49,700	100,000	0	0	42,000	317,600	509,300
1926	0	0	99,400	100,000	0	50,000	0	39,500	288,900
1927	0	0	0	100,000	0	0	0	79,000	179,000
1928	0	0	0	0	0	50,000	0	19,650	69,650
1929	0	0	0	150,000	0	50,000	0	0	200,000
1930	0	0	0	50,000	0	0	0	39,300	89,300
1931	0	0	1250	0	0	250,050	0	0	251,300
1932	0	0	250	0	0	0	0	0	250
1933	0	0	0	0	0	0	0	00	0
1934	0	0	2,500	0	0	0	0	0	2,500
1935	0	0	2,750	200,000	$100,000	0	0	0	302,750
1936	0	0	18,144	200,000	420,000	0	0	19,650	657,794
1937	0	0	84,000	0	0	0	0	0	84,000
1938	0	0	60,500	0	0	0	0	38,900	99,400
1939	0	0	2,450	0	0	0	0	0	2,450
1940	0	0	20,250	0	0	0	0	19,450	39,700
1941	0	$37,500	20,250	0	130,000	0	0	0	187,750
1942	0	0	4,050	0	0	0	0	0	4,050
1943	0	0	20,250	0	0	0	0	19,400	39,650
1944	0	0	24,300	0	0	0	0	19,400	43,700
1945	0	0	40,500	0	0	0	0	38,800	79,300
1946	0	74,500	202,500	0	0	0	137,500	77,600	492,100
1947	0	0	0	0	0	0	0	77,600	77,600
1948	0	0	16,875	0	0	0	0	77,600	94,475
1949	0	74,500	112,500	0	0	0	0	0	225,800
1950	0	0	0	0	0	0	0	38,800	38,800
1952	0	0	0	0	0	0	0	58,200	58,200
1953	0	74,500	3,000	0	0	0	0	38,200	38,200
1954	0	0	12,780	0	0	0	0	18,925	31,705
1955	0	0	12,780	100,000	0	0	0	18,925	131,705
1956	0	7,450	0	50,000	0	0	0	0	57,450
Total	0	268,450	1,280,594	1,350,000	650,000	600,050	499,500	1,224,040	5,796,39

Note: No data available for 1951.

Source: U.S. Congress, House Judiciary Committee, *Organized Baseball, Hearings before the Subcommittee on Study of* Monopoly Power, 82nd Cong., 1st Sess., 1951, serial 1, part 6 (Washington, DC: Government Printing Office, 1952), 1600; U.S. Senate, House Judiciary Committee, *Organized Professional Team Sports: Hearings before the Subcommittee on Antitrust and Monopoly of the Committee of the Judiciary*, 85th Cong., 2nd Sess. (Washington, DC: Government Printing Office, 1958), 651.

with three straight hundred-victory seasons and three world championships. In 1929, the A's carried the second highest payroll in the AL, and fourth highest in MLB ($255,231), and still ended up making $276,483. Overall, from 1921 through 1930, they were slightly better than average in attendance (13.21), earning $1,182,628, with dividends of $350,000.[28]

The White Sox, decimated by the Black Sox scandal, were still quite profitable, making $1,025,312 in the Roaring Twenties. Comiskey spent liberally, but unsuccessfully, to rebuild the team, which typically finished in sixth place. Yet the loyal South Side fans kept turning out, standing by the "Noble Roman." The Cleveland Indians, playing in the fifth largest market made $795,893 in the 1920s, over three-fourths of which came in 1920 when they won the World Series and the following season, when the fans still felt a lot of euphoria.

The St. Louis Browns were seventh in attendance in the 1920s, as they had been in the 1910s, but still made $812,799. Historically mired in the second division, the Browns peaked in the early 1920s. In 1922, they missed the pennant by just one game (93–61), setting their all-time attendance record of 712,918, earned a record profit of $260,498, and distributed $240,000 in dividends. The club led the AL in both batting (.313) and ERA (3.38). MVP first baseman George Sisler hit .420 with 246 hits, while teammate Ken Williams led the league in homers with thirty-nine and total bases with 367. The Browns had another $122,000 in dividends over the next three years, but there were no more dividends until 1946 when the stockholders shared $137,500.[29]

The Boston Red Sox were at the bottom of the dotted line. There are no team records for the early 1920s, but owner Harry Frazee reportedly made money in each of his seven years of ownership. Then in 1923, he sold the team for $1.3 million. The 1920s Sox finished last every year except 1924, when the club made it to seventh. This was a huge deterioration from its outstanding clubs in the 1910s when the team was one of the finest in the major leagues. Boston's poor play helped keep it under 10 percent of AL attendance from 1921 until 1935. In 1929, when Sunday ball was finally introduced to Bean Town, its share of attendance rose from 6.62 percent to 9.40 percent, the highest since 1920. Between 1923 and 1941, Boston ended up barely in the black in 1925 ($2,573) and 1930 ($7,674). The team lost $242,349 from 1923 through 1929 when every other MLB team made money, and it never declared a dividend through the mid-1950s.[30]

In 1929, 87.6 percent of all MLB revenue came from baseball games; this included 62.4 percent from home games, 21.1 percent from road games, and 4.2 percent from exhibition games and World Series receipts. The remaining revenue came from concessions (5.5 percent) and "other" (6.9 percent), which included rentals of ballparks for such events as boxing matches and football games. The typical team devoted 35.3 percent of expenditures to salaries for players, coaches, and managers ($140,000), 10.3 percent to subsidize their minor league farm system, 1.4 percent for their minor league teams' operating losses, 8.9 percent to buy contracts, 1.8 percent on income taxes, and 52.6 percent for other expenses.[31]

In the 1920s, there was an extremely strong correlation between AL attendance and size of city (Rs = 0.8095), a solid association between profits and population (0.6429), but none between performance and overall attendance. The NL had a weaker correlation between attendance and size of city (Rs = 0.619), but there was virtually no relationship between size of city and profits or attendance and profits; however, there was an extremely strong correlation between profits and success on the playing field (Rs = 0.8264). This suggests that good teams could make money from sources other than the regular-season gate, such as the Pirates revenue from World Series appearances and the Cardinals development of a farm system.

DEPRESSION ERA BASEBALL

The baseball business was booming at the end of the Roaring Twenties, and continued into 1930, the first year of the Depression, with high attendances, big profits, and large salaries (see tables 5 and 6). In 1929, the Yankees and Cubs both had payrolls that exceeded $300,000. The Bambino was making $80,000, stars were earning between $15,000 and $25,000, and the average big leaguer made about $5,300. In 1929 and 1930, MLB teams made $1.36 million and $1.965 million in 1929 and 1930, respectively, with profit margins of 11.3 percent and 16.4 percent. The NL alone made $750,590 in 1929 and nearly doubled a year later to $1,461,988, the highest of any league until 1946. The AL in 1929 made $585,152, a 500 percent improvement over 1928, but dropped a year later to $503,019. The NL made $718,300 in dividends, second highest for any league until 1946.[32]

The Depression hit the economy forcefully soon after the Great Crash, but came later to baseball. When millions of people were losing their jobs, one of the last things they gave up were their diversions so they could temporarily escape the bad times. As historian Charles Alexander points out, major league baseball was more popular than ever at the gate, and financially sound. According to *Baseball Magazine,* the sport seemed to be "an impregnable industry . . . strongly entrenched and . . . vitally necessary to the public welfare."[33]

Opening Day in 1931 drew a record 247,162, including 80,403 at Yankee Stadium. According to Fred Lieb of the *New York Evening Post*, "Perhaps the public is tired of talking depression and welcomes the opportunity to change the conversation to Babe Ruth's homers, Bill Terry's quest for new batting championships and Babe Herman's antics in the outfield." The *Chicago Herald and Examiner* was certain that "no one in the crowd at the opening game was aware that any area of depression existed within a thousand miles of the baseball park." Attendances, however, dropped 17 percent and MLB teams earned just $217,000, a profit margin of 2.3 percent.[34]

In 1931, NL teams earned $373,121, but only St. Louis, Chicago, and Pittsburgh finished in the black, yet the owners issued $366,600 in dividends. Cubs attendance of 990,000 was down by over half a million from the prior season. The Cards drew only 333,000, barely more than their Columbus farm team, yet made over $345,000, double the Cubs who were second. The AL lost $149,409, with only Philadelphia and New York in the black. The A's made $109,123, and were the only team to declare a significant dividend ($250,050). Owners began to lower salaries and cut rosters by two men. The full depression hit MLB in 1932 when the NL lost $482,900, the first time it was in the red since accurate statistics were gathered, and the AL lost $718,390. An average team's gross operating expenses then were about $471,000.[35]

The AL had four straight losing seasons (1931 through 1934), including a loss of $1,063,518 in 1933, by far the largest loss of a league in MLB history. The NL lost $587,292, which came to a combined deficit of $1,650,810 (equivalent to a negative margin of 23.9 percent). The NL lost heavily from 1932 to 1935, which was tied to a 40 to 45 percent drop in attendance since 1929. MLB in four years lost $2,925,354, but returned to the black in 1936. Profit margins, starting in 1936 through 1942, averaged 4.4 percent.[36]

Baseball held up better than most recreations during the Depression. Between 1929 and 1933, most entertainment sales dropped to 47 percent, but baseball only dropped to 68 percent, exceeded only by the movies, which maintained 72 percent of their business. Baseball recovered relatively rapidly in the second half of the depression (1935 to 1939), and enjoyed a higher profit margin than the movies, although it was a much smaller industry.[37]

NATIONAL LEAGUE

The NL's most profitable team during the Depression was the New York Giants, who were second in attendance and in performance. They made $1,033,711, and paid out $1,008,348 in dividends, which meant they were not

TABLE 5. CONDENSED PROFIT-AND-LOSS STATEMENTS, NATIONAL LEAGUE, 1929

	Boston	*Brooklyn*	*Chicago*	*Cincinnati*	*New York*	*Philadelphia*	*Pittsburgh*	*St. Louis*
Games at home	$253,357	$576,501	$1,285,894	$241,778	$700,144	$181,284	—	$320,36
Games away	124,474	308,781	188,585	138,279	147,389	148,255	—	170,333
Exhibition games	2,462	4,751	62,022	11,092	31,473	22,190	—	18,988
Radio	0	0	0	0	0	0	—	0
Concessions (net)	13,315	46,037	132,162	37,000	87,578	5,000	—	41,211
Gross operating income	461,649	796,328	1,668,520	449,189	1,077,594	357,736	$855,317	601,054
Gross operating expenses	485,262	586,553	849,761	544,110	828,646	318,525	629,693	508,814
Net operating income	(23,813)	209,775	818,759	(94,941)	248,948	39,211	225,624	92,239
Cost of player contracts	(43,000)	76,900	301,600	108,150	71,297	14,600	59,850	(17,80
Net income before taxes	19,587	132,875	517,159	(203,091)	177,651	24,611	165,774	110,03
Farm losses	0	0	32,900	0	0	0	0	44,974
Consolidated net income before taxes	19,587	132,875	484,259	(203,091)	177,651	24,611	165,774	65,065
Income taxes	0	8,815	57,385	0	17,068	0	18,392	14,481
Consolidated net income	19,587	124,060	426,874	(203,091)	160,583	24,611	147,382	50,584
Dividends	0	184,000	100,000	0	125,000	0	171,000	0
Retained earnings	19,587	(59,940)	326,874	(203,091)	35,583	24,611	(23,818)	50,584

Note: (1) No data is available.

Affiliated baseball real estate companies of Brooklyn and Pittsburgh are consolidated with parent clubs.

Source: U.S. Congress, House Judiciary Committee, *Organized Baseball, Hearings before the Subcommittee on Study of Monopoly Power,* 82nd Cong., 1st Sess., 1951, serial 1, part 6 (Washington, DC: Government Printing Office, 1952), 1606.

reinvesting in the team. On top of that, owner-president Charles A. Stoneham paid himself a princely $45,000 salary. The Giants lost money ($214,813) only in 1932, the year when the team came in seventh and McGraw resigned as manager. The team rebounded the next year to win the World Series, led by hall of famers Carl Hubbell and Bill Terry. The squad made $59,416 in a year when only one other team broke even. From 1933 through 1937, the club won at least ninety games, as well as pennants in 1936 and 1937. The Giants earned a team record $301,870 in 1936, and topped that a year later at $331,186. In 1939, the team found a new source of profit in radio broadcasts, worth $110,000, double the league average ($57,063), at a time when a little over 7 percent of MLB revenues came from broadcasting (see table 7).[38]

ABLE 6. CONDENSED PROFIT-AND-LOSS STATEMENTS, NATIONAL LEAGUE, 1939

	Boston	*Brooklyn*	*Chicago*	*Cincinnati*	*New York*	*Philadelphia*	*Pittsburgh*	*St. Louis*
ames at home	$190,779	$752,523	$562,201	$915,238	$542,453	$185,240	$350,224	$301,386
ames away	129,303	134,353	193,858	182,879	142,029	96,867	138,204	151,315
xhibition games	15,314	43,068	50,457	109,819	24,744	7,941	5,812	24,581
adio	45,000	87,500	41,000	27,500	110,000	96,500	66,000	33,000
oncessions (net)	22,889	73,899	76,564	309,001	91,169	10,935	77,237	71,955
ross operating come	408,926	1,159,195	910,669	1,345,615	1,067,372	348,388	660,568	636,320
ross operating penses	412,586	767,933	810,460	693,857	903,897	367,688	591,209	563,450
et operating come	(3,660)	391,362	100,209	651,758	163,475	(19,300)	69,309	72,871
st of player ntracts	(51,350)	232,050	121,737	167,250	133,817	49,950	104,800	19,250
et income before xes	47,890	159,312	(21,528)	484,508	29,658	(69,250)	(35,491)	53,621
rm losses	19,287	14,833	0	80,730	(80,600)	0	0	(58,197)
nsolidated net come before taxes	28,403	144,679	(21,528)	423,778	110,258	(69,250)	(35,991)	109,818
come taxes	6,003	1,042	0	88,568	15,344	0	4,825	20,352
nsolidated net come	22,400	143,637	(21,528)	335,210	94,914	(69,250)	(40,316)	89,466
vidends	0	0	0	108,620	23,502	0	27,550	101,520
tained earnings	22,400	143,637	(21,528)	226,590	71,412	(89,250)	(67,886)	(12, 054)

te. Affiliated real estate companies of Brooklyn and Pittsburgh are consolidated with parent club. Spring training receipts t included for Pittsburgh exhibition games.

urce: U.S. Congress, House Judiciary Committee, *Organized Baseball, Hearings before the Subcommittee on Study of* onopoly Power, 82nd Cong., 1st Sess., 1951, serial 1, part 6 (Washington, DC: Government Printing Office, 1952), 1607.

The Cards earned $788,777 and paid out $558,400 in dividends in the thirties. Capturing the World Series in 1931 and 1934, they had the third best record in the NL, but only the fifth best attendance. They earned a lot of money from player sales from their vast minor league farm system, including $144,700 in 1934 alone. The general manager, Branch Rickey, was the highest paid executive in baseball during the Depression, with a $35,000 salary, plus $14,470 in bonuses from 10 percent of all Cardinals player sales. He surpassed Commissioner Kenesaw M. Landis, who took a voluntary paycut in 1933 from $65,000 to $40,000. Cardinals president-owner Sam Breadon drew an $18,000 salary in 1934, raised to $25,000 a year later. By the early 1940s, Rickey was making about $80,000 (including bonus).[39]

The third most profitable team was the Cubs who won pennants in 1932, 1935, and 1938, which helped bring in the NL's largest attendance, even as fans enjoyed free radio broadcasts. The Cubs made $649,572 in the 1930s, most of it coming in 1930 ($523,651), the year after they had won their first pennant in more than a decade. The profits that season comprised an NL record until 1946, and had only previously been surpassed by the 1927 Yankees of Murderer's Row fame. Despite the Depression, Wrigley was generous to himself, distributing $730,000 in dividends, and also to his players, who had the highest payroll in the NL (and second highest in MLB) in 1929 and 1933, and third highest in 1939.[40]

The Reds and Pirates comprised a second tier of teams. The Reds had been losing money since 1928 and were stuck in the red through 1934. Nevertheless, they came out of the era with a profit of $261,564, under the leadership of the foresighted Larry MacPhail, who introduced night baseball in 1935 and rebuilt the team's roster. In 1939, the Reds took the pennant and were second in attendance, which produced a team record $335,210 profit, wiping out a decade of losses.[41] The Pirates were fourth in performance, consistently in the first division, but sixth in attendance. They made $252,827, and distributed about $333,000 in dividends.[42]

The third tier was comprised of the Phillies, Dodgers, and Braves. The Brooklyns had the fifth best record in the NL, but drew the third best attendance because of its large population base and loyal fans. Nonetheless, the club lost $129,637 during the Depression. They started the decade in fourth place, drawing a team record of over a million spectators. The Dodgers made $426,976 in 1930, a franchise record that lasted until 1947, and declared themselves a dividend of $175,000; but the Bums lost money for eight straight years, including four years of over $100,000. By 1938, the badly run team was $1.2 million in debt. The Dodgers, however, turned the corner in 1939 with a third-place finish, their best in seven years, and started a five-year reign as NL attendance champion, earning $143,637.[43]

The Phillies had the worst team in the NL, finishing seventh or last eight times in the 1930s, and the lowest attendance in the NL from 1928 to 1942. This was part of an even longer trend, since from 1918 until 1950 the club was never better than fifth in attendance. Yet the team virtually broke even during the Depression by operating under a tight budget and keeping down losses, which never exceeded $70,000. The only anomaly was the 1932 team that came in a surprising fourth (the *only* winning season between 1917 and 1950), even that failed to bring out the fans, and the Phillies attendance was just 268,914. The Boston Braves also continued to struggle, the second poor

TABLE 7. SOURCES OF MAJOR LEAGUE REVENUE AND EXPENDITURES

REVENUES

	Home Games	Away Games	Exhibitions	Concessions	Other	Media
1929	62.4	21.1	4.2	5.5	6.9	0
1939	55.9	19.2	4.6	7.0	6.0	7.3
1950	57.2	14.1	2.8	9.2	6.2	10.5

EXPENDITURES

	Salary	Minor Leagues Subsidy	Contract Purchasing	Farm Oper. Losses	Income Taxes	Others
1929	35.3	10.3	8.9	1.4	1.8	52.6
1939	32.4	7.5	9.6	(2.1)	2.3	57.8
1950	22.1	12.6	4.1	8.5	6.0	59.3

team in a small two-city town. The Braves had the second worst team in the NL, behind the Phillies, and drew the second smallest crowds. The club enjoyed just one profitable year between 1931 and 1938, losing $225,606 in the Depression.[44]

AMERICAN LEAGUE

The Yankees again dominated on the playing field and at the box office. The Yanks average finish was 1.6, including a Series win over the Cubs in 1932 and four straight titles to finish the decade (1936 to 1939). The club continued to spend freely, and outspent everyone by a wide margin. In 1933, a season when every AL team lost money, the Yankees gross operating income ($753,211) was more than double every other team except for pennant winner Washington. The Yankees drew at least 650,000 every year, and hosted 22.43 percent of total AL attendance, peaking at 30.71 percent in 1933. They were a great attraction with such players as Ruth and Gehrig in the early 1930s, and Gehrig and DiMaggio in the late 1930s. The Yankees led the league in profits ($1,434,679), but even the Yankees were not Depression proof, and they lost money in 1932, 1933, and 1935. In 1935, the Yankees, for the first time, issued dividends of $100,000, raised a year later to $420,000.[45]

In the 1930s, the Tigers were a close second to the Yankees in profits with $1,345,531. The Tigers made more money at home than the Yankees, but were nearly doubled by them in revenue from away games ($267,499). Detroit surpassed its proportion of attendance with an 18.9 percent share, second highest in the AL, and four times from 1934 through 1940 was first or second in AL attendance. The team drew over one million spectators in 1934, and made $521,202, a record that lasted for years. The team started out with low expenses since the 1929 Tigers payroll of $185,771 was third lowest in the majors, and in 1933 had the lowest at $138,758. Yet in 1934, the team won the World Series with 101 wins, and won another pennant the next year. The Tigers ended up with the decade's second best AL record, which pushed up salaries by 1939 to $298,154, second only to the Yankees. Detroit's owners issued generous dividends, $600,000 in the 1920s and 1930s, including $200,000 in 1935 and 1936. Its owners were already among the highest paid baseball executives. In 1934, president Frank Navin made $40,000 and paid his brother a $30,000 salary. After Navin died, the team was sold to automobile parts magnate Walter O. Briggs, whose salary as CEO was $24,000 a year.[46]

The Cleveland Indians were third attendance (13.02 percent), and generally came in third or fourth in the pennant races. During the 1930s, they made $225,868 and distributed $171,844 in dividends. In 1932, the city opened the massive $3 million Municipal Stadium, built in hopes of getting the Olympics, but it turned out to be the "mistake by the lake." The team played there from mid-1932 through 1933 and thereafter only on Sundays and holidays until 1947.[47]

The Senators opened the 1930s with a powerful team that averaged over ninety-four wins a year over four years, culminating in the 1933 pennant. Then they fell precipitously the next year, losing thirty more games than the year before, and finishing seventh. The team had the overall fourth best record in the AL, but the second smallest attendance in the league. When Washington was competitive, it drew well, nearly 15 percent of the AL total in 1932, but it had a very small population base of 621,000. Owner Calvin Griffith was pretty tight with a buck, and after the 1932 season fired manager Walter Johnson, the all-time Senators hero, and brought in 26-year-old shortstop Joe Cronin as player-manager, mainly to save money. Apparently Griffith knew what he was doing because Cronin made the All-Star team and led the Senators to the pennant. The team made just $29,268 in the decade, yet declared dividends of $97,850, albeit one-sixth of the dividends of the 1920s.[48]

The A's started out the 1930s brilliantly, with one of the best teams ever, but fell on hard times. The team followed up the 1929 World Series Championship with another in 1930. The team was led by MVP Lefty Grove, who won the pitcher's Triple Crown (28–5, 2.54 ERA, and 209 strikeouts), and Al

Simmons took the batting title at .381 with 152 runs scored. The team made $162,542, second only to the Yankees. The A's followed this up with 107 victories and another pennant in 1931, but lost the Series to the Cards. The club made $102,123, triple that of the Yankees, the only other AL team to make money.

In 1932, the A's finished a distant second to the Yankees, and after the season, Mack then shocked the baseball world by breaking up a great team for the second time. He began by selling off second baseman Jimmy Dykes and superstar outfielder Al Simmons to the White Sox, enabling him to finish with a profit of $10,023, the *only* AL team in the black. Mack, who relied on the team for income, claimed these sales were necessary because of financial problems, some of which he attributed to the absence of Sunday baseball in Pennsylvania, which was only achieved in 1934. Even that was somewhat balanced off by a rise in state taxes that made Athletics tickets the most expensive in the majors.

The sale helped him cut his payroll for 1933 by 35 percent less than it had been in 1929 when it was second highest in the AL. During the Depression, Mack cut his payroll more sharply than any other owner. His gross operating expenses dropped from $629,400 in 1929 to $477,548 in 1933, when the team fell to third. The A's lost $21,047, which was actually the second best financial result behind the pennant-winning Senators. Thereafter Mack traded and sold most of his remaining stars for $245,000.[49]

Mack's economizing by 1939 produced the second lowest payroll in the AL, which finished seventh or eighth place every year from 1935 through 1946. The A's went from having the third best attendance in the 1920s to the third worst. After the glory years of the early 1930s, the A's were in the red from 1933 through 1940, and lost a total of $17,144 in the 1930s. Mack's stock may not have appreciated, but he was still earning a good living, with a $50,000 salary as manager. He also added the title of team president in 1937.[50]

The White Sox, Browns, and Red Sox suffered heavy financial losses during the Depression. The head of the family-owned White Sox, Charles Comiskey, died in 1932, and was succeeded by son J. Louis. The Pale Hose had been very profitable in the 1920s, but lost $668,947 in the 1930s, which reflected their less than mediocre play and the loss of their large fan base. The team was sixth worst in the league on the diamond and fifth in attendance, only twice drawing its proportionate share of AL attendance.[51]

During the Depression, the Browns only twice drew over 150,000 spectators, topping out at 179,126 in 1931. Three times they had fewer than

100,000, including a record low 80,922 in 1935. They had the poorest attendance in the majors, only 4.61 percent of the AL attendance from 1931 to 1940, and were last in the AL from 1926 to 1943. The Browns were abysmal on the field, with six finishes in last or next to last in the 1930s. Long-time owner Phil Ball, who became rich building refrigeration plants, had been willing to pick up financial losses, but died in 1933 and his executors refused to subsidize the losing venture. In 1936, a syndicate led by Bill DeWitt, a Rickey protégé, bought the team, but it lacked the capital to carry out his innovative plans. The Browns lost $899,348 in the 1930s, making money just once.[52]

At the financial floor of the AL were the Red Sox, who lost a staggering $1,887,721 in the Depression. The team lost money every year from 1923 through 1940 except for 1930 when it made a miniscule profit. In 1933 alone, the seventh place club lost $537,000, drawing a meager 268,715. In 1929, the team had the lowest payroll in the AL ($171,260), and second lowest in the majors behind the Pirates. Four years later, the Sox remained next to last in payroll in MLB ($145,806), behind the Browns. Then in 1933, Tom Yawkey, heir to a lumber and iron fortune, bought the team for $1.5 million. He soon opened his wide pockets and spent liberally, but not always unwisely, to improve his team. Yawkey's money did help the Red Sox become competitive again, finishing in second in 1938 and again in 1939, by which time they had the ninth highest payroll in the majors, after finishing in second place the year before. The fans were coming out to the ballpark, and the team ended up fourth overall in AL attendance. But the third highest expenditures in the AL, including higher salaries and the most money spent acquiring new players, kept the team in the red.[53]

By 1939, MLB's gross operating income was $12 million, back where it had been in 1930. The gate that season comprised 79.7 percent of revenue, with homes games accounting for 55.9 percent, away games 19.2 percent, and other games 4.6 percent. This was a drop from 87.6 percent of revenue coming from the box office a decade earlier. A new factor contributing revenue was media, which accounted for 7.3 percent, with concessions up slightly to 7.0 percent compared to 5.5 percent in 1929, and "other" down to 6.0 percent from 6.9 percent. In regards to expenditures, salaries in 1939 comprised 32.4 percent of expenses, down from 35.3 percent in 1929. Minor league subsidies declined to 7.5 percent, with minor league contract costs at 9.6 percent, while farm systems actually making 2.1 percent to operate. Income taxes were 2.3 percent of expenditures, compared to 1.8 percent in 1929 and nothing in 1933. The nebulous category of "other expenses" (which includes dividends and retained earnings) was up about 10 percent since 1929 to 57.8 percent.[54]

BASEBALL IN THE WAR ERA AND AFTER

During World War II the major leagues struggled to survive as millions of baseball fans went overseas to serve their country, joined in time, by hundreds of major league ballplayers. There was concern the government would curtail the national pastime as had occurred in World War I, but President Franklin Roosevelt chose to let baseball continue for the purpose of keeping up morale. The quality of play declined as hundreds of players served in the military. In 1944, the AL batting champ George "Stuffy" Stirnweiss hit only .309, and Nick Ettan led with only twenty-two homers. MLB had to rely on men who were 4-F, older players, younger players, and even one-armed Pete Gray, who played for the Browns in 1945. Gray had actually been a stellar minor leaguer, the year before, batting .333 for Memphis of the Southern Association, stealing sixty-eight bases, which tied the league record, and being selected MVP. Cubs owner Philip K. Wrigley was so concerned about the state of baseball that he organized the All American Girls' Professional Baseball League to sustain interest.[55]

The sport struggled financially during the war, and in 1943 lost money for the first time since 1935 ($135,318 for the NL and $104,705 for the AL). Yet, despite the lower quality of play, attendance during the war regained its pre-Depression level, and overall MLB made money. Between 1940 and 1945, MLB averaged a profit of about $570,442 ($35,653 per team), which included a profit of over $1 million in 1945, when operating income exceeded $15 million, about 25 percent more than in 1939.[56]

Once the war ended, baseball, like many other consumer sectors, enjoyed a huge boom, with attendance doubling compared to the war years. There was an enormous pent up interest for consumer goods, homes, and entertainment. Baseball enjoyed a triumphant popularity, aided by the elevated quality of play as hundreds of veterans tried to regain their jobs, and by the slow integration of MLB. Fans were excited to see their old heroes return and compete against new blood. Major league attendance rose from 10.8 million in 1945 to 18.5 million in 1946, while there was an even bigger boom in the minors. Minor league audiences rose from 10.7 million in 1945 to 32.7 million a year later. The minors peaked in 1949 with fifty-nine leagues and an attendance of 41.9 million.[57]

From 1946 through 1949, MLB averaged over $4 million in profits, a 400 percent increase over the already profitable 1945 campaign. The NL made 48.5 percent and the AL 51.5 percent. Overall, for the entire 1940s, MLB averaged $1,966,479 earnings, and the typical team made $122,905 per annum. Operating income nearly doubled from 1945 to $27.5 million in 1946, and then surpassed $30 million the next four years. MLB made a healthy 8 percent return on operating income in 1944 and 1945, and then shot up to 17.7 percent in 1946, with a record profit of $4,886,931. Teams were becoming much more valuable. The average franchise sold in the late 1940s for $1,563,000, compared to $673,000 in the 1930s and $1,019,000 in the 1920s.[58]

NATIONAL LEAGUE

The top team in the NL in the 1940s was the high-flying St. Louis Cardinals, who won four pennants (1942 to 1944, 1946) and three World Series, came in second five times and third just once. St. Louis in the 1940s was the eighth largest city in America, only smaller than four other major league cities (Boston, Pittsburgh, Washington, and Cincinnati). Nonetheless, the team made $3,3439,621, second only to the Yankees, and was the only team in the war never to lose money. In 1949, when the Cards lost the pennant by one game, the franchise made $857,553, a MLB record. They paid nearly $1 million in dividends, including $670,032 in 1947.[59]

The Cardinals were not making their money from the box office, since the team was only fourth in NL attendance. Their highest ranking came in 1949 when they were third, the best the Cards had done since 1935. In 1946, the year the Cardinals won the World Series, the club made nearly $700,000, despite a gross operating income ($1,817,898) that was only fourth highest in the NL, but just sixth in operating expenses ($873,562). The Red Birds were only fourth in revenue from games at home, and seventh in media ($30,000). Yet they were a close second in money from away games, made $153,382 from exhibitions (including the World Series), and led the majors by a wide margin in concessions ($323,080), nearly double the NL average of $174,000. Expenses were low because the rich farm system promoted strong competition for the twenty-five roster spots in St. Louis and the team did not have to spend much for new talent. The Cardinals payroll in 1946 was fifth in the NL, whose team salaries had little variance, ranging from $302,000 to $349,000. NL salaries were substantially below the AL whose payrolls averaged $62,500 more. There was also a wider standard deviation as the variance ranged from $511,000 for Boston to $222,000 for the Browns. Four years later, the Cards had become a high expense team, paying their squad $495,683, the most in the NL and fifth in MLB. The squad that year was more experienced, averaging twenty-nine years of age, two years older than the 1946 team. Nonetheless, the club was still quite profitable, earning $263,202, second only to the pennant-winning Phils.[60]

In the early 1940s, the Dodgers enjoyed great success under the direction of Larry MacPhail, who became president in 1938, and then his successor Branch Rickey. Historically second divisioners, the "Bums" in the 1940s had the second best record in the NL, including pennants in 1941, 1947, and 1949, and the third best record in all MLB. MacPhail's team in his four years (1939 to 1942) drew over one million fans, one-third more than the other New York clubs. They led the NL in attendance in the 1940s by a wide margin (18.56 percent), including first five times, and drew over a million eight times. In 1945 and 1946, the Dodgers had 20 percent of the entire NL attendance. In 1946, the Dodgers drew nearly 1.8 million, most in the NL, and had by far the highest return from homes games in the NL, $1.8 million compared to the average of $1.3 million. They were only third in concessions, but their media contract of $150,000 was 2.5 times the league average of $58,094. The club made over $400,000, and radio revenue and box office yields were major factors.[61] Attendance peaked a year later at 2,807,526, with Jackie Robinson and a pennant-winning team. The Dodgers had relied heavily in the past on their large population base and loyal fans, like Hilda Chester, but in the 1940s, spectators were also drawn to Ebbets Field to see an excellent product. The Dodgers made $2,480,634 in the 1940s, including an average of $529,318 in 1946 through 1949. Actually, the Dodgers net income was understated according to Congressman Emanuel Cellar, chairman of the House judiciary subcommittee that investigated organized baseball to see if it was violating antitrust laws. The data did not reflect certain salaries and bonuses of club officials, notably GM Rickey's bonuses that surpassed $730,000![62]

The Dodgers success in the early 1940s enabled the team to retire its $1.25 million debt. The well-compensated MacPhail paid out little in the way of dividends, spending $500,000 rehabilitating Ebbets Field, putting $1 million into the club and its farm system, and ending up with $250,000 in the bank. He joined the military in 1942 and was replaced by Branch Rickey, the former Cardinals executive, who was much more generous to the stockholders, declaring a $21,000 dividend in 1943, and an additional $173,250 between 1948 and 1950. Rickey built up the Dodgers farm system, which included about four hundred players in 1946, which he used to staff the Dodgers. The surplus was sold off for $1,413,325 in 1945 to 1948. Rickey's base salary was $65,000, plus 10 percent of profits, and a bonus when attendance exceeded six hundred thousand. In 1944, Rickey, John Smith of Pfizer, and team attorney Walter O'Malley together bought a quarter of the stock, and one year later secured three-fourths of the shares; however, they did not work well together, and despite big profits and pennants in 1947 and 1949, Rickey was not rehired as president in 1950. The Mahatma subsequently sold his shares in the club to O'Malley for $1.05 million, triple what he had paid for them.[63]

The Giants fared less well in the 1940s, earning just $290,170, sixth highest in the NL. The Giants managed to be the NL's second best draw, mainly because of its New York location, since they were only the fifth best team in the NL. The team lost money in five seasons, including nearly $250,000 in 1943, and in 1946 and 1949 were the only NL club to operate on a deficit. In 1946, when the team came in eighth and Giants lost $211,546, they had the second highest gross operating income in the NL, but also the second highest gross operating expenses, nearly double that of the World Champion Cardinals. The Giants did have the NL's second best media contract ($87,000), but it was 42 percent less than their cross-town rivals, the Dodgers. The team paid $344,635 for salaries, which was in line with other teams, but its biggest debit, the cost of player contracts ($563,780), was way out of line. Perhaps those acquisitions helped, because the Giants rose to fourth in 1947, and set a team record attendance of 1,600,793, earning nearly $530,000, second in the NL to the Cardinals $630,978 income. Still, the Giants made just $115,892 in the profitable 1946 to 1949 period, second lowest in the NL. Nonetheless, Stoneham rewarded himself and the other stockholders, with $293,775 in dividends for the decade, including $141,012 for 1946 to 1949, which exceeded the team's earnings.[64]

The Cubs had the second worst record from 1941 to 1950 with winning seasons only in 1945, when they won the pennant, and a third-place finish in 1946. Yet they finished third in NL attendance, highlighted by their first million attendance since 1931 in 1945, tops in the league that year. The Cubs made $942,792 in the 1940s despite starting the decade with three years of losses amounting to $347,053. Nearly all profits were reinvested, with only dividends of $210,000 between 1946 and 1948. Owner P. K. Wrigley was not a profit maximizer, and only charged $41,000 for radio rights in 1946, just $1,000 more than the lowly Pirates. In 1950, after the advent of television, the Cubs got $189,718 for media privileges, just fifth best in the NL. The team did shine in the area of concessions. Back in 1929, the first year for which there were records, they earned $132,162 in this category when only one other team (the Giants at $87,576) surpassed $46,000 (see table 5). The

Cubs ranked number one in concessions in 1933, fourth in 1939 (see table 6), first in 1943, second in 1946, and first in 1950. This reflected their large attendances, and the thirst and hunger of Cubs fans.[65]

The Reds had the lowest attendance in the NL, yet surpassed the Cubs financially in the 1940s, making $1,049,049 with dividends of $442,550. The Reds started the decade like gangbusters, following up the 1939 pennant with a world championship in 1940, but faded thereafter, and ended with the fourth best record in the league. The Reds typically had gross profits less than the league average, but also among the lowest operating expenses. The Pirates finished right behind the Reds in attendance with a respectable 12.59 percent, very good considering the size of the city and its average 5.15 finish in the pennant race. The team earned $554,406, and distributed $185,500 in dividends.[66]

The lowly Braves, who typically finished in the second division, lost money every year during the war, but made out positively afterwards, and finished the decade ahead by $231,719. The team had the league's third worst attendance (9.25 percent), though it picked up a lot after the war, more than doubling to 969,673 in 1946 as the team became more competitive. The Braves surpassed the million mark in 1947 and then set a team record of 1,455,439 in the glorious 1948 season when the Braves, led by Spahn and Sain ("and hope for rain"), made the World Series for the first time since 1914, but lost to the Cleveland Indians.[67]

The Phillies, the other historic tail-ender, had the worst team in the league, and drew the smallest crowds, less than 9 percent of NL attendance. The team lost money ever year from 1937 through 1945 except for a tiny profit in 1943, a year all other NL clubs lost money. The Phillies had dreadful ownership until the Carpenter family took over in 1943 and worked to right the ship. The Philadelphians enjoyed a huge bump in attendance in 1946 to over one million, more than triple the previous year, and surpassed that mark in 1950 with 1,217,035. During the 1940s, the team was down $453,283, but recouped most of it in the pennant-winning 1950 season when the Phils earned $309,579.[68]

AMERICAN LEAGUE

The AL's financial situation in the 1940s was similar to the prior decade with the Yankees and Tigers doing well, and Boston and Philadelphia struggling, but there was one notable change: the emergence of the Cleveland Indians. In this decade there was a very strong correlation (Rs = 0.8095) between attendance and rank in league play.

In the 1940s, the Yankees made $3,156,554, the most in MLB. They made at least $135,000 every year except for the pennant-winning 1943 campaign when they lost $88,521 (see table 3). The club drew one-fifth of all AL home attendance, surpassing the 2 million mark from 1946 through 1950. The Yankees led the AL in attendance every year from 1946 through 1959, save for 1948, when the Yankees set a club record of 2,373,901.

In 1946, *Fortune* published a financial statement about the Yankees and its farm system, probably the most detailed up to then (see table 8). The team identified its main assets as its franchise ($300,000, the amount the original Baltimore franchise designated as their share of the working capital when the AL was founded), the plant and equipment ($2,152,276), and cash ($347,252, plus another $469,513 for the farm teams), which put the Yankees in a great cash flow situation. The team's receipts were nearly $1.6 million, more than half of which came from home receipts. The team's expenses came to $1.3 million, mainly from playing expenses ($365,158), taxes ($341,199), and general and overhead costs ($326,212). The major league club made a net profit of $306,490, but farm club losses of $104,609 brought the total profit to just over $200,000.[69]

After the war, Ruppert's heirs and executive Ed Barrow, who owned a 10 percent share, sold the team to Dan Topping, Lee MacPhail, and Del Webb for $2.85 million, a bargain since the team was worth $7 million. In the ensuing four years, the team netted about $2.52 million, almost what the team had cost them in the first place. In 1946, the club's gross operating income was $3,455,173, over $1.3 million more than the Tigers, who were second in income. The team earned $808,866, almost as much as the entire AL had made the year before. About $300,000 in profits came from ticket sales and concessions at home and the club's share of road admissions. The Yankees also made about $250,000 from their farm system; about $100,000 from renting their ballparks in New York, Newark, Kansas City, and Norfolk to Negro League teams; and $45,000 from radio. In addition, the Yankees earned $75,000 from local television, the first ML team to make money from the new medium. The revenue derived from the black teams undoubtedly influenced MacPhail's opposition to integrating baseball and harming the Negro Leagues. The Yankees won the World Series in 1947, and set a MLB record for earnings with $846,737.[70]

Eight major league teams made money during the war from Negro League games, mainly New York, Washington, Detroit, and Chicago, who hosted the annual Negro League All-Star Game that attracted around forty thousand spectators. In 1942, after the demolition of Dyckman Oval, a popular site

TABLE 8. YANKEES 1945 CONSOLIDATED OPERATING STATEMENT AND BALANCE SHEET

RECEIPTS	New York	Farm Clubs	Total
Home receipts	$859,909	$275,623	$1,171,532
Abroad receipts	262,122	96,529	358,651
Play-offs and exhibitions	5,740	41,431	47,171
Training trip receipts	16,635	5,979	22,614
Park privileges	159,376	95,098	254,474
Stadium rentals	55,587	43,790	99,377
Radio	65,000	16,400	81,400
Miscellaneous	6,618	2,455	9,073
Sale of player contracts	130,000	68,100	198,100
Total	$1,596,987	$645,405	$2,242,392
EXPENSES			
Stadium operating	$118,473	$78,060	$196,533
Playing	365,158	190,580	555,738
Abroad	38,903	50,222	89,125
Scouting	—	109,890	109,890
Training	16,680	17,912	34,592
General and overhead	326,212	92,549	418,761
Taxes	341,199	183,912	525,111
Miscellaneous	—	2,800	2,800
Depreciation	63,910	18,799	82,709
Interest	19,962	294	20,256
Purchase of player contracts	—	4,996	4,996
Total	$1,290,497	$750,014	$2,040,511
Profit	$306,490	($104,609)	$201,881
ASSETS			
Cash	$347,252	$469,513	$816,765
Notes receivable	2,000	—	2,000
Plant and equipment	2,152,276	580,183	2,732,459
Franchise	300,000	32,797	332,797
Deferred charges	28,668	7,762	36,430
Player contracts	1	1	2
Open accounts, etc.	62,748	40,684	103,432
Total	$2,892,945	$1,130,940	$4,023,885
LIABILITIES			
Funded debt	$1,150,000	—	$1,150,000
Accounts payable	123,156	$54,507	177,663
Accrued taxes	64,571	77,584	142,155
Reserve for depreciation	424,741	45,702	469,813
Capital stock	300,000	134,200	434,200
Surplus	830,476	819,578	1,650,054
Total	$2,892,944	$1,130,941	$4,023,885

Source: "The Yankees," *Fortune* 34 (July 1946): 171.

for New York semipro baseball games, the Yankees began renting out their ballpark for Negro League Sunday double headers. In Detroit in 1944, four games played at Briggs Stadium drew nearly eighty-five thousand, about 10 percent of the Tigers entire attendance. Major league teams typically charged lessees 20 to 25 percent of the gross receipts, though the Tigers and Browns asked 40 percent. Some teams required guarantees, like the Dodgers, who in 1940 required $500 to rent Ebbets Field while the Yankees in the late 1940s demanded $2,500 to $3,000 upfront to lease Yankee Stadium.[71]

The second most profitable team was the formerly struggling Cleveland Indians, who made $2,189,636, virtually all after the war. Attendance doubled in 1946 to over a million despite a sixth-place finish. Then in 1947, the Indians became a contender. Owner Bill Veeck moved all games to spacious Memorial Stadium, and attendance skyrocketed to over 1.5 million. The Indians won the World Series a year later, and set a major league attendance record of 2,620,627. From 1946 through 1949, the Tribe earned $1,700,517, with dividends of $461,475.

The Tigers also did well in the 1940s, with 17.29 percent of league attendance, and an average finish of 3.25. The team made $1,404,988, and reinvested all profits. The club struggled at the start of World War II, with superstar Hank Greenberg in uniform. They lost a little money in 1941, broke even in 1942, and then made about $530,000 in the next three years, culminating in the 1945 world championship season when the Tigers drew over one million spectators. The euphoria of the championship pushed attendance the following year to over 1.7 million and produced a $467,283 profit the following year.[72]

The Washington Senators were a surprise success in the 1940s, making $1.45 million, and distributing $407,450 in dividends. Washington, the smallest city in the AL, was sixth in attendance and sixth in the pennant races. The club came in second in 1945, which led to a big year at the box office the following season, with over one million spectators. Another factor that bolstered attendance was the installation of lights for night games in 1941, which paid for themselves in two years. Griffith also rented out the ballpark to the Washington Redskins for $100,000, and to Negro League teams, "our bread and butter," in the words of his nephew Calvin Griffith. The Homestead Grays paid between $50,000 and $100,000 in 1943 for fourteen games, and sometimes outdrew the Senators. These extra sources of revenue were the difference between profit and loss. Despite operating in the smallest market in the AL, Griffith had twenty-five straight profitable years, and kept several family members on the payroll at hefty salaries. When

Clark Griffith died in 1955, the team was worth $4 million, and his nephew took over. The family held on to the team until 1984 when it was sold for $36 million.[73]

Most of the lesser AL teams also made a profit in the 1940s. The big-market White Sox, who had struggled in the 1930s, stepped up in the 1940s with $934,209 in profit and $186,500 in dividends. They still had a poor product on the field, with the seventh worst team in the AL and only the fifth best attendance. Another big-city team, the Athletics did not do the City of Brotherly Love proud, and were usually mired in last place. They were seventh in attendance despite playing in the nation's third largest city, but still made $445,388 in profits with very low expenses.

Normally the St. Louis Browns was a bottom feeder, but in the 1940s the team made $1,158,015, and was in the black from 1942 through 1950. This was remarkable because the team was fifth in quality and eighth in attendance. In 1942, local businessman Richard Muckerman invested $300,000 in the team, and became vice president. His financial infusion helped the Browns rebuild, and they amassed their first wining record in thirteen years. Then they captured the pennant in 1944 and made third a year later. The championship season attracted 508,644, a 58 percent increase over 1943, and their highest attendance since 1924; but this renaissance was short lived. Muckerman spent liberally to fix up Sportsman's Park and even brought in two African American ballplayers in 1947 to bolster fan interest, but the Browns remained at the nadir of league attendance from 1946 to 1953.[74]

Only the Red Sox finished in the red, $256,041 in the 1940s. The Boston team remained a financial black hole through the end of the war. From 1923 through 1945, the team finished in the black only four times. Until then, the best the team ever did was to make $57,342 in the banner 1941 season, when the team had its third second-place finish in four years—but the first to be profitable. The team on the field was excellent, third best in the AL over the decade, led by Ted Williams, Jimmy Fox, Bobby Doerr, and Dom DiMaggio. These stars brought out the fans, and the attendance was third in the league (13.64 percent). The team finally had a big profit, $405,133 in 1946, when the Sox went to the World Series. The team made $224,198 from preseason and postseason games, notably the World Series, and was the biggest out-of-town attraction, pulling in $510,598, one-third more than the league average. Yet overall the team was a financial mess because of high expenses. The Sox in 1943 had the second highest operating expenses in the AL, but the second lowest operating incomes. They had the third highest payroll in the AL ($212,982) and fifth highest in the majors, and their farm system cost them over $100,000, twice as much as the Yankees. In 1946, their $511,025 was the highest payroll in MLB, and it was still second highest in 1950 ($561,482).[75]

THE SILVER AGE OF BASEBALL: THE 1950S

The early 1950s was a period of outstanding baseball when the major leagues had finally integrated, and when most top professional athletes were ballplayers. The dominant franchise was the Yankees, who won five consecutive World Series (1949 to 1953). They lost the pennant in 1954 despite winning 103 games, and followed that up with four more consecutive pennants (1955 to 1958). The NL had great teams as well, particularly the Boys of Summer, who won four pennants in Brooklyn (and a fifth in Los Angeles), and lost the 1950 and 1951 pennant races on the last day of the season. There was, incidentally, an extremely high correlation between team's position in the pennant race and payroll (Rs = 0.802).

The conventional wisdom has been that MLB was doing very well in this period. By 1956, MLB's gross income reached $42,836,327, about a one-third increase from 1950 ($32,035,481), and teams in the 1950s sold for an average price of $3.52 million, double the typical sale price of $1.56 million in the prior decade. Major league attendance peaked in 1948 at 20.9 million, fell as low as 14.4 million, and only reached the 20 million mark in 1960. Organized baseball's total attendance, which had reached 62 million in 1948, slid to 44 million by 1951, a 20 percent drop in the majors and about two-thirds for the minors. The minors suffered huge financial losses, $3.7 million in 1952 when there were 163 teams reporting to the IRS, $3.3 million in 1953, and $2.8 million in 1956 when 114 of 132 teams reported a loss.[76]

The American League faired well in the early 1950s (1950, 1952 to 1956), earning $3,320,048, but the National League had serious financial problems. The NL went from a $2 million profit in 1949 to a loss of $756,207 the following year, and then amassed over a $1.7 million deficit for 1952 to 1954 (no data exist for 1951). Overall, in the years 1950, and 1952 to 1956, the NL made just over $100,000 (see table 9). Historian Robert Burk attributed the financial issues to TV saturation, shifting demography with the rise of Sunbelt and suburbs, imbalance among teams, competition from other sports, paternalistic owners, particularly sportsmen like P. K. Wrigley, and management's scant awareness of marketing. Despite exciting pennant races, NL attendance in the early 1950s did not keep up with population growth, and actually declined outside of Cincinnati and Milwaukee.[77]

Major league revenues in 1950 came from some different sources compared to the previous twenty years. In 1950, baseball games supplied 74.1 percent of gross income, compared to 87.6 percent in 1929 and 82.5 percent as recently as 1946. Overall, 57.2 percent of the gross came from home games, 14.1 percent from road games, and 2.8 percent from preseason and postseason games. Ticket revenue was tied to the inelasticity of ticket prices, as grandstand tickets were still one dollar, unchanged from over a generation. The main change was the big increase that media revenue provided as part of the gross income. Radio and television was up to 10.5 percent compared to about 7 percent in the early 1940s and 3.0 percent in 1946, and it would rise to 17 percent in 1956. In absolute terms, media revenues for MLB rose from $4.16 million in 1952 to $7.3 million, an over 70 percent appreciation. Between just 1952 and 1956, concessions comprised 9.2 percent, close to what it had been for a decade. The remaining source of revenue was "other," at 6.2 percent.[78]

The distribution of gross operating incomes (GOI) looked a lot different in 1950 than it had before. Salaries comprised 21.6 percent of expenses, very similar to 1946 (20.5 percent), but far different from the years 1929, 1943, and 1946 when salaries were about 30 percent of GOI, and especially 1933 when it was 44.2 percent. The mean salary in 1950 was $13,288 (median was about $11,000), compared to $7,306 in 1939 and $11,294 in 1946. The salary increase (which amounted to just 1.1 percent of GOI) did not have much of a negative impact on net income, which dropped sharply from 17.3 percent in 1946 to just 2.1 percent four years later. There was a very big change in four years in minor league subsidies (12.4 percent compared to 4.5 percent), and farm-operating loss (8.4 percent) compared to a small profit (0.3 percent) in 1946. This was understandable considering the record number (fifty-nine) of minor leagues in the late 1940s. At this time MLB had its biggest disparity ever between teams making the most and the least. Economist Andrew Zimbalist found a significant gap in the maximum–minimum ratio of highest to lowest team revenue (5.716), slightly higher than in 1939 (5.436), and twice as high as in 1990 (2.882).[79]

By the mid-1950s, the financial situation had improved. The NL nearly broke even, and the AL made a whopping $1,524,968. In 1955, the average team made nearly $89,000, and nearly $119,000 the following year. The NL surpassed the junior circuit in profits that year, which reflected a more even balance of power in that league. The average club in the mid-1950s netted about $2.45 million. This included $1.35 million (55.1 percent) in home receipts, $275,000 in road receipts, $400,000 in media revenues (16.3 percent), $300,000 from concessions and advertising privileges (12.2 percent), and $150,000 from park rentals, parking fees, and other related sources. The Yankees were at the high end of the spectrum with revenues exceeding $4.5 million, based on leading attendances, high revenues from media, and World Series money each year. Teams then had payrolls of about $400,000 (twenty-five players, coaches, manager, and trainer); $400,000 in administrative expenses and salaries; $250,000 for spring training, travel, and equipment; a similar amount for ballpark rent and maintenance; and $600,000 for player recruitment and development.[80]

NATIONAL LEAGUE

Financial problems in MLB led to the first team shifts since the forfeited Baltimore Orioles franchise moved to New York in 1903 where they became the Highlanders. The first team to move was the Braves from Boston to Milwaukee in 1953. Their years of futility as the second team in Boston and renewed losses in the early 1950s following a brief turnaround in the late 1940s, convinced the Braves to move, and the NL to approve it. They secured a terrific deal from the city of Milwaukee, who provided the Braves with the publicly owned County Stadium as a new home. This was a big innovation since only the Cleveland Indians then were not playing in a privately owned stadium.[81]

Once the Braves moved to Milwaukee, they became the most profitable team in the NL. They made a huge, instant turnaround from losing $459,099 in Boston in 1952, to making $637,798 the next year in Milwaukee (see Table 1). The Braves earned $2,316,701 from 1953 through 1956 ($579,175 a year), peaking in 1955 at $807,395. These excellent returns came mainly from box office receipts. In 1953, the Braves drew a dazzling 1,826,397 in Milwaukee compared to 281,278 the year before in Boston. Milwaukee had the highest attendance in the NL for six straight years, surpassing a couple-million in 1954 to 1956, and in 1955 and 1956 produced one-fourth of the entire NL attendance. In 1956, the Braves made $2,603,354 from home ticket sales compared to a league average of $1,442,818, while making about $85,000 for each visiting team, which far exceeded the league norm. Once inside the ballpark, fans spent liberally, enjoying their beer and bratwursts. The team in 1956 made $542,406 from concessions, about twice that of all other NL clubs except for the Dodgers (see table 9).

However, the Braves fell to second in profits, surpassed by the Dodgers. The Braves that year had the highest total expenses in the NL, although the Dodgers, winners of the 1955 World Championship, had higher salaries. The

ABLE 9. STATEMENTS OF PROFIT AND LOSS FOR NATIONAL LEAGUE, YEAR ENDING IN 1956

	Brooklyn	*Chicago*	*Cincinnati*	*Milwaukee*	*New York*	*Philadelphia*	*Pittsburgh*	*St. Louis*
NCOME:								
Games at home	$1,790,275	$793,859	$1,498,568	$2,603,354	$1,008,183	$1,307,937	$1,254,142	$1,296,226
Games away	430,797	245,986	303,566	342,443	300,326	237,611	240,381	277,521
xhibition games	30,399	(1)	48,060	(1)	(1)	(1)	4,223	(1)
adio and television	888,270	226,803	267,275	125,000	730,593	301,630	158,500	327,450
oncessions (net)	315,407	283,444	234,599	542,406	196,141	188,961	193,518	266,449
ther income	425,676	97,101	73,569	83,864	236,529	242,372	222,027	87,492
Total income	3,880,824	1,646,993	2,415,637	3,697,067	2,471,772	2,278,511	2,072,791	2,255,138
XPENSES:								
layers' salaries	2,598,666	[3]380,752	[4]441,355	469,924	[6]530,640	448,220	6,346,822	412,094
layers' bonuses 7	5,500	122,304	(1)	148,952	12,383	(1)	45,644	21,666
layers' contracts purchased (sold), net	(8,000)	113,719	148,250	97,900	(41,117)	30,894	87,000	
fficers' salaries	111,200	56,000	94,326	93,500	142,500	49,800	112,000	72,738
ther expenses	1,676,945	1,085,157	1,238,063	1,637,987	1,768,800	1,627,223	1,472,557	1,131,244
otal expenses	2,384,311	1,757,922	1,921,994	2,448,263	2,413,166	2,156,137	2,064,023	1,658,242
et income (loss) including companies other than farm clubs, before taxes on income	1,496,513	(110,929)	493,643	1,248,804	58,606	122,374	8,768	596,896
et income (loss) of farm club subsidiaries, before taxes on income	(376,260)	(48,783)	38,522	(205,227)	62,530	(123,708)	(58,620)	(267,401)
et income (loss) before taxes on income	1,120, 253	(159, 712)	532,165	1,043,577	121,136	(1,334)	(47, 852)	329,495
ovision for federal and other taxes on income	632,791	——	230,949	629,179	39,721	76,729	——	——
Net income (loss)	487,462	(159,712)	301,216	414,398	81,415	(78,063)	(47,852)	329,495
(DEDUCT):								
vidends paid	——		(60,770)	——	——	——	——	——
her earned surplus transactions (net)	——		(1,569)	——	(21,768)	——	——	——
Net increase (decrease) in earned surplus	487,462	(145,712)	238,877	414,398	59,647	(78,063)	(47,852)	329,495

Not segregated.

Also includes manager's, coaches', trainers', and clubhouse salaries.

Also includes coaches' salaries.

Also includes coaches' and manager's salaries and bonuses.

Represents team salary expense.

Also includes manager's and coaches' salaries.

ncludes all bonuses paid to players. See separate exhibit for bonuses paid to bonus players.

urce: U.S. Congress, House Judiciary Committee, *Organized Professional Team Sports, Hearings before the Antitrust* *ocommittee of the Committee on the Judiciary*, 85th Cong., 1st Sess. (Washington: Government Printing Office, 1957), 358.

Braves outspent the Dodgers by $105,000 when it came to purchasing contracts and even more so for player bonuses ($148,952 to $5,500) for new talent, which soon paid off with pennants in 1957 and 1958.[82]

The Braves, however, made out poorly when it came to media revenues. Milwaukee had a small nodal zone, with Chicago on one side and Minneapolis on the other. The Braves left a media goldmine in Boston, where the club earned $316,324 from radio and television in 1952, which exceeded ticket sales ($312,069), and was only surpassed by the Dodgers and Giants in the lucrative New York market. But in Milwaukee, the team only got $141,200 in 1954, which declined two years later to $125,000, lowest in the NL (which averaged $378,165). Nine years later the Braves moved to Atlanta, drawn by lucrative TV opportunities.[83]

The Braves instant success in Milwaukee encouraged other teams to follow their example. In 1954, the St. Louis Browns moved to Baltimore, and then in 1955, the Philadelphia A's moved to Kansas City, which were both also "second franchises" in two team cities. Shortly thereafter, the sports world was shocked by the announcement that the highly profitable Dodgers and the struggling Giants were bound for the West Coast in 1958.[84]

While the Milwaukee Braves made out like gangbusters at first, several other NL clubs struggled in the early 1950s. The Cubs poor play on the diamond (they languished deep in the second division from 1947 through 1966) resulted in the NL's fifth-place attendance between 1950 and 1956, very poor for a team in the nation's second metropolis. The bottom line was also hurt by Wrigley's disinterest in negotiating TV rights. In 1956, the benevolent Cubs had the fourth lowest media contract in MLB at $226,603. They lost $559,736 in the six years for which we have data. The Reds were up $260,836, which mostly came in their exciting 1956 campaign, when they came in third, their first contending season since 1944. The Reds drew a million fans for the first time, setting a team record that lasted until 1970. The Phillies started out the decade famously, making $309,579 in their pennant-winning season of 1950 when they drew 1,217,035 to lead the NL and set a team record. However, despite winning seasons in 1952 and 1953, their finances took a nosedive. The team was down $24,178 for the period 1950 to 1956. The Cards and Pirates did even worse. The Cardinals, led by hall of famer Stan Musial, were competitive, with a winning record from 1950 to 1954, and were fourth in attendance then; but they were no longer making big money from their farm system, and finished in the red by $744,888. The dismal Pirates somehow made $138,220 in 1950 despite going 57–96, mostly from fans going to see slugger Ralph Kiner who had hit fifty-four homers the year before. They were a dreadful team, losing over one hundred games from 1952 to 1954, and in seven years amassed a deficit of $1,809,083. Attendance dropped from nearly 1.2 million in 1950 to under 470,000 in 1955.[85]

The Giants, led by the mercurial Willie Mays, managed to make $78,488 in the early 1950s, a very modest amount for a New York City team, having suffered a total of about $550,000 in losses in 1950 and 1952 to 1953. They presumably did well in the electrifying 1951 season that drew 1,059,539, second in the NL, and ended with Bobby Thomson's home run (although only 34,000 were at the game that day!). It was the sixth straight year with over one million spectators, but did not reach that mark again until 1954 when the Giants won the World Series. They made $395,113 that year, but dropped to $151,113 in 1955 and just $81,415 in 1956. Stoneham was making $70,000 a year as team president and his son was also on the payroll. They paid themselves $141,012 in dividends in the early 1950s, and were one of only two NL teams to pay dividends between 1952 and 1956.[86]

In 1946, the Giants home and away gate was nearly 80 percent of baseball-related income, and radio brought in only 5 percent, but in 1950, the gate was down to 70 percent of baseball-related income, while media (including television) was up to 15 percent, which was more than the road game income. By 1952, the Giants had the league's second highest gross income, thanks to home attendance of nearly a million and broadcasting revenue, but also the highest expenses by a wide margin. In 1956, when the team came in sixth, it was third in gross income even though attendance had dropped to just 629,267, the lowest in the NL. Broadcasting had risen to $730,593, second to the Dodgers, and more than double any other NL team. It accounted for 30 percent of revenue, which helped keep the team profitable. The team was still making money. The team had a big cash flow, but was third in expenses ($2.41 million), just behind Milwaukee ($2.44 million), but earned one-fifth as much as Milwaukee ($414,398). Historian John Fetter blames the declining finances on the slow move to night baseball, the dated Polo Grounds which was in disrepair, the large number of cheap seats and small number of expensive box seats, and a location adjacent to Harlem that turned off many fans. In addition, Stoneham was not putting enough money into the team, which resulted in a declining lineup. The Giants had fallen to third in the hearts of New Yorkers. Fans mainly came out just for games with the Dodgers, which comprised 34 percent of the total gate. The numbers certainly explain why the Giants were ready to follow the Dodgers to the West Coast where they could monopolize broadcasting rights.[87]

While the Giants were struggling, their cross-town rivals, the Dodgers, were doing sensationally, earning over $300,000 a year in 1950 and 1952 to 1956. The Boys of Summer were a great team, coming in first or second every year from 1949 through 1956. They drew at least one million every year, and were second in NL attendance. The team stumbled financially in the thrilling 1950 season, when they lost the pennant on the last day of the season, losing $8,057. The bottom line included the writing off of a $167,000 loss attributed to the club's professional football team. Then from 1952 to 1956, the Dodgers averaged $372,149 in profits, or a grand total of $1,852,688, the highest in MLB. Despite this, Walter O'Malley was very jealous of the Braves success. Between 1953 and 1955, when his team won the pennant in 1953 and the World Series two years later, the Braves doubled his profits every year. Finally in 1956, when the Dodgers repeated as pennant winners, they topped the Braves, $487,462 to $414,398. The Braves that year had a bigger home gate, but the Bums were a bigger draw at away games, made nearly seven times more money from media ($888,270), and quintupled the Braves in the category of "other income."[88]

The Dodgers, along with the Giants, got about 30 percent of their revenue from the media, while most teams got only 10 percent. In 1954, the Dodgers earned $609,000 from media sources, with the Giants a distant second at $490,192. In 1955, after winning the World Series, the Giants went up to $645,640, but the Dodgers appreciated to $787,155, $110,000 more than the Yankees. In 1956, the Giants increased to $730,593, the Dodgers rose to $888,270, and the Bronx Bombers skyrocketed to $900,000, but Cleveland surpassed all of them at $1,053,171, up 46.1 percent over the previous year.[89]

Despite the Dodgers excellent returns, O'Malley was an unsentimental profit maximizer, and was concerned about the team's future financial viability. His plan was to move from the small Ebbets Field, which was becoming less accessible as his customers moved to the suburbs, to a new and profitable location in downtown Brooklyn; however, the municipality refused to help him secure his chosen site through exercising eminent domain. So O'Malley turned his focus to greener pastures in Los Angeles, where he moved in 1958.[90]

In the six years for which we have data in the 1950s, NL teams averaged $195,219 in profits, or just $32,537 a year. There was quite a variance, with four teams profiting, two of which made over $1.5 million (although the Braves surely lost heavily in 1951, the year for which we have no data), and four losing money, led by the Pirates who dropped a staggering $1.8 million.

AMERICAN LEAGUE

The Yankees dominated the AL on the field, winning eight pennants and seven world championships between 1947 and 1956, making 58 percent of AL profits in 1950, and from 1952 to 1956. The other teams were jealous of the Yankees, but looked forward to their visits because they were a huge box office attraction. The pinstripers actually fared less well from 1952 to 1956 when their average profit was $288,868, compared to $603,177 for 1947 to 1950. Not surprisingly, they led the AL in attendance every year from 1949 through 1959. The lack of competitiveness in a league was generally presumed to be very deleterious, but the AL did well financially in the early 1950s even though hometown fans had little hopes for a pennant. In fact, the other seven teams in the league looked forward to visits by the Yankees who were a huge box office attraction.

The Yankees large home gate was a major factor in the team's bottom line, which in 1950 and 1952 to 1956 was third in MLB ($1,518,004). In 1950, the team's receipts exceeded $2.5 million from home games alone, nearly $800,000 more than Cleveland, which was second. By contrast, the lowly A's took in just $345,634 at home, which provided encouragement to move. The Yankees also benefited greatly from the media, especially since by 1950 half of New York homes already had television sets. In 1954, the Yankees made $675,000 from media revenue, slightly ahead of the pennant-winning Indians at $635,762, but well above the league average of $352,225. Overall, MLB's media revenue grew from $4,164,939 in 1952 to $7,306,259 in four years, a 40 percent appreciation; but there was a huge difference from team to team, which in 1956 ranged from $210,000 for Kansas City to $1,053,171 for Cleveland.[91]

The Yankees historically paid higher salaries than other clubs, which had been a major segment of team expenses, but were just 17.8 percent in 1956. Surprisingly, in the early 1950s, when the Yankees were omnipotent on the playing field, they were not the highest paid team in the AL. The Cleveland Indians paid higher salaries in the AL between 1952 and 1956, except for 1954, when, ironically, they captured the pennant. The Indians payroll rose from $18,040 a man in 1954 ($487,050 for the team) to $22,680 ($567,000) in 1955, when the league average was $12,726, while the Yankees declined from $18,890 ($510,000 for the team) to $15,830 ($411,500). The Yankees were probably underpaid because the general manager, George Weiss, was such a difficult negotiator and considered their annual World Series check part of their regular remuneration. By 1956, the Yankees had the highest payroll in MLB ($492,000), just ahead of the Dodgers ($472,000). There was still a wide variance, with the Senators the lowest paid at $215,150.[92]

Other expenditures also differed across the league. For instance, in 1954, the Yankees spent only $2,200 on signing bonuses for new players, whereas the Indians spent $137,510. The Yankees made $85,000 on the sale of contracts because they had an abundance of players through their farm system, whereas the White Sox spent $220,000 and the Orioles $176,950 to buy players. Another big expense was the farm system, which cost Detroit $360,050, while Cleveland actually made $117,482. In the catch-all category of "other expenses," the Yankees spent over $3 million, whereas Washington spent only $740,630. Salaries of team officers also varied widely. Chicago's executives made $196,126, but the Baltimore front office earned just $17,667.[93]

AL profits were unevenly divided. Close behind the Yankees were the Indians, who made $1,385,353, including $583,283 in their great 1954 campaign when they won 110 games. Next came the Chicago White Sox who came in third every year from 1952 to 1956, making $477,543, and declaring $81,950 in dividends, and the Tigers, who made $216,477, with $150,000 distributed in dividends. The Tigers were a second division team that suffered a huge drop in attendance from 1.95 million in 1950 to 884,658 four years later. The Senators made just $9,055, but managed to pay out $173,050 in dividends.

The Philadelphia A's and the Boston Red Sox fared poorly, losing, respectively $540,785, and $849,796. Mack's sons took over the A's in 1950, and according to historian Bruce Kuklick, ran the franchise into the ground. They remodeled the ballpark at a cost of $300,000, leased the valuable concessions, and mortgaged Shibe Park, a poor decision at a time of declining cash flow. The team was solvent in 1952 only because of diminutive pitcher Bobby Shantz, who won twenty-four games before suffering a fractured wrist. He brought in 44 percent of the home attendance in the sixteen home games he pitched. Otherwise the A's were a poor draw, bottoming out at 304,666 in 1954. The squabbling Mack family sold the team to Chicago businessman Arnold Johnson, who moved the club in 1955 to Kansas City. The novelty brought in nearly 1.4 million fans, second most in the AL, which more than quadrupled the last year in Philadelphia, and was the most the team ever drew in Kansas City. The result was a meager profit of $28,214, but that was about $200,000 better than the year before. The A's drew one million again the next season, and the team broke even. Thereafter the excitement of MLB in the heartland wore off, and the club never drew one million again until 1973 when it was in Oakland.[94]

The Red Sox had good players, most notably Ted Williams (who missed nearly all of 1952 and 1953 for the Korean War), and generally finished in fourth place in the pennant race and in attendance, but expenses outpaced revenues. In 1954, when the Sox made $27,4546, the seventh biggest profit in the AL that year, the team was sixth in income and fourth in expenses (just $60,000 out of second), including third in salaries.[95]

The doormats of the AL were the St. Louis Browns, who typically ended up in seventh place, with the lowest attendance in the AL. In 1950, when the team's $7,000 (median) payroll was the smallest payroll in MLB by $3,000, pitcher Al Widmar almost refused his promotion from Triple-A because he had to take a $2,000 pay cut. The Browns tried to survive by selling off their best players, but that was only a short-term fix.[96] In 1951, the team was sold to Bill Veeck, whose 80 percent ownership of the stock gave him special tax benefits, such as player depreciation. He tried countless promotions, such as "bat day" and hiring midget Eddie Gaedel to play for the team to publicize the team. The Browns drew 518,796, fifth highest in team history, but in 1952, Veeck got only $22,000 from his media contract. One year later he got $44,427 for radio rights, but could not get a TV contract. The maverick owner tried to move the franchise, but the lords of the AL turned him down. He ended up selling to a Baltimore syndicate in 1954 for $2.4 million, which gave Veeck and his partners a $1 million profit.[97]

Baltimore did all it could to accommodate the AL, providing Memorial Stadium for a home park. The team got the parking and food concessions, and the city spent $2.5 million in stadium improvements and picked up all the maintenance costs. The Orioles emulated the Braves as models for how teams could squeeze their new cities for all they were worth. The Orioles made $643,407 in its first season, which helped accelerate the idea of franchise relocation. The Orioles were fifth in attendance in the AL, with over a million spectators, compared to fewer than 300,000 in 1953 in St. Louis. They were fourth in gate receipts at $1,572,143 in gate receipts, over a million dollars more than they had made the year before from the home gate in St. Louis. They also made out much better with media rights which were sold for $312,795, but that was still seventh in the AL, but the euphoria was short lived, and the team lost $86,715 the following year.[98]

CONCLUSION: MAJOR LEAGUE PROFITS, 1920–1956

The most profitable baseball teams in the period 1920 to 1956 were the New York Yankees and the Brooklyn Dodgers, who drew large crowds playing in the nation's largest market, especially when they had competitive teams. The

TABLE 10. MAJOR LEAGUE PROFITS, 1920–1956

NATIONAL LEAGUE	1920–1950	1952–1956	Total
Brooklyn Dodgers	$3,843,973	$1,860,744	$5,704,717
St. Louis Cardinals	5,962,681	(1,094,374)	4,868,307
New York Giants	2,891,698	342,602	3,234,300
Chicago Cubs	2,613,456	(426,612)	2,186,844
Cincinnati Reds	1,571,093	325,709	1,896,802
Pittsburgh Pirates	3,767,713	(1,947,303)	1,820,410
Milwaukee Braves	(297,890)	1,857,602	1,559,712
Philadelphia Phillies	(12,702)	(733,757)	(746,459)
AMERICAN LEAGUE			
New York Yankees	8,496,995	1,444,339	9,941,334
Detroit Tigers	4,702,262	442,621	5,144,883
Cleveland Indians	3,670,091	867,305	4,537,396
Washington Senators	2,746,889	161,318	2,908,207
Chicago White Sox	1,346,839	815,389	2,162,226
Baltimore Orioles	1,016,517	410,636	1,481,788
Kansas City Athletics	1,139,593	(341,963)	797,630
Boston Red Sox	(2,356,578)	(395,271)	(2,751,849)

Source: U.S. Congress, House Judiciary Committee, *Organized Baseball, Hearings before the Subcommittee on Study of Monopoly Power,* 82nd Cong., 1st Sess., 1951, serial 1, part 6 (Washington, DC: Government Printing Office, 1952), 1611; U.S. Senate, Committee on the Judiciary, *Organized Professional Team Sports: Hearings before the Subcommittee on Antitrust and Monopoly of the Committee of the Judiciary,* 85th Cong., 2nd Sess. (Washington, DC: Government Printing Office, 1958), 353.

Yankees won the most pennants, had the highest overall rank in pennant races, and the largest attendance. The team's net income was $9,941,34, averaging $276,148, nearly double the Tigers, the second closest AL team. The Yankees only paid out $650,000 in dividends over this period fourth highest in the league, retaining nearly $9 million which was reinvested in the team. The Dodgers made $5,804,467, despite playing in small Ebbets Field, and struggling mightily during the Depression (see table 10). They made a fortune after the war, especially from 1952 to 1956 ($1,860,744). They also distributed a generous $1,308,250 in dividends prior to 1951. When

TABLE 11. AVERAGE ANNUAL PROFITS PER TEAM, 1920–1956

Years	*Current Dollars*	*Adjusted for Inflation for 2002*
1920–1929	$115,000	$1,172,540
1930–1939	14,375	188,316
1940–1949	116,250	1,177,380
1950–1956	35,713	239,920

Source: Andrew Zimbalist, *Baseball and Billions: A Probing Look inside the Big Business of Our National Pastime* (New York: Basic Books, 1994), 62; U.S. Senate, Committee on the Judiciary, *Organized Professional Team Sports: Hearings before the Subcommittee on Antitrust and Monopoly of the Committee of the Judiciary*, 85th Cong., 2nd Sess. (Washington, DC: Government Printing Office, 1958), 353.

the Yankees and Dodgers had astute ownership, they made a lot of money by selling surplus players; vending media rights; marketing liquid refreshment, food, and other products to fans; and renting their ballparks to other entertainments such as the Negro leagues, football, and prize fighting. The team earned the most of any major league team in the early 1950s, but apparently not enough to stay in Brooklyn.

Yet, while the Yankees and Dodgers led in profits, overall there was not a strong correlation between size of city and profits (Rs = 0.4471). There was a strong correlation in the American League between attendance and profits (Rs = 0.7619) from 1920 to 1950, but not in the National League, where the Cardinals and Pirates were among the most profitable teams despite middling attendances, whereas the Cubs, who led in attendance, were not efficiently run by the Wrigleys, who were not profit maximizers. In the American League, the most financially successful teams after the Yankees were the Detroit Tigers ($5,144,883), the Cleveland Indians ($4,537,396), and surprisingly the Washington Senators ($2,908,207). These three teams also distributed dividends of over a million dollars. Washington was the third smallest city in MLB, and did not have a great record on the field, yet was seventh in profits among all major league teams, just behind the Giants ($3,234,300) of the NL.

In the NL, the Giants distributed the most of any major league team ($3,006,761), spending nearly everything the team made. The Cardinals, on the other hand, made nearly $4.7 million, but only distributed $1,762,331 in dividends. The Giants were third in the NL after the Dodgers and the

TABLE 12. MAJOR LEAGUE PROFITS (LOSSES), 1950, 1952–1956

Year	National League Profit (Loss)	American League Profit (Loss)
1950	($76,207)	$764,856
1952	(1,033,360)	(197,799)
1953	(672,651)	(176,296)
1954	(29,610)	1,524,968
1955	591,873	831,052
1956	1,328,359	573,267
Total	$108,404	$3,320,048

Source: U.S. Senate, Committee on the Judiciary, *Organized Professional Team Sports: Hearings before the Subcommittee on Antitrust and Monopoly of the Committee of the Judiciary*, 85th Cong., 2nd Sess. (Washington, DC: Government Printing Office, 1958), 353.

St. Louis Cardinals ($4,868,307), who played in the sixth largest market, which they shared for many years with the Browns, one of the least profitable nines. The Red Birds were third in the NL in team performance in the 1920s and 1930s, and first in the 1940s. Their profits were not heavily drawn from attendance since they were never among the leading teams in any decade, and only in the 1940s did they draw more than the league average. Their big profits came from Branch Rickey's farm system, which enabled them to earn a lot from player sales. Then in the early 1950s, their weak teams and their small-town problems caught up with the Cardinals who lost over a million dollars in six seasons.[99]

Major league teams in two-team cities outside New York were significantly less successful businesses. Chicago's nines both made nearly $2.2 million, but not as much as their large population base warranted. The Cubs earned about twice as much as the White Sox from 1920 to 1950 ($2.6 million), but suffered big losses in the early 1950s with poor teams and modest media revenues, when the Sox were on the way up, finally. The Cubs were at times outstanding draws, setting a major league attendance record in 1929, and led the NL in attendance in the 1920s and 1930s (with pennants in 1929, 1932, 1935, and 1938), but as already noted, the Wrigleys treated the club as a hobby rather than as a business. Still they siphoned off nearly $1.4 million in dividends while the Sox just $268,450.[100]

The two Philadelphia teams did much worse, far below what their metropolitan size should have warranted. The Phillies were a total disaster, with an annual loss of $20,734, the worst in the NL. They had terrible teams and even worse ownership, probably the most incompetent in the history of baseball. The Athletics, on the other hand, had the most consistent leaderships in baseball under owner-manager Connie Mack, but he did not have deep pockets. They also enjoyed one of the greatest teams in baseball history, the 1929–1931 A's. The Athletics earned $754,570 during the Mack tenure, which included years of big profits and big losses, reflecting their ups and downs on the diamond. The Macks were paid handsomely and also took in $600,050 in dividends, leaving little for reinvestment.[101]

Finally, Boston was too small to support two terrible teams that both lost money. The Red Sox bled money, losing $2.75 million, the only AL team to lose money in the period between 1920 and 1956, and the biggest loser in MLB. The Sox had the worst attendance in the AL in the 1920s, but achieved a respectable fourth in the 1930s and 1940s. The Red Sox had been a top team in the 1900s, the best team overall in the 1910s, and then after disastrous transactions, notably the sale of Babe Ruth to the Yankees, the worst AL team in the 1920s. They improved to fifth in the 1930s, and third in the 1940s, led by a great lineup that featured Ted Williams. Owner Tom Yawkey spent freely to build a good team, which he did not achieve until after World War II. Their cross-town rivals, the Braves, lost $756,989, an average of $23,656, worst in the NL. The Braves had one of the most spacious ballparks in the majors, but had horrible teams. The club had the worst attendance in the NL in the 1920s, and was near the bottom in the 1930s and 1940s. The Braves were historically one of the worst teams in the NL. Their best decade was the 1940s when they had an average finish of fifth place. The city was too small to support two teams, and it was understandable that the Braves would move on. They turned things around in Milwaukee, which set off a flurry of team migrations, most regrettably the Dodgers to Los Angeles and the Giants to San Francisco. But baseball is business after all, even though players play it.[102]

Profitability, which included actual profits, dividends, and salaries taken by owners, varied from team to team, but overall baseball was a good investment for shrewd executives. Between 1920 and 1950, MLB collectively had just three years with a negative profit margin, 1933 and 1934 in the heart of the Depression, and 1943, during World War II.[103] Owners had to take an active role in wisely managing the club or hire astute executives to operate the team, or it could likely falter, as happened to both the Pirates and Cardinals in the early 1950s. Nonetheless, a baseball team was a solid investment that weathered bad times, like the Great Depression, better than most businesses. Furthermore, Major League Baseball was a monopsony, and an owner could reasonably expect that the value of the franchise would regularly appreciate and provide a handsome profit when the time to sell arose. The new owners who came into baseball in this era were not going to be former baseball players or politicians as they had often been in the early twentieth century, but increasingly men of means, including millionaires. The owners were not yet conglomerates, such as CBS, who bought the Yankees in 1964, and more recently such companies as the Tribune Company, Doubleday, or Walt Disney. Owners were mainly businessmen who regarded their ball club as a business to make money, though there were exceptions like Yawkey, Wrigley, and Ruppert, who treated their franchise as a hobby, with mixed success. Still, over the long haul, there were probably better places to park one's capital. From 1929 to 1950, the value of all industries rose by 214 percent (mainly because of the great postwar boom), the value of all recreational industries other than motion pictures rose by 191 percent, and MLB rose by 184 percent.[104] Of course, it is a lot more fun to own a baseball team than a textile mill or a department store.

NOTES

1. In 1883, the Chicago White Stockings reportedly earned $20,000, $15,000 in 1886, and $80,000 in 1887, by which time the franchise had accumulated a surplus of about $100,000. This was followed by a $60,000 profit in 1888. Albert G. Spalding won five pennants in seven years (1880–1882, 1885–1886), with dividends that often exceeded 20 percent of the original investment. However, in 1890, the White Stockings lost $65,000 in fighting the new Players League sponsored by the players union, the Brotherhood. See, Bessie Louise Pierce, *A History of Chicago, 1871–1893*, vol. 3 (Chicago: University of Chicago Press, 1957), 478; Peter Levine, *A.G. Spalding and the Rise of Baseball: The Promise of American Sport* (New York: Oxford University Press, 1985), 36–37, 64; Harold Seymour, *Baseball*, vol. 1, *The Early Years* (Ithaca, NY: Cornell University Press, 1960), 119; David Q. Voigt, "Cash and Glory: The Commercialization of Major League Baseball as a Sports Spectacle, 1865–1892" (Ph.D diss., Syracuse University, 1963), 524–25. There are scattered data on early major league profits and losses. In 1879, NL champion Providence reputedly made $1,500, while seventh-place Troy lost $5,000. Providence made $3,350 in 1880, $3,098 in 1882, and $10,000 in 1884. The Boston Red Stockings were among the more profitable teams. The club made a $150 profit in 1881, $3,750 the following year, and then $40,000 and $48,000 in 1883 and 1884, respectively. See *Syracuse Evening Herald*, October

10, 1879, 8, cited in U.S. Congress, House Judiciary Committee, *Organized Baseball, Hearings before the Subcommittee on Study of Monopoly Power,* 82nd Cong., 1st Sess., 1951, serial 1, part 6 (Washington, DC: Government Printing Office, 1952), 1440 (hereafter cited as *Organized Baseball*). According to Voigt, the club made $300,000 during the 1880s. David Q. Voigt, *American Baseball,* vol. 1, *From Gentlemen's Sport to the Commissioner System* (Norman, OK: University of Oklahoma Press, 1966), 232. On early American Association profits, see Voigt, *American Baseball,* 130; ibid., "Cash and Glory," 505, 529–30; *Sporting Life,* October 22, 1883, 8. The NL claimed in 1889 that the teams had collectively made $750,000 between 1885 and 1889, 80 percent of which reputedly was reinvested in the franchises. The league report claimed these were the only years of profitability, which is questionable. See *New York Sun,* November 22, 1889, cited in *Organized Baseball,* 1440–41. On the Giants, see *New York Tribune,* January 25, 1895; *New York Times,* October 26, 1904, December 5, 1915, April 13, 1917, April 7, 1941; *Brooklyn Eagle,* January 18, 1896; Blanch S. McGraw, *The Real McGraw* (New York: D. McKay, 1953), 90–91, 170; Seymour, *Baseball,* vol. 1, 238.

2. Financial data from this era must be used with caution. The *World* estimated the average team made $29,333, while the *Herald,* a more modest $8,750.

ESTIMATED NATIONAL LEAGUE PROFITS IN 1899

NL Club	*New York World*	*New York Herald*	*Chicago Times-Herald*
Brooklyn	$50,000	$15,000	profit
New York	12,000	–40,000	loss
Boston	60,000	20,000	50,000
Philadelphia	75,000	40,000	15,000
Baltimore	15,000	10,000	15,000
Louisville	12,000	–10,000	profit
Pittsburgh	15,000	–10,000	15,000
Chicago	35,000	0	20,000
St. Louis	50,000	20,000	50,000
Cleveland	0	–30,000	loss
Cincinnati	20,000	–5,000	profit
Washington	8,000	–10,000	profit
Total	$352,000	0	$210,000 +

Source: *Sporting Life,* October, 21, 1899; *Chicago Times-Herald,* October 15, 1899; *Sporting News,* February 17, 1900.

3. *New York Times,* September 10, 1908, February 3, 1920; Edward Mott Woolley, "The Business of Baseball," *McClure's* 39 (1912): 251–55; George Ethelbert Walsh, "The Gilt-Edged Diamond," *The Independent* 75 (July 31, 1913): 261–63.

4. Lindberg, *Who's on 3rd? The Chicago White Sox Story* (South Bend, IN: Icarus, 1983), 17–22; Lindberg, "Yesterday's City: The South Side's Baseball Factory," *Chicago History* 18 (1989): 61; Seymour, *Baseball*, vol. 2, *The Golden Age* (Ithaca, NY: Cornell University Press, 1971), 71; Eugene Murdock, *Ban Johnson: Czar of Baseball* (Westport, CT: Greenwood Press, 1982), 149, 154; *New York Times*, September 28, 1919; *Organized Baseball*, 1591, 1593.

5. Edward Mott Woolley, "The Business of Baseball," *McClure's* 39 (July 1912): 245; *Chicago Tribune*, March 18, 1916. Seymour, *Baseball*, vol. 2, 420; Joe Tinker, "Putting Across the Federal League," *Everybody's Magazine* 30 (May 1914): 583; Seymour, *Baseball*, vol. 2, 34–36; Warren Brown, *The Chicago Cubs* (New York: G.P. Putnam's Sons, 1946), 64–65; *The Federal Baseball Club of Baltimore, Inc. v. The National League of Professional Baseball Clubs and the American League of Professional Baseball Clubs* (1922), 259 U.S. 200.

6. Henry D. Fetter, *Taking on the Yankees; Winnings and Losing in the Business of Baseball, 1903–2003* (New York: W.W. Norton, 2003), 200. On bucket shops, see David Hochfelder, "'Where the Common People Could Speculate': The Ticker, Bucket Shops, and the Origins of Popular Participation in Financial Markets, 1880–1920," *Journal of American History* 93 (September 2006): 335–58; Jonathan Ira Levy, "Contemplating Delivery: Futures Trading and the Problem of Commodity Exchange in the United States, 1875–1905," *American Historical Review* 111 (April 2006): 307–35.

7. Bruce Kuklick, *To Every Thing a Season: Shibe Park and Urban Philadelphia, 1909–1976* (Princeton, NJ: Princeton University Press, 1991), 14–18, 34.

8. Ibid., 36, 49–50; David M. Jordan, *The Athletics of Philadelphia: Connie Mack's White Elephants, 1901–1954* (Jefferson City, NC: McFarland, 1999), 69.

9. Hugh C. Weir, "Baseball: The Men and the Dollars Behind It," *World Today* 17 (July 1909): 752–61; "Fortunes Made in Baseball," *Literary Digest* 45 (July 20, 1912): 119–20; Edward Mott Woolley, "The Business of Baseball," *McClure's* 39 (July 1912): 241–56; "The Business Side of Baseball," *Current Literature* 53 (August 1912): 170; *Sporting Life*, January 13, 1900; *New York Times*, April 19, 1925; *New York Tribune*, April 19, 1925; *Sporting News*, January 3, 1920. Ebbets had to sell half the team when he overextended himself building Ebbets Field in 1913, and sold a half share in the team for $100,000. Fetter, *Taking on the Yankees*, 27; Michael Haupert, "The Economic History of Major League Baseball," http://www.eh.net/graphics/encyclopedia/mlb.htm (accessed March 1, 2006).

10. *Sporting News*, August 1910, quoted in David Pietrusza, *Major Leagues: The Formation, Sometimes Absorption, and Mostly Eventual Demise of 18 Professional Baseball Organizations, 1871 to Present* (Jefferson City, NC: McFarland, 1991), 183–84.

11. Robert F. Burk, *Never Just a Game: Players, Owners & American Baseball to 1920* (Chapel Hill, NC: University of North Carolina Press, 1994), 206.

12. *Organized Baseball*, 1591–92.

13. Compiled from table entitled "Margin of Profit on Gross Operating Income, Major League Clubs, 1920–1950," *Organized Baseball,* 1615.

14. Michael Haupert, "Purchasing the Pennants: The New York Yankees Then and Now. Part 1: Yankee Revenues and Expenses," *OTC (Over the Line),* newsletter of the SABR Business Committee (Winter 2005).

15. *Organized Baseball,* 1591, 1617, 1619.

16. David Q. Voigt, *American Baseball,* vol. 2, *From the Commissioner to Continental Expansion* (Norman, OK: University of Oklahoma Press, 1970), 246.

17. *Organized Baseball,* 1591–92, 1600–01, 1606; Michael Haupert, "Economic History of Major League Baseball," 2.

18. Voigt, *American Baseball,* vol. 2, 243; *Organized Baseball,* 1591–1601; *Sporting Life,* January 13, 1900; *Sporting News,* January 3, 1920; *New York Times,* April 19, 1925; *New York Tribune,* April 19, 1925. Both the *Times* and *Tribune* inaccurately estimated profits in 1920 at over $500,000.

19. Fetter, *Taking on the Yankees,* 141–42; *Organized Baseball,* 1591–92, 1600–01.

20. Ibid.; John David Cash, "The St. Louis Cardinals," in *The Encyclopedia of Major League Baseball,* vol. 1, *The National League,* ed. Steven A. Riess (Westport, CT: Greenwood Press, 2006), 401–37; *Organized Baseball,* 1591–92, 1600–01. Rickey's first Cardinal contract in 1918 called for a $25,000 base salary and a 10 percent share of club profits. Robert F. Burk, *Much More than a Game: Players, Owners & American Baseball Since 1921* (Chapel Hill, NC: University of North Carolina Press, 2001), 36.

21. Robert S. Fuchs and Wayne Soini, *Judge Fuchs and the Boston Braves, 1923–1935* (Jefferson, NC: McFarland, 1998), 26.

22. *Organized Baseball,* 1591–92, 1600.

23. Ibid., 1591–92, 1600–01; Fuchs and Soini, *Judge Fuchs and the Boston Braves,* 42. Judge Fuchs owned the team from 1923 to 1935. He bought the team for $300,000 from fellow New York politician George Washington Grant, who had bought the team in 1919 for $400,000.

24. Fetter, *Taking on the Yankees,* 69–83; Michael Haupert, with Ken Winter, "'Yankee Profits and Promise': The Purchase of Babe Ruth and the Building of Yankee Stadium," in *The Cooperstown Symposium on Baseball and American Culture, 2003–2004,* ed. William Simons (Jefferson, NC: McFarland, 2005), 199, 201; *Organized Baseball,* 1620. When Devery died, his estate was $1,023 in debt; Farrell ended up with just $1,072. See "The Yankees," *Fortune* 34 (July 1946): 134. In 1923, Ruppert bought out Huston for $1.5 million, a big appreciation in team value. Haupert, "Purchasing the Pennants."

25. *Organized Baseball,* 1591, 1618, 1620; Burk, *Much More than a Game,* 23.

26. *Organized Baseball,* 1592, 1620; Burk, *Much More than a Game,* 23, 211–12.

27. Brad Snyder, *Beyond the Shadow of the Senators: The Untold Story of the Homestead Grays and the Integration of Baseball* (Chicago: Contemporary Books, 2003), 56–67; *Organized Baseball,* 1591–92, 1600.

28. Robert F. Lewis, "Oakland Athletics," *Encyclopedia of Major League Baseball*, vol. 2, *American League*, ed. Steven A. Riess (Westport, CT: Greenwood, 2006), 757–77; Jordan, *The Athletics of Philadelphia;* Kuklick, *To Every Thing a Season.*

29. *Organized Baseball*, 1599–1600, 1618, 1620. For the statistics on the Browns, see "1922 St. Louis Browns," in *Baseball-Reference.com*, http://www.baseball-reference.com/teams/SLB/1922.shtml (accessed March 4, 2006).

30. Ibid. Robert K. Barney and David E. Barney, "Boston Red Sox," in *Encyclopedia of Major League Teams*, vol. 2, ed. Riess, 499–527.

31. *Organized Baseball*, 1610. Visiting teams then got 25 percent of revenues. On average team payrolls, see *NYT*, May 21, 1952, 32.

32. *Organized Baseball*, 1599, 1615.

33. *Baseball Magazine* (September 1930): 434, cited in Charles Alexander, *Breaking the Slump: Baseball in the Depression Era* (New York: Columbia University Press, 2002), 17.

34. *The Sporting News*, April 23, 1931, 2, quoted in ibid., 40. See also ibid., 77.

35. *Organized Baseball*, 1599–1600, 1610, 1617; Alexander, *Breaking the Slump*, 61. Cleveland business manager Billy Evans said the average annual cost of running a major league team in 1932 was $535,000, with at least $235,000 for salaries. Spring training cost $10,000; rail, hotel ($5 a night for doubles), and meals ($3.50 to $4.00) $30,000; scouting $50,000, and new players $50,000. He estimated teams would need to draw 500,000 at home and 500,000 on the road to break even.

36. *Organized Baseball*, 1599, 1610; Andrew Zimbalist, *Baseball and Billions: A Probing Look inside the Big Business of Our National Pastime*, updated ed. (New York, Basic Books, 1994), 62.

37. *Organized Baseball*, 1636.

38. Ibid., 1600–01, 1606–07; Burk, *Much More than a Game*, 68.

39. Ibid., 1599–1600; "Year in Review: 1936," *Baseball Almanac*, http://www.baseball-almanac.com/yearly/yr1936a.shtml (accessed November 18, 2006). During the mid-1930s, corporations were required to report all annual salaries above $15,000, and they were published in *The Sporting News*. Douglas Pappas found a source of data based on government reports of corporate salaries in the years 1934 to 1937 at the National Baseball Hall of Fame, Cooperstown, New York. See Douglas Pappas, "1934–1937 Salaries," in "Doug's Business of Baseball Articles," http://roadsidephotos.sabr.org/baseball/sabrmain.htm.

40. *Organized Baseball*, 1591–92, 1600–01, 1610. William Wrigley claimed in 1934 that his team had lost about $600,000, but congressional records set the losses for 1933 to 1934 at $417,661. The team also declared dividends of $110,000 in 1934. See William Wrigley, Jr., "Owning a Big-League Baseball Team," *Saturday Evening Post* 203 (September 13, 1930): 25; Alexander, *Breaking the Slump*, 35; *Organized Baseball*, 1601.

41. *Organized Baseball*, 1606. The Reds were the one of the first to charge for radio broadcasts, $2,000 in 1933. According to MacPhail's biography, three stations were

each paying $2,000 for the privileges. See Don Warfield, *The Roaring Redhead: Larry MacPhail—Baseball's Great Innovator* (South Bend, IN: Diamond Communications, 1987), 51.

42. *Organized Baseball,* 1591–92, 1600–01; Alexander, *Depression Baseball,* 100.

43. Ibid., 1591–92, 1600–01, 1617; John Helyar, *Lords of the Realm: The Real History of Baseball* (New York: Ballentine Books, 1994), 40.

44. Ibid., 1591, 1600, 1601, 1610. Despite its negative ledger, Judge Fuchs reportedly turned down a $600,000 offer to sell the team to Joseph P. Kennedy and Herbert B. Swope of the *New York World.* See Fuchs and Sorini, *Judge Fuchs and the Boston Braves,* 109.

45. Ibid., 1591–92, 1602–03, 1610, 1618, 1620.

46. Ibid., 1599–1600, 1610. Pappas, "1934–1937 Salaries."

47. Ibid., 1591, 1592, 1599, 1600, 1610.

48. Ibid., 1600, 1620; Tom Deveaux, *The Washington Senators, 1901–1971* (Jefferson, NC: McFarland, 2001).

49. *Organized Baseball,* 1602–03.

50. http://baseball-reference.com/teams/PHA/1933_trans.shtml; *Organized Baseball,* 1591, 1599, computed from 1610; Fetter, *Taking on the Yankees,* 170; Jordan, *Athletics of Philadelphia,* 117, 119; Kuklick, *To Everything a Season,* 62, 112–13.

51. *Organized Baseball,* 1591–1591, 1599–1600. Louis Comiskey took a salary of $23,996. See Pappas, "1914–1937 Salaries."

52. *Organized Baseball,* 1591–92, 1599–1600, 1620; James Edward Miller, *The Baseball Business: Pursuing Pennants and Profits in Baltimore* (Chapel Hill, NC: University of North Carolina Press, 1990), 23.

53. Glenn Stout and Richard A. Johnson, *Red Sox Century: One Hundred Years of Red Sox Baseball* (Boston: Houghton Mifflin, 2000); *Organized Baseball,* 1599, 1603, 1610.

54. *Organized Baseball,* 969, 1610–11.

55. Benjamin G. Rader, *Baseball: A History of America's Game,* 2nd ed. (Urbana, IL: University of Illinois Press, 2002), 188.

56. *Organized Baseball,* 1599, 1615, 1636; Zimbalist, *Baseball and Billions,* 62, 68.

57. Ibid., 1616. On postwar baseball, see William Marshall, *Baseball's Pivotal Era, 1945–1951* (Lexington: University Press of Kentucky, 1999).

58. Rader, *Baseball,* 188; *Organized Baseball,* 1599, 1615, 1636. The movies had a higher profit margin than baseball from 1941 to 1943, but baseball went ahead from 1944 through 1949. Zimbalist, *Baseball and Billions,* 62, 68.

59. *Organized Baseball,* 1601, 1608–10.

60. Ibid., 1608, 1610; "1946 St. Louis Cardinals Statistics and Roster," http://www.baseball-reference.com/teams/STL/1946.shtml; "1950 St. Louis Cardinals Statistics and Roster," http://www.baseball-reference.com/teams/STL/1950.shtml (accessed October 26, 2006).

61. *Organized Baseball,* 1608; "The Yankees," 171.

62. Ibid., 1591–92, 1600–01; *NYT,* November 8, 1951.

63. Ibid., 1608; Steven Gietschier, "The Los Angeles Dodgers," in *The Encyclopedia of Major League Baseball,* ed. Steven A. Riess (Westport, CT: Greenwood Press, 2006), 181–217; Helyar, *Lords of the Realm,* 47.

64. Ibid., 1591–92, 1600, 1608, 1610.

65. Ibid., 1591–92, 1600, 1606–09.

66. Ibid.

67. Ibid., 1591–92, 1600–01, 1619.

68. Ibid.

69. "The Yankees," 139, 171, 175. There is a discrepancy of less than $1,000 between the profit reported by *Fortune* and the amount reported by the congressional investigation of baseball in 1952. See *Organized Baseball,* 1602.

70. Warfield, *Roaring Redhead,* 162. On MacPhail's report to baseball that criticized integration, see *Organized Baseball,* 484–85; Snyder, *Beyond the Shadows of the Senators,* 232. In 1964, the Yankees were sold for $13.2 million to CBS. Zimbalist, *Baseball and Billions,* 68. On TV, see Haupert, "Economic History of Major League Baseball," 9.

71. Neil Lanctot, *Negro League Baseball: The Rise and Ruin of a Black Institution* (Philadelphia: University of Pennsylvania Press, 2004), 127, 148–50, 200.

72. *Organized Baseball,* 1590, 1591, 1599, 1600.

73. Snyder, *Beyond the Shadows of the Senators,* 95, 182, 207, 232, 233, 250.

74. *Organized Baseball,* 1591–92, 1600–01; Miller, *Baseball Business,* 23, 24.

75. Ibid., 1591, 1600–01, 1603–05, 1610.

76. Ibid., 1616, 1636; Burk, *More than a Game,* 109; Haupert, "Economic History of Major League Baseball," 9; *Organized Professional Team Sports,* 370.

77. Ibid.,1599; Burk, *More than a Game,* 107, 109–12; Haupert, "Economic History of Major League Baseball," 9.

78. Ibid., 1610–11; U.S. Senate, Committee on the Judiciary, *Organized Professional Team Sports: Hearings before the Subcommittee on Antitrust and Monopoly of the Committee of the Judiciary,* 85th Cong., 2nd Sess. (Washington: Government Printing Office, 1958), 803 (hereafter cited as *Organized Professional Team Sports).*

79. *Organized Professional Team Sports,* 800; Burk, *More than a Game,* 112. The share of revenue from media rose from about 3 percent in 1946 to 10 percent in 1950, and 17 percent in 1956. Zimbalist, *Baseball and Billions,* 85, 87, 98. See also Joseph M. Sheehan, "Baseball Clubs as Big Business," *NYT,* June 9, 1957, 172.

80. Sheehan, "Baseball Clubs as Big Business," 172.

81. Glen Gendzel, "Competitive Boosterism: How Milwaukee Lost the Braves," *Business History Review* 69 (1995): 530–66.

82. Fetter, *Taking on the Yankees,* 275, 354–55, 358; U.S. Congress, House Judiciary Committee, *Organized Professional Team Sports. Hearings before the Antitrust Subcom-*

mittee of the Committee on the Judiciary, 85th Cong., 1st Sess. (Washington: Government Printing Office, 1957), 353 (hereafter cited as *OPTS*).

83. *OPTS*, 353; *Organized Baseball*, 1599; Arthur L. Olszyk, "The Struggle over Braves Broadcasting Rights," *Milwaukee History* 19:2 (1996): 49–53.

84. Rader, *Baseball*, 186–97; Neil Sullivan, *The Dodgers Move West* (New York: Oxford University Press, 1987).

85. *OPTS*, 353. 800–03; "Ballparks of Baseball: The Fields of Major League Baseball," http://www.ballparksofbaseball.com/1950–59attendance.htm (accessed August 26, 2006).

86. *Organized Baseball*, 1608–09.

87. Ibid., 1608–09; *OPTS*, 353, 358; Fetter, *Taking on the Yankees*, 261–65, 268; Sullivan, *The Dodgers Move West*, 116.

88. Fetter, *Taking on the Yankees*, 354–55, 358; *NYT*, November 8, 1951.

89. *OPTS*, 354–58, 648–49, 800–03; Fetter, *Taking on the Yankees*, 230; Burk, *More than a Game*, 111.

90. *Organized Baseball*, 1600; *OPTS*, 353. On the Dodgers migration, see Sullivan, *The Dodgers Move West;* Lee Lowenfish, "A Tale of Many Cities: The Westward Expansion of Major League Baseball in the 1950's," *Journal of the West* 17:3 (1978): 71–82.

91. *OPTS*, 800–03.

92. Ibid., 798–800. Payroll reports in government documents often included managers and coaches. For a report on the payrolls for just major and minor league players in 1950, see *NYT*, October 23, 1951, 36. The Yankees had the highest payroll of $488,500, followed by the Boston Red Sox ($450,000) and the St. Louis Cardinals ($385,500). The Browns were the lowest at just $192,750. The Yankees were in the World Series nineteen times and in the first division from 1921 through 1952 every season but 1925, which meant World Series money for the players. During that period, the average Yankee made $3,148 per season, while only the Cards and Giants made more than $1,000. In 1946, the front office published a booklet for prospective recruits that included a chapter that highlighted the financial advantages of joining the Bronx Bombers. *NYT*, October 21, 1952, 40.

93. "Revised Statements of Profits and Loss for Years Ending in 1952," *OPTS*, 648.

94. Ibid., 651; Jordan, *Athletics of Philadelphia*, 119, 184. Scholars have given careful attention to the demise of the Athletics in Philadelphia and the ending of the Mack family control. They have often been the poster child for issues of baseball profitability, especially since their entire income was derived from the team. In 1954, the Macks sold the team and Shibe Park to Roy Johnson. Connie got $604,000 for 302 shares, and his sons Roy and Earle $50,000 each for their 163 shares a piece, plus Johnson assumed a $2 million debt. See also Kuklick, *To Everything a Season*, 114, 116–17, 119, 123.

95. *OPTS*, 648.

96. Miller, *Business of Baseball,* 24–25.

97. Ibid., 26–27, 34–35.

98. *OPTS,* 353, 359–61, 648–49.

99. *Organized Baseball,* 1591–92, 1601.

100. Ibid., 1599–1600; *OPTS,* 353.

101. Ibid.

102. Ibid.

103. Ibid., 1615.

104. *OPTS,* 798. In 2006, there were nine teams owned by corporations, five of whom have had better records than under private control. One of the teams, the Toronto Blue Jays, never had private control. However, a survey by the *Chicago Tribune* found that corporate teams have underperformed when measured by championships. Corporations owned major league teams for 17 percent of the seasons played by the current teams since 1970, but captured just 11 percent of league titles and 14 percent of World Series championships. *Chicago Tribune,* November 19, 2006, V, 1, 10–11.

MARK DYRESON

MAPPING AN EMPIRE OF BASEBALL

AMERICAN VISIONS OF NATIONAL PASTIMES AND GLOBAL INFLUENCE, 1919 TO 1941

On an August night in 1936, a crowd estimated at as many as one hundred and twenty-five thousand people turned out "to witness America's National Game."[1] The enormous congregation, by contemporary accounts the largest assembly ever to watch a baseball contest, surprised some observers, particularly since it gathered in a stadium far removed from the sport's homeland. On a makeshift field sketched in athletic tape over the green grass of a soccer pitch illuminated by the blinding rays of gargantuan searchlights, two teams garbed in red, white, and blue uniforms and composed mainly of American collegians, the World's Champions and the U.S. Olympics, battled for seven innings. A dramatic home run in the bottom of the seventh won the contest for the World's Champions. Though unfamiliar with baseball the huge throng roared as the horsehide sphere flew into the stands.[2]

This dramatic demonstration of the American national pastime occurred at one of the most spectacular and controversial sporting events of the twentieth century, the 1936 Olympic Games in Berlin.[3] German organizers, following Olympic protocol that required host nations to go beyond the standard Olympic menu and select one "foreign" demonstration sport as well as one "native" exhibition, had picked baseball as their exotic entry.[4] Some observers offered less than charitable assessments of the German reaction to baseball. An Associated Press correspondent asserted that the spectators' huge cheer at the end of the contest came not from their joy at witnessing a walk-off home run but from their delight that their ordeal had finally concluded.[5]

Most contemporary analysts offered far more generous interpretations of the event. Avery Brundage, the head of the American Olympic delegation in Berlin, crowed after the exhibition that baseball had conquered the world in Olympic Stadium.[6] The game impressed not only Americans but foreign observers as well. Carl Diem, the German organizer of the Berlin Games, rushed to the makeshift diamond after the contest ended. "I have come officially to advise you that this has been the finest demonstration of any sport that any nation has ever put on at any Olympic Games," Diem declared. "We congratulate you—and speaking for my people, you have made over 100,000 friends here tonight and as they go home America's baseball players' praises will be sung by all," he promised.[7]

The Berlin baseball demonstration impressed not only Nazi Germany but also the leadership of the militaristic dictatorship in Japan. At the conclusion of the Berlin Games the Japanese announced the inclusion of baseball in the program for the 1940 Tokyo Olympic Games.[8] The Berlin exhibition also sparked the creation of an International Baseball Congress. Member nations—though not all were nations by contemporary political reckoning—included Egypt, France, Hawaii, Cuba, China, Peru, South Africa, North Africa, Belgium, England, Canada, the Philippines, Holland, Sweden, Germany, Costa Rica, India, Spain, Mexico, Japan, and the United States. The new organization announced that it had scheduled a global baseball series that would pit Japan versus the United States in Tokyo in 1937, Panama versus the United States in the Canal Zone in 1938, and Japan versus the United States again, this time in Honolulu in 1939. These international contests would culminate in a "World's Tournament" scheduled for the 1940 Olympics. In the wake of baseball's enthusiastic reception at the Berlin Games, nine nations had already lined up to compete in the Tokyo Games—China, the Philippines, Hawaii, England, Germany, Mexico, Cuba, the United States, and host Japan.[9] With the Philippines, Hawaii, and the United States on the roster, the American empire would count for one-third of the "national" entries.[10]

Leslie Mann, the American baseball booster who almost single-handedly put the game on the 1936 Olympic program, was the guiding force in putting together the International Baseball Congress and promoting these new international contests. Mann had enjoyed a sixteen-year stint in the major leagues as a well-traveled outfielder with the Boston Braves, Chicago Whales, Chicago Cubs, St. Louis Cardinals, Cincinnati Reds, and New York Giants. He hit a respectable .282 for his career.[11] After retiring from professional baseball Mann became a fervent promoter of including baseball in the Olympic program. In that quest Mann recruited the man who during that era symbolized the game to the world to serve as the "commandant" of the American baseball delegation in Berlin. In a ploy that revealed Mann's genius for public relations he announced that Babe Ruth would head the American delegation.[12] Ruth failed to make the trip to Germany but Mann soldiered forward with his plans to add baseball to what was then the world's most popular sporting event.[13] In the afterglow of the Berlin Games, Mann proclaimed that "baseball was given its chance on the Olympic program and came through successfully." Mann predicted that "it is the type of game that will be taken on internationally and by 1940 our national game will be on the active program of the World's Greatest Athletic spectacle—the Olympic Games."[14]

The Berlin Olympic baseball exhibition represented the high tide of American aspirations to use their national pastime to build a more peaceful and a more American world. In retrospect, those visions seem more like delusions, given the history that rapidly unfolded in the wake of the 1936 Olympic Games. After all, baseball did little to quell the rush to war. Japan's 1940 "World's Tournament" was swallowed up by war, as were the Tokyo Olympic Games. An overly cynical reading of the Berlin exhibition through contemporary lenses, however, masks the importance of the event and blunts the central historical message of the game. This episode highlights the enormous, if naive, faith that many Americans between World Wars I and II invested in the power of their national pastime to transform the globe. That faith represents an important component of American culture during the 1920s and 1930s. Nurtured by the work of baseball promoters, popular journalists, and even government officials, Americans mapped a pacific empire united by a common faith in baseball and the American institutions the game supposedly invigorated, especially democracy, meritocracy, and egalitarianism. Ultimately, that empire failed to coalesce, but its boundaries reached farther than most historians imagine.

The *National Geographic Magazine* in 1919 provided the original map of those boundaries. In a world survey of sporting customs, the journalist J. R. Hildebrand charted the athletic traditions of the globe's cultures, arguing that "sports and games ever were magic touchstones of geography and those allied sciences which provide the surest clues to how peoples live, and work, and think." Hildebrand insisted that the Anglo American nations had the most developed sporting cultures in the world and credited that fact with the Allied victory in World War I. In the new world order that had emerged after the war Hildebrand gave the United States the crucial leadership role over its Anglo American cousins, arguing that American sports had more potential than British pastimes for transforming the world.[15]

Hildebrand identified baseball as the key to his map for remaking the world through sport. "It has been noted that the sports of a nation afford an almost invariable barometer of its progress in civilization," he asserted. "Baseball is one of the most complicated and highly organized pastimes known to any people," he declared. "It is a veritable instrument of the most delicate precision in the world of sport," he explained. "A South Sea islander no more could play it than he could operate a linotype machine or deftly handle the paper money in a bank teller's cage," argued Hildebrand in linking baseball directly to the civilizing process. Of course, Hildebrand noted, while South Sea Islanders might not be able to master baseball on their own, they could under American tutelage certainly learn both the game and the rudiments of civilization it inevitably conveyed.[16]

The *National Geographic*'s essay on "The Geography Games" concluded with an aerial photograph of Paris's Pershing Stadium, built by the U.S. military for the 1919 Inter-allied Games.[17] The Americans made certain that they included baseball in the program at those "Military Olympics," as they were popularly known, since those contests were designed to set the frame for the postwar world's sporting habits.[18] Those visions of baseball's power to Americanize the world were shared between the wars by an American multitude of baseball writers, baseball players, baseball entrepreneurs, and baseball fans, a history that the baseball scholar Richard Crepeau has deftly explored. Crepeau uncovers a widespread conversation which proclaimed that American League President Ban Johnson's trip to Mexico, New York Yankee sluggers Lou Gehrig's and Babe Ruth's tours of the Far East, and regular press commentaries about the spread of baseball represented the most powerful weapons in America's foreign policy arsenal. Those dialogues convinced many that the national pastime might be more effective than politicians in the quest for world peace. "The baseball community was certainly as active as the business community in expanding American influence in the world in the decades between the wars," Crepeau contends.[19]

The baseball community, as Crepeau details, played a major role in pushing for a *Pax Americana* during the 1920s and 1930s. In drawing a map of a league of nations governed by fealty to baseball, however, the federal government also played a key role. This endeavor constituted a powerful irony since the U.S. government failed to join the League of Nations that it had originally designed. Excavations of an alternative set of sources reveal that during the 1920s and 1930s the U.S. Departments of Commerce and State sought to link the baseball and business communities together in a coalition designed to export both U.S. influence and U.S. products. Government documents reveal the breadth and depth of American dreams for a baseball empire, including fantasies of baseball taking root in distant lands, hopes that baseball might temper conflicts with rival nations, visions of grand new markets for baseball goods, rumors that Fascist dictators might convert to the gospel of baseball, and tales of magical baseball bats that would never splinter.[20]

The fact that the federal government mapped out a plan for Americanizing the world through baseball reinforces the game's central role in U.S. culture. Neither the baseball community nor the business community undertook this venture on its own. Contrary to historian Allen Guttmann's recent contention that during the 1920s and 1930s only Fascist, Communist, and Nazi states actively used sport as an instrument of statecraft, the U.S. government's crucial role in drafting a map of baseball's potential empire demonstrates that liberal-democratic governments also "instrumentalized sports."[21] The U.S. government played a key role in promoting baseball as an instrument for spreading American ways of life throughout the world.[22] The federal bureaucrats understood baseball in the same way as *National Geographic,* as "a veritable instrument of the most delicate precision."[23] With that instrument they believed they could transform the world.[24]

The federal government began mapping an American baseball empire in the 1920s, as the United States became the world's economic colossus. American industrial and technological prowess sparked "fables of abundance" that dazzled global audiences. American society loomed as the global model for affluence that made the United States the leading exporter not only of products but also of culture. American tastes in fashion, movies, and music became global fads.[25] The global depression that began at the end of the 1920s and wreaked havoc on the world's economies during the 1930s tarnished but did not destroy those "fables of abundance." In the midst of the bleakest crisis in modern economic history the United States remained at the center of the new world system.[26]

In the early 1920s in the warrens of the Departments of Commerce and State, federal bureaucrats began to chart the possibilities of an American dominion based on sport. America's national pastime played an essential role in their imperial schemes. A request from a consortium of sports businesses for the federal government's aid in opening foreign markets provided the original impetus for the project. In 1923, the Chicago-based National Sports Promotion Association, a fledgling sporting goods manufacturing cooperative that included baseball equipment makers Thomas E. Wilson & Company and the Western Sporting Goods Manufacturing Company, petitioned the federal government for help in finding foreign consumers for U.S. athletic goods.[27] The sporting goods firms contended that the invasion of American troops into Europe during World War I had "resulted in the education of a large number of people to American games—this field, if properly cultivated should result in a large business."[28] Indeed, Hildebrand's 1919 story in the *National Geographic* had reported that during the war the

U.S. shipped an enormous cache of baseball equipment to Europe. "At the government's behest, one welfare organization alone sent 25,000 baseballs and 15,000 baseball bats to France before half our men arrived there," Hildebrand revealed. "Even the sport-loving Britons are said to have admired and wondered at the American dough-boy, whacking out three-baggers amid the booming of Big Berthas, issuing occasional rain-checks in mid-inning when the downpour of bursting shell became too distracting," the *National Geographic*'s correspondent marveled.[29]

The sporting goods conglomerate's request reached U.S. Secretary of Commerce Herbert Hoover, then in the midst of using federal power to open the world's markets to American firms.[30] Hoover thought the idea of pushing the export of sport had considerable merit. He sent the proposal to the Specialties Division of his agency's Bureau of Foreign and Domestic Commerce. Henry Morse, the chief of the Specialties Division, also eagerly endorsed the contention that American games such as baseball would open the floodgates for the export of U.S. goods and values.[31]

Taking their cues from the National Sports Promotion Association, Department of Commerce experts designed a trade survey to test the prospects for exporting baseball and other American games to foreign markets. Their "Questionnaire No. 84" instructed U.S. overseas operatives to gather data on sports around the world. The Washington headquarters of the Department of Commerce shipped the questionnaire to the far corners of the globe.[32] A few years later, after the United States won the right to host the 1932 Winter and Summer Olympic Games, U.S. Department of Commerce and State analysts refined the survey as "Questionnaire No. 302" and amassed a second set of sports data from around the world.[33] The information collected in the two surveys led Commerce Department leaders to boast to the U.S. Congress that their projects resulted in the "accumulation of a vast amount of data on the development of sports in foreign countries."[34]

The surveys and the trade reports they generated should have sobered the bureaucrats, the baseball industry, the press, and the millions of fans who had imbibed of the narcotic vision of an American empire of influence built on baseball. In spite of a strong tradition of American athletic prestige around the world, based in large part on American success in the Olympic Games, the analyses revealed formidable obstacles arrayed against the plan to push American culture and American commerce through American games. First, the United States faced intense competition, primarily from Great Britain but in some regions from other industrial powers, in the sporting goods marketplace. Second, in many parts of the developing world the laboring masses could not even afford the cheapest American-produced baseball bats, gloves, or balls. Federal trade experts remained confident that in most cases these first two obstacles were surmountable. They believed, even after the Great Depression inflicted enormous damage on individual spending power, that the world's working masses would quickly become consumers. They also believed that American firms would conquer British and other foreign rivals in the competition to supply the world's athletic desires.

The third obstacle, however, represented an exceptionally daunting challenge. Both of the questionnaires had concentrated on collecting information about the world's leading national pastimes. Indeed, as Commerce Department memorandums outlining procedures for conducting the first survey insisted, the key to the exercise was to determine in each nation the answer to a basic question: "What is the National game or sport that predominates?"[35] The answers to that query presented a colossal impediment to American desires to make baseball the world's game.

The State and Commerce Departments' reports on the scope of national pastimes in that era confirm West Indian historian and revolutionary C. L. R. James's declaration in *Beyond a Boundary* that the twentieth-century's "common people" were consumed by an ardent desire for sport.[36] People around the world loved athletic contests. Even among the developing world's poverty-stricken masses too poor to afford modern sporting goods, a deep passion for modern sport had already been kindled. The pastimes most of the world loved, however, were not American games. In James's West Indian homeland and in much of the rest of the English-speaking world, people preferred cricket paddles to baseball bats. In the rest of the world, association football—soccer in American parlance—had already seized the mantle of the "world's game."[37]

American ambassadors, attachés, and analysts simply could not ignore the pervasive popularity of soccer. The game ranked as the "leading sport" in almost every European and Latin American nation and in quite a few African and Asian nations. Soccer shared laurels as a co-national pastime with cricket in much of the English-speaking world—even on James's home island of Trinidad.[38] Undeniably, the "Esperanto of the ball," in Uruguayan essayist Eduardo Galeano's magical phrase, flourished even at the margins of modernity by the third and fourth decades of the twentieth century.[39]

American foreign service officers were not particularly fluent in this version of the new global language. The emerging international soccer football culture was not a world that very many Americans, including the presumably cosmopolitan diplomatic corps, inhabited. The architects of the blueprint to Americanize the world through sports thus faced a conundrum. The globe's masses craved sports; however, outside of a few areas with strong political or economic ties to the United States, such as Cuba, some of the other Caribbean nations, parts of Latin America, the Philippines, and Japan where baseball was becoming a "transnational" national pastime, the world was not particularly interested in the American national pastime.[40] The federal bureaucrats clearly recognized a fundamental difference between American and other national sporting cultures around which some twenty-first-century scholars toiling in the domain of "sport studies" have erected a cottage industry. American resistance to soccer, a clear marker of American exceptionalism, created problems for the United States in international relations.[41]

Government officials believed those problems might have a solution—the deliberate distribution of baseball. The U.S. government's topographies of world sport initially revealed a rather inhospitable global terrain for the advance of baseball. Faced with soccer's burgeoning hegemony over the globe's sporting habits, federal experts maintained their faith that in the end baseball would win over the world.[42] Certainly the bureaucrats manifested an intense devotion to those beliefs. "American goods could only be popularized if American games were played here," wrote U.S. Vice Consul Alfredo Demorest from Trinidad—to reiterate, James's cricket-loving and soccer-worshiping home island. Demorest hoped that somehow baseball would sweep British games off the island.[43] From the Irish Free State, U.S. Vice Consul Edwin King echoed those sentiments, opining that the real problem in selling American sporting goods in Ireland was the absence of baseball in Irish sporting traditions.[44] A host of reports reveal similar opinions.

Faced with data that contradicted their desires, the federal officials in the Departments of Commerce and State made certain to highlight on their sporting map of the world every spot where even the faintest interest in baseball flickered. Without ignoring the reality that soccer had conquered large swaths of the globe, they kept their faith that the American national pastime would compete for dominion. Corporate elements of the baseball community shared their convictions, eagerly waiting for any tidbit about potential baseball markets that federal agents could develop. From baseball specialists such as bat manufacturers Hillerich & Bradsby to general sporting goods producers with baseball lines such as A. J. Reach and A. G. Spalding & Brothers, American corporations eagerly clamored for the maps of the nascent baseball empire sketched by the Departments of Commerce and State.[45]

Those maps revealed a very strange set of contours for the potential global spread of America's national pastime. As might be expected, the places furthest from American geographic gazes in that era also yielded the least sports data in the official charts. The athletic maps of Africa and the Near East drawn by the U.S. government officials depicted a vast wasteland devoid of prospects for baseball. Commerce and State Department reports from the 1920s and 1930s reported almost no sporting activity or interest in huge swaths of those two areas. U.S. officials noted that soccer football represented the only national pastime with any hope of gaining even a small foothold among the African and Middle Eastern masses. Baseball seemed to have no chance whatsoever.[46]

The experts blamed a lack of economic development, the failure of modernization, the vestiges of colonialism, and equatorial temperatures for the antisporting climate. In a particular reference to Africa, U.S. bureaucrats also regarded race as an impediment. "Africa is populated almost entirely by blacks, who for the most part still have very primitive methods of living and virtually no purchasing power whatsoever," contended the Department of Commerce's trade bulletin detailing the *Market for Sporting and Athletic Goods in Africa and Near East*. "They have not inherited any athletic tradition and except for the business of hunting and fishing have never participated in athletic sports—at least not any kind which would call for the type of athletic equipment produced in the United States," the Commerce bulletin insisted.[47]

Perhaps the strict segregation in the American national pastime contributed to the racial attitudes of the government officials in charge of surveying the prospects for building a baseball empire.[48] Regardless, the foreign service officers could not see any prospect for baseball growing in African or Middle Eastern soils. Where bat-and-ball games did appear in those provinces, they were the pastimes of European, particularly British, colonials. In that climate only cricket flourished, at least among the white masters of colonial dominions.[49]

Given their assumptions, the upper echelons of the Department of Commerce reacted with great surprise when in 1933 Samuel H. Day, the American commercial attaché in Johannesburg, reported a case of baseball fever in South Africa. Day's missives to Washington made it clear that the game had begun to flourish among white colonials and not the black masses. Still, given that South Africa was a British colony with very little immigration from the United States, the appearance of baseball was a huge shock. Day advised his superiors that "local baseball interests" from the Wanderers Club of Johannesburg had approached him for help in securing a scoreboard for their new baseball stadium.[50] Day made a point of identifying the Wanderers as the "chief sports club" in South Africa.[51]

A South African magnate sponsored the project to spur the development of baseball. "It appears that a local man of means, who is desirous of seeing baseball well established and well patronized by South African sports crowds, has agreed to put up a fair-sized scoreboard, provided, of course, the expense is not too great," Day revealed. Day noted that this patron, J. C. Perring, was also secretary of the Transvaal Cricket Union. South Africans, Day informed his stunned Washington supervisors, viewed baseball as a complement to their cricket traditions. "It is decidedly encouraging to note the progress already made and to see the appeal which it has made to the cricketers," Day observed. "One international cricketer, who is enjoying a very fine season, attributes a fair amount of his improved batting to his baseball experience last Winter." Day confirmed that several leagues had sprung up around Johannesburg. He contended that the game had spread to the rest of the colony and even into Rhodesia. The commercial attaché predicted that "with some support" baseball "should evolve into one of the major sports of the country."[52]

Although shocked by the news, Department of Commerce managers in the United States proved eager to help South African baseball develop. Eric T. King, chief of the Specialties Division, informed Day he would do everything in his power to help baseball grow in South Africa. "Should the market develop to such an extent that you need American equipment, please let us know," King insisted.[53] King immediately sought help in procuring Day's specific request, a bid for a scoreboard for Johannesburg's baseball leagues, or at least blueprints so the South Africans could build their own. King wired Commerce Department offices in Boston, Chicago, Milwaukee, New York, and St. Louis. After considerable searching and many delays the district offices eventually discovered prospective scoreboard suppliers in Massachusetts, Illinois, and Wisconsin.[54]

The slow pace of the scoreboard acquisition efforts in the United States frustrated trade attaché Day and his South African buyers. "I was prompted to send this cable as I have been several times approached by the original inquirers, who were anxious to get started on this project, inasmuch as the baseball season is something over one month old," Day telegraphed Washington. Day warned that the South Africans were going to have to build the scoreboard locally.[55]

Responding to Day's cable, Commerce's Washington leadership redoubled their efforts. The Wisconsin prospect turned out to be a dead end—a contact with an assistant athletic director at the University of Wisconsin who knew nothing about manufacturing such devices.[56] A Massachusetts entrepreneur,

W. W. Colson, sent the South Africans plans for an electronic scoreboard.[57] The Champaign, Illinois-based Remotomatic Scoreboard Company sent catalogues of their wares to the South Africans. Chicago's Tablet and Ticket Company sent a bid for a complete scoreboard package.[58] Tablet and Ticket proved an ardent suitor, hounding the Department of Commerce for word of a South African contract.[59] Day informed his bosses in Washington that the American bid had come too late in the South African baseball season. The South Africans planned to build their own scoreboard for the next season, quashing Ticket and Tablet's hopes for a sale.[60]

Day refused to give up on the South African baseball market. In 1935, he informed Washington about a new plan devised by the Wanderers Club. Day reminded his bosses that the club "has been particularly useful to us in connection with the growing interest in South Africa of baseball." He explained that they wanted to exchange their *Wanderers' Club Monthly Magazine* for similar subscriptions from American sporting clubs.[61] Once again, the Department of Commerce went to work in an effort to help baseball take root in South Africa. Through inquiries to their regional offices they managed to get two sporting goods industry journals, the *Sporting Goods Dealer,* based in St. Louis, and *The Sporting Goods Journal,* based in Chicago, to agree to an exchange with the *Wanderers' Club Monthly.* Both of the American publications hoped to use their South African connection to develop an African market for baseball equipment.[62]

If, with the exception of South Africa, Africa and the Middle East appeared as vast sporting deserts on U.S. athletic maps, Europe stood as a potentially lucrative market in which great barriers to the expansion of baseball loomed. The continent's modernity and enthusiasm for sport titillated American surveyors, but Europe's fierce embrace of other national pastimes diminished their enthusiasm. Baseball, it seemed, would never find a haven on European playing fields.

Appraisals of Europe revealed little sign of the American national pastime. By all accounts, soccer football represented the most popular national pastime in almost every European nation. C. J. North, who compiled the Department of Commerce's trade bulletins on sports during the 1920s, admitted that "soccer has become the national game of most of the countries of Europe, in the same sense that baseball is the national game in the United States and, generally speaking, practically everybody there either plays the game or watches someone else play it."[63] Where bat-and-ball games flourished, particularly in Greater Britain, cricket ovals rather than baseball diamonds dominated the sporting landscape.[64]

Still, the Department of Commerce dared to dream that baseball might carve a European niche. Trade analysts recognized that Europe comprised a profitable territory filled with sport-smitten consumers. American agents searched diligently for any sign, no matter how small, that baseball had any chance in Europe. Sightings came from strange places. Foreign service officers from Poland and Turkey divulged that they had seen a bit of baseball in their locales.[65] A State Department official in Lithuania also caught a glimpse, reporting that the Lithuanian Physical Training Union, founded in 1920, encouraged baseball, among other games, in its extensive youth sports program.[66]

Strangest of all were the sightings from inside the Soviet Union of factories that allegedly churned out baseball gloves and bats. These rumors surfaced in the early 1930s when a New York City sporting goods chain, Davega United Sport and Radio Shops, contacted the Department of Commerce for information about how to sell bats and gloves to Bolsheviks. The retail chain had heard tales of a Soviet baseball craze.[67] The head of Commerce's Russian Section, E. C. Ropes, responded to the inquiry. "You are doubtless aware of the fact that this government has no relations with that of the Soviet Union," Ropes dryly informed the sporting goods retailers. Still, Ropes admitted that "on this particular point, the only information that we have is the statement recently by a Moscow correspondent of an American paper that the Russians had taken up baseball enthusiastically, under the coaching of some of the many Americans working there, and that all supplies were being manufactured in the country." Explaining that since the United States had no relations with the Soviet government his agency had no agents in country to confirm or deny the sprouting of Soviet baseball, Ropes guessed that Russian factories were probably making baseball gloves, bats, and uniforms. His speculations gave the impression that leather and lumber had been diverted from the most recent Soviet five-year plan to satiate the baseball hunger. Ropes sternly informed United Sport and Radio Shops that the Soviets would never permit the importation of any American baseball products to Mother Russia, effectively ending the effort to open a Russian front in baseball's imperial quest.[68]

Sightings of baseball also came from sunnier climes than the Soviet Union. Southern Europe seemed to offer potentially hospitable territory. From Portugal, U.S. Consul General W. Stanley Hollis marveled that baseball was "beginning to secure a hold" along Europe's Atlantic coast. Hollis's colleague stationed next door in Spain, Consul General Ralph J. Totten, confirmed the Iberian sightings with a report that a few diamonds were sprinkled on Spanish soil. Totten admitted that in terms of mass appeal Spanish baseball had "not yet caught the popular fancy."[69] Still, the Portuguese and Spanish sightings inspired optimism.

From another southern European nation came a startling revelation that seemed to imply baseball's conquest of Europe was not a hopeless dream. In Italy, a nation where during the 1930s soccer played a major role in defining national identity, baseball made a sudden and unexpected appearance. In the winter of 1931, rumors spread that Benito Mussolini's Fascist government was poised to declare baseball Italy's new national pastime. A story to that effect in the Paris-based *International Herald Tribune* created a firestorm of interest among U.S. sporting goods manufacturers, particularly the tidbit that the Italian government planned to purchase a huge supply of baseball equipment to outfit Italians for their new national pastime. A special report from foreign correspondent Arnaldo Cortesi to the *New York Times* announced that the Fascists had sponsored a general sports boom in Italy. "Scores of thousands of Italian youths who formerly considered it the height of bliss to spend their time flirting in cafés now enjoy building up their bodies on the playing fields or in the gymnasiums," claimed Cortesi. He revealed that the Fascist Party had created a government school to train sports instructors on how to inculcate a devotion to the strenuous life among the masses of former café patrons. Forty-three instructors from the Italian national sports academy planned a six-month trip to the United States. In America they would "learn to play baseball, which the Fascist authorities have recently been making an attempt to introduce into this country," Cortesi asserted. The special correspondent contended that the Italians had no other summer pastimes, save the "aristocratic game" of tennis, since the soccer football season ended in the spring. "Baseball, it is thought, would be ideal for filling this deficiency, being far superior in popular appeal to cricket, which is also receiving some consideration as a possibility," Cortesi concluded.[70]

News of the Italian conversion to baseball spread rapidly. The Merchants Association of New York immediately contacted the Department of Commerce with an offer to satisfy the Italian government's plans for a spending spree on bats, balls, and gloves.[71] Commerce's commercial attaché in Rome launched an investigation into whether the reliability of press reports that baseball would by fiat become the new love of the Italian masses held any merit. The attaché, Mowatt M. Mitchell, reported back to Washington: "I am sorry to say that the story to the effect that baseball is to be adopted as the Italian national sport, which appeared on the 13th in the Paris Edition of the New York Herald-Tribune [actually the *International Herald Tribune*], and which was undoubtedly wildly reproduced at home, is absolutely false." Mitchell had checked with Italian ministers at the national Department of Physical Education and found that they knew nothing about the baseball rumor. Indeed, the Italians hinted that someone had planted the story in the press to cause trouble. "I trust that the story, if printed at home, has not aroused the hopes of too many sporting good manufacturers," Mowatt observed. He noted that an American sporting goods entrepreneur, Donald J. Moore, the export manager of the Draper Maynard Company, had been in Milan when the rumor broke and had immediately cabled his overseas office in London to send their traveling baseball equipment exhibit to Italy. "We were sorry to have to explain to him that there was absolutely nothing doing," Mowatt groused.[72]

With considerable regret, the Commerce Department's trade specialists crushed the New York merchants' dreams of an Italian baseball bonanza. The head of the Specialties Division at the department informed Gotham's sporting goods sellers that the news reports were hoaxes. "We were advised by our Rome Office that there appears to be no foundation for the report that baseball is to be adopted as the Italian national sport," admitted that Specialties Division chief.[73]

Department of Commerce investigations notwithstanding, the rumor that the Italian Fascists planned to mandate baseball as the new national pastime refused to die easily. Several weeks after the federal bureaucrats thought they had quashed the chatter about Italian baseball a new report emerged that some Italian instructors were in Florida on a mission to learn baseball secrets and procure baseball supplies. The Specialties Division in Washington contacted their office in Jacksonville, Florida, in an attempt to check the veracity of the new claim. They warned their Florida field agents that it was a hoax that had already been exposed. "Apparently, however, Bernarr Macfadden is pulling a stunt without Italian official sanction," they contended, fingering the self-proclaimed "father of physical culture" and tabloid publisher, who routinely sold fitness fads to the American public, as the source of the fraud.[74] "We are interested in getting some check up on the possible results of this delegation's visit for the information of our trade," Commerce's Washington brain trust instructed. "Should they show themselves in Jacksonville please try to get in touch with them and learn their subsequent itinerary and something of their purposes."[75]

The Jacksonville bureau launched a search for the alleged Italian baseball delegation. "I have checked this matter over with a number of persons who should know of the presence in this state of such a delegation, but nothing can be learned which would indicate that they are here at this time nor are they expected at a later date," reported the Florida commercial attaché to Washington. He promised to contact his supervisors immediately should he stumble across any Italian baseball afficionados in the future.[76] In the meantime, the tale that Mussolini was looking to score a large quantity of baseball bats had reached Louisville. The Hillerich & Bradsby Company, makers of the famous "Louisville Slugger," phoned the local branch of the Commerce Department in Kentucky to make sure that the Italian procurement team visited their factory. The Louisville field office phoned Washington at Hillerich & Bradsby's request.[77]

Once again, officials in the Department of Commerce's Washington headquarters quelled the hopes of American merchants. They informed Hillerich & Bradsby that they had investigated the matter thoroughly and found no truth in the reports. They did admit that officials at the U.S. Chamber of Commerce had related a story that a delegation of "about forty Italians is in this country at the present time, and are believed to be in Florida or one of the other Gulf States." The Italians were supposed "to be visiting this country under the auspices of the Macfadden Publications." Commerce officials tried to contact Bernarr Macfadden for details about the Italian visit but could not locate him. The Department of Commerce assured Hillerich & Bradsby that should the government learn of any actual Italian interest in baseball bats they would immediately contact the Louisville firm.[78]

Though the Department of Commerce could locate neither him nor his Italian guests, for six months in 1931 Macfadden had hosted forty Italian naval cadets. The "guru" of healthy living and intense exercise had traveled to Italy earlier in 1930 and met with Benito Mussolini. Harboring both political and publicity ambitions, Macfadden set up the trip to prove to *Il Duce* and the world that his system of physical training could energize a modern nation. The group toured New York, Connecticut, Ohio, Kentucky, and Tennessee. Macfadden put them through a rigorous regimen of exercise, nutrition, and sport. In a book about the experiment released by Macfadden's publishing empire, the American fitness mogul maintained that baseball quickly became the favorite sport of his Italian subjects.[79] On their return to Italy, they failed, in spite of their alleged love for the American national pastime, to replace soccer with baseball.

Beyond Europe on the government maps of baseball's possible reach lay more fertile territories. Though Latin America had been gripped by the same soccer mania that engulfed Europe, baseball seemed to have a far greater chance to make an impact. In his preface to a 1924 trade bulletin on Latin

America, the director of the Bureau of Foreign and Domestic Commerce, Julius Klein, argued that baseball had already opened doors to U.S. influence in many parts of the region. "While the United States dominates the athletic-goods market in Cuba, Mexico, and Central America, where baseball is rapidly becoming the national game, it is possible by proper merchandising effort to extend sales in the markets of Argentina, Brazil, and other South American countries," Klein insisted, even though soccer fever raged in those nations.[80]

Some of the information in the Latin American bulletin contradicted Klein's optimistic stance. In the South American regions furthest from the United States, soccer so consumed the populace that baseball was played only "spasmodically," as the U.S. consul to Chile, George A. Makinson, reported. Government diplomats in Argentina reported a similar pattern. Baseball held little appeal to Argentines, but the American and Japanese communities in the country had developed a thriving set of leagues. Expatriates also played the game in Brazil, while native Brazilians showed no interest in any other national pastime than soccer. Baseball made only fleeting appearances in Paraguay, Uruguay, Peru, and Bolivia. In the Andean republics nearer to the United States, baseball seemed poised to take off. Data from Colombia, Venezuela, and Ecuador indicated a burgeoning interest in the game. "There are signs that baseball may become somewhat popular, although it can not be said at present that indications are more than slight," reported American agents in Ecuador in perhaps the most honest appraisal of baseball's appeal in South America during that era.[81]

Even those slight indications were more than enough to generate excitement amongst Department of Commerce officials. When the U.S. vice consul to Ecuador, J. N. Spangler, informed his superiors in Washington that the Ecuadorean national sports federation had solicited catalogues to price American baseball equipment, the Department of Commerce sent a flurry of hot market tips to U.S. companies. Commerce agents contacted P. Goldsmith and Sons, National Sporting Goods Manufacturing, Wilson-Western Sporting Goods, Draper Maynard, A. J. Reach, Wright and Ditson, Stall and Dean Manufacturing, and A.G. Spalding & Brothers.[82] The Spalding corporation responded eagerly and promised to ship lists of their voluminous inventory of baseball gear to Ecuador.[83]

Slight indications also sparked optimism about Venezuela. Halbert Watkins, a commercial attaché stationed in Caracas, wrote to Washington headquarters that the Venezuelan government had significantly lowered tariffs on sporting goods. "Venezuelans are enthusiastic over out-door sports,"

Watkins insisted. He claimed that baseball reigned as their favorite pastime. Watkins informed his Washington superiors that a huge new sporting goods store was about to open in Caracas. He wanted to make sure that U.S. firms had a foothold in the new sports emporium.[84] In Washington, Eric T. King, the chief of Commerce's Specialties Division, received the news enthusiastically. He churned out a "Special Circular" that announced, "Market for Sporting Goods in Venezuela Increasing." With a "well directed advertising campaign," King predicted, Venezuela would soon join the empire of baseball.[85]

Off the Atlantic shores of Venezuela, U.S. analysts hoped that an advertising campaign might bring the entire Caribbean into baseball's orbit. U.S. observers discovered a mixture of favorable and unfavorable signs in the Caribbean. Cricket dominated the landscape of the British West Indies, but American observers sighted baseball games in the Bahamas, Barbados, and Bermuda.[86] On other islets such as Trinidad and Tobago, U.S. investigators saw absolutely no signs of baseball—though they witnessed abundant evidence of cricket.[87] Games organized by American expatriates or military personnel in Haiti and Martinique represented the only sign of baseball in the French West Indies.[88] The American consul general to Haiti noted that the U.S. Marines, who regularly occupied the nation during the early twentieth century, had tried to convert Haitians to the pleasures of baseball but only a few native boys showed any interest in the game. The consul general did recognize that the large contingent of Marines in Haiti might make a good market for U.S. purveyors of baseball goods.[89]

In the Spanish Caribbean, baseball reigned as the national pastimes of Cuba and the Dominican Republic. State Department officials disclosed that "baseball is the most popular game in the [Dominican] Republic and the market for this type of supplies is on the increase." They admitted, however, that the island's poverty severely limited sales prospects for American manufacturers.[90] A later survey by U.S. Consul Reed Paige Clark argued that "while Base Ball is decidedly popular, it is believed that Basket Ball and Volley Ball, in addition to Golf and Tennis, may be classed as the most popular local sports." Clark gave credit to Protestant missionaries for popularizing basketball and volleyball.[91] Clark's mention of golf and tennis indicated that he probably spent more time looking at the pastimes of the local elites and American military officers than at the leisure preferences of the Dominican masses. His claim that the two missionary sports had surpassed Dominican ardor for baseball seems also to be a misreading of the situation.[92]

Cuba manifested a love for *béisbol* every bit as strong as the Dominican Republic's ardor.[93] From Havana, U.S. Consul A. C. Frost informed his superiors that baseball fever was so intense on the island that "it is doubtful if even in the United States there exists a more widespread enthusiasm for this form of recreation." Cuban Spanish reflected the nation's love for baseball. Frost revealed that "the reader who is used to classic Castilian is likely to be confounded by the common appearance of such terms a 'tubey' (two-bagger), . . . 'jonron' (home run), [and] 'beisbolero' (baseball player)." Cubans religiously followed their countrymen who played in U.S. professional leagues. Cuban boys dreamed of growing up to become major leaguers. Frost concluded that a huge market for American baseball equipment existed in Cuba.[94]

U.S. officials in the American territory of Puerto Rico also saw evidence that baseball had flowered on another island of the old Spanish Caribbean. Darwin DeGolia, Puerto Rico's assistant trade commissioner, confided that especially in urban areas, "the people are what your advertising hands would call 'sport conscious.'" DeGolia saw Sunday morning sandlot contests in every vacant lot in San Juan. "Baseball is quite a coming game," he announced.[95]

Elsewhere along the western edge of the Gulf of Mexico, baseball thrived. Even in British Honduras (now Belize) baseball had made some inroads against cricket.[96] From Costa Rica, U.S. Vice Consul Roderick W. Uncles reported that baseball was "gradually becoming quite popular." Indeed, it rivaled soccer for national affection.[97] From Honduras, U.S. Consul Robert L. Kaiser also confirmed a strong interest in baseball. Later reports confirmed a "growing demand" for the American national pastime.[98] In Nicaragua, U.S. Consul Harold Planter marveled that "baseball has made enormous strides in the past few years" and had triumphed over soccer as the Nicaraguan national pastime.[99] When American analysts conducted their Nicaraguan surveys, U.S. Marines occupied the country in an effort to hunt down rebel leader Augusto César Sandino.[100] While they struggled to capture Sandino, the Marines had clearly augmented the development of Nicaraguan baseball. The data noted that the large number of American military and local baseball teams in the country provided an excellent market for American manufacturers.[101] Reports from Panama also indicated optimism about the spread of baseball. Once again, the significant American military and civilian presence in the Canal Zone amplified local interest in the game and expanded the local market for baseball equipment.[102]

Military connections also opened baseball trade avenues in Guatemala. The commercial attachés to the U.S. Legation in Guatemala City notified the Department of Commerce that the Guatemalan army sought to purchase a large quantity of uniforms for its baseball-playing soldiers.[103] Commerce officials contacted several major American suppliers of baseball haberdashery, A.G. Spalding & Brothers, Alex Taylor & Company, A. J. Reach, Wright and Ditson, Wilson-Western Company, and Ken-Wel Sporting Goods.[104] When Ken-Wel made a major sale to the Guatemalan military they thanked the Department of Commerce profusely for its assistance.[105]

The Department of Commerce also helped an American firm make a uniform sale in El Salvador. The Draper-Maynard Company of Boston outfitted El Salvador's national team. A shot of the team in Draper-Maynard's pinstripes graced the cover of El Salvador's leading sports magazine after the Salvadorans beat Honduras and Guatemala to win the Central American championship.[106] El Salvador's success in Central American baseball tournaments apparently inspired a strong grassroots interest in the sport. American agents discovered that baseball had become the leading sport in the nation's schools.[107] When they took to local sandlots most Salvadorans were not as well-dressed as the national team. A State Department official observed that the nation's poverty-stricken masses played their games without uniforms or gloves, with sticks for bats, and with balls conjured from rags, paper, or wood scraps.[108]

Baseball thrived not only in Central America but also on both borders of the United States, in Mexico and Canada.[109] U.S. Consul to Mexico Claude I. Dawson reported a baseball boom in that nation. "The growth of baseball, which is now the most popular outdoor sport among Mexicans, may be attributed largely to the American influence," Dawson attested. He claimed that baseball "bids fair to gaining favor with the coming generations, since it has now become popular with the small boys." Baseball's conquest of children made it a power to be reckoned with in postrevolutionary Mexico. Aflame with baseball faith Dawson extolled the game as one of Mexican society's most potent democratic and egalitarian forces.[110]

On the northern border of the United States, government trade experts divulged that baseball was at least as popular in Canada as it was on the southern border. In his introduction to a trade bulletin for Canada, Julius Klein, director of the Bureau of Foreign and Domestic Commerce, declared that "in nearly every respect the Canadian market for sporting goods is like that of the United States." Canadians loved baseball nearly as much as Americans—and they were nearly as affluent as Americans when it came to purchasing power. Canada represented "the best customer" in the world for U.S. exporters of athletic goods Klein disclosed.[111] While admitting that hockey, lacrosse, and even cricket enjoyed strong Canadian followings, the commerce bulletins insisted that baseball knit Canada to the United States. Federal trade surveys charted Canadian baseball interest province by province. Baseball's Canadian stronghold lay in the maritime provinces of Labrador, and Newfoundland. Quebec also had a strong interest in baseball. From the national capital in Ottawa, Vice Consul Gilson G. Blake Jr. divulged that in Ontario "the popularity of baseball seems to grow each year." Baseball maintained its strength from the prairies through the mountains to the West Coast, from Manitoba to Saskatchewan to Alberta to British Columbia. Indeed, "Louisville Sluggers" from Hillerich & Bradsby proved a popular brand in British Columbia. Only on Vancouver Island did baseball fervor wane. From Victoria, U.S. Vice Consul R. M. Newcomb explained the city's lack of interest in baseball as the result of enormous British influence in the city.[112]

Unlike Africa, the Middle East, and Europe, the Americas seemed to provide hospitable territory for spreading baseball and U.S. influence. Even with soccer passion running rampant in South America, baseball had established a presence from Cape Horn to the Bering Sea. American diplomats were confident that baseball could help to maintain the old dictums of the Monroe Doctrine. Certainly prospects for a baseball-united league of American nations seemed more likely than the chances for a European or African or Middle Eastern union centered on diamonds.

Westward across the Pacific lay vast and rich markets that the United States had long coveted. Commerce and State Department officials hoped they might win these regions to American ways of life through the spread of baseball. The Pacific and East Asia held tantalizing opportunities, both for baseball and for commerce. As in Latin America, baseball already had a considerable history in parts of those regions.[113] Baseball had established crucial beachheads in the Pacific, most importantly in Japan. Indeed, by the 1920s, the Far East had already become the second largest customer for American sports in the world. That fact led off the Department of Commerce trade bulletin on the *Far Eastern Market for Sporting and Athletic Goods*. Based on that data, Bureau of Foreign and Domestic Commerce boss Julius Klein pushed for more U.S. action along the Pacific Rim. "Judged then, as a whole, the Far Eastern market for athletic goods is well worth cultivating, for, while obstacles are numerous, the potential reward for sound merchandising and selling are probably greater than those other sections of the world which have been more intensively cultivated," Klein maintained.[114]

American trade analysts presented a bullish report on baseball's prospects in the Far East. They identified very strong markets for baseball in Australia, New Zealand, and the Philippines. They noted growing potential in China, India, and even Siam (now Thailand). Most significantly, they zeroed in on

Japanese baseball traditions. Japan represented a possible partner in their visions of an empire of baseball. They recognized Japan as a potentially dangerous rival both in baseball commerce and in Asian influence.[115] Japan, they feared, could destroy their maps for making baseball the world's game.

Japan's baseball interests and their other designs on China particularly worried American foreign service officers. From Manchuria, soon to be a Japanese puppet-state, U.S. Consul J. W. Ballantine warned that Japanese baseball equipment dominated the province even though "it is of distinctly inferior quality to similar goods" made by American firms. Reports from Beijing, Shanghai, Hong Kong, and Canton also revealed strong Japanese influence. Japanese expatriates competed with American expatriates to push their particular versions of the same national pastime onto the Chinese. Both nations sought to inculcate their version of the game in the Chinese school system. Shanghai and Hong Kong developed particularly strong rivalries between U.S. and Japanese baseball interests. In spite of Japanese competition, the fact that baseball seemed to be finding a niche in China heartened U.S. diplomats.[116]

Baseball did not develop a following in most of the Asian provinces of the British Empire beyond Hong Kong. In Singapore, Malaysia, and Sumatra baseball failed to grow, crowded out by the thickets of cricket and soccer.[117] Curiously, in the most British nations in the Pacific, New Zealand and Australia, U.S. experts discovered a lively interest in baseball. That fascination was all the more unexpected given that both of the antipodean members of the British Commonwealth were major cricket powers.[118]

From New Zealand, U.S. Vice Consul John E. Moran asserted that baseball, though novel, generated considerable interest. New Zealand military veterans brought the game back with them from the Great War. Some New Zealand schools, Moran claimed, had even replaced cricket with baseball. All in all, New Zealand seemed a solid prospect for inclusion in the global baseball union.[119]

U.S. agents unearthed an even stronger absorption in baseball in Australia. During the 1920s and 1930s American observers regularly noted that Australia had one of the most severe cases of sporting fever in the world. In spite of the "Ashes" and a host of other evidence that placed Australia near the top of the list of cricket-loving nations, Commerce and State Department officials maintained that baseball threatened the hold of the British bat-and-ball game on sports-mad Australians.[120] In 1925, the American vice consul to Australia, John Vebber, reported to Washington that while "baseball is still in its infancy in Australia," the game held a strong attraction. Vebber observed dozens of leagues that played both summer and winter schedules in all the Australian cities. He noted that "special matches" between the leading nines of Australian states generated considerable public enthusiasm. A baseball craze had also infected the schools, especially the girls' schools. Vebber marveled at the Australian schoolgirls' passion for the American national pastime. The vice consul suggested "that the introduction of the 'indoor' baseball would greatly aid the game among those schools, as the average girl has a tendency to be afraid of the hardness of the ball."[121] Perhaps Vebber had forgotten how poorly indoor baseball fared among American schoolgirls.[122]

Most of the equipment used in Australian baseball, Vebber revealed, was manufactured in the United States, indicating that a strong potential market existed "down under." The vice consul recommended a South Pacific tour by American teams as a "great impetus" for fueling the glowing sparks baseball had already ignited in Australian sports culture.[123] Vebber made no mention that more than three decades earlier Albert Goodwill Spalding's around-the-world baseball tour of major league "missionaries" promoting Americanization through the national pastime had attempted to kindle the same Australian tinder.[124]

Given other U.S. foreign service reports on Australian baseball over the next few years, vice consul Vebber somewhat overstated the American pastime's threat to cricket in the Southern Hemisphere. In 1930, the assistant trade commissioner of the U.S. Commerce Department stationed in Sydney, H. P. Van Blarcom, reported that the secretary of the New South Wales Baseball Association told him that the vast unfamiliarity of Australians with the American game dramatically impeded the spread of the sport. The Australian baseball promoter asked Van Blarcom if he could somehow secure a few American publications that gave basic instructions on how to play each position on the diamond. "He stated that if he could get a series of this kind it probably would be of great assistance to him in increasing the popularity of the game in New South Wales," Van Blarcom advised his superiors in Washington.[125]

The Washington bureaucrats immediately thought of the A. G. Spalding & Brothers series of baseball instructional booklets.[126] Memorandums on the request flew back and forth between the Department of Commerce's headquarters in the District of Columbia and its field office in New York City, where the government attempted to persuade Spalding's publishing arm, American Sports Publishing, to provide the New South Wales baseball afficionados with how-to-play pamphlets.[127] The Spalding corporation quickly agreed to send free copies to the New South Wales group. The sporting goods company also relayed the information that they had an Australian division headquartered in Melbourne and a Spalding retail branch located at 352 Kent Street in Sydney.[128] The pamphlets, described in Commerce memorandums as the "How to Play Each Position in Baseball" series, were shipped to Australia.[129]

Australian baseball enthusiasts thanked the Department of Commerce agents and A.G. Spalding & Brothers profusely for the publications. In a follow-up to Washington, assistant trade commissioner Van Blarcom noted that the pamphlets were not currently available at Spalding's Sydney store and that high tariffs would make ordering them prohibitively expensive. He also relayed the New South Wales Baseball Association's request for more pamphlets. They planned to ship them to rural areas along the coast and in the outback in the hopes that local newspapers would publish material from the how-to guides and ignite baseball fever in Australia.[130]

Washington officials passed along the request for additional baseball manuals to Spalding headquarters.[131] Spalding executives responded that while their altruism had limits, they would "be as liberal as they can" in furnishing additional pamphlets to the Australians. They also commanded their Australian branch to "give the New South Wales Association every possible cooperation and assistance in developing and popularizing Baseball in their territory."[132] Certainly motives beyond benevolence animated Spalding's largesse. Should baseball flourish in Australia the corporation stood ready to garner an important new market. Making money and Americanizing Australia, as Commerce officials clearly understood, went hand in baseball glove in these endeavors.

If most Australians were so unfamiliar with baseball that they needed how-to pamphlets to get involved, then another series of missives between U.S. government officials in Australia and in the United States reveals that at least one Australian inventor knew the game well enough to develop and patent an allegedly "unbreakable" baseball bat. This nugget of information was once again uncovered by assistant trade commissioner Van Blarcom. He breathlessly reported to Washington that in his explorations of Australian baseball he had discovered a Sydney firm, Palmer's Ltd., which had engineered a baseball bat that was "guaranteed unbreakable." The bat was fashioned from seven pieces of Alpine Ash cut in the interior of New South Wales and cemented by special glues. The bat's creator promised it would not splinter even when confronted by the wickedest fastball a pitcher could hurl. "In talking with the chap who invented this bat I learned that he was very much interested in disposing of his manufacturing rights in the United

States to some American company who could put the thing over," Van Blarcom confided. "Should you know of anybody who might be interested in this possibility I feel quite sure that I will be able to obtain some sample bats for their inspection and trial," he vowed.[133]

The "unbreakable" bat intrigued Eric T. King, chief of the Specialties Division at the U.S. Department of Commerce. He assured Van Blarcom that "I was very much interested in your . . . description which you give of the construction of this bat, I have no doubt that it is 'unbreakable,' or nearly so." King pledged that "we are bringing this matter to the attention of the leading manufacturers of baseball bats, and should any of them express any interest in taking over the manufacturing rights in the United States, we will be glad to write you."[134] He relayed word of the "unbreakable" bat to Department of Commerce offices in Louisville, New York, St. Louis, Cincinnati, and Philadelphia. "Will you please bring this to the attention of contacts who may be interested, requesting them to advise us of any action they may take," King instructed.[135]

The New York office responded that a local firm, Alex Taylor & Company, had a strong interest and wanted "an opportunity to examine this new invention."[136] However, returns from the other Department of Commerce offices chilled enthusiasm for the "unbreakable" bat. One commerce agent quoted a letter from acclaimed bat maker Hillerich & Bradsby Company, manufacturer of the renowned Louisville Slugger. "We are familiar with this type of bat, but its use is not permitted in the United States," Hillerich & Bradsby officials contended. The Louisville Slugger manufacturer informed the Department of Commerce that baseball's rules required bats to be hewn out of a single piece of wood rather than being fashioned together from composite pieces.[137] Other manufactures concurred with Hillerich & Bradsby that Australia's "unbreakable" bat violated baseball's regulations and had no place in the U.S. national pastime.[138] Perhaps the Australian inventor had not yet read the section in Spalding's "how-to-play" booklets on regulations for bats.

A dismayed head of Commerce's Specialty Division sent the bad news back to Sydney.[139] King also warned the New York office to inform Alex Taylor & Company that the bat was not only unbreakable but illegal.[140] From Australia,Van Blarcom replied that the unbreakable, illegal bat was in fact not even available for inspection. He had been "informed that tests made with the seven piece bat indicated that the handle vibrated upon impact with the ball, and in order to overcome this vibration the company was making further investigations and planned to put out a four piece bat which they think will overcome this difficulty." The Australians were unwilling to send a seven-piece prototype to the Americans. Still, in spite of Van Blarcom's warnings about the lack of a "market" for the illegal bat, the Australian inventor of the "unbreakable" cudgel persisted in his endeavors. "I have explained to him the difficulties with regard to the official baseball rules, but he seems to feel that although organized baseball might not approve of the bat, it could be used and probably would find a fairly large sale among some of the lower schools and amateur leagues," Van Blarcom marveled. "Personally, I feel that unless there was some change in the regulation there would not be a very great market."[141] Washington commerce officers dutifully passed along the news to the Alex Taylor & Company.[142] Van Blarcom never managed to get a sample of either the seven-piece or four-piece "unbreakable" bat. He did send a sample of the seven-layer wooden composite block out of which the bats were made to the Department of Commerce. They passed the sample along to Alex Taylor & Company, which decided it had no more interest in the venture.[143]

While gauging the true level of interest in baseball in Australia remained as difficult as sorting out the details of the unbreakable bat, the American surveyors of baseball's empire easily located a thriving baseball culture in the Philippines. Ever since they annexed the islands during the Spanish-American War, U.S. officials who governed the protectorate had used baseball to pacify and Americanize Filipinos.[144] By the interwar period, baseball reigned as the Philippine national pastime. Reporting from Manila, trade commissioner John A. Fowler insisted baseball ruled the nation while also opening some lucrative trade opportunities for the U.S. sporting goods firms. Fowler contended that baseball's stronghold on native Filipinos as well as on a large number of U.S. military personnel posted to the islands provided a thriving market for baseball goods. American firms, he proudly maintained, dominated the trade. The Japanese had yet to make any inroads into Filipino baseball.[145]

Japan loomed over outlines of the American baseball empire sketched by government surveyors, the great unknown in this and many other American foreign policy schemes. In their surveys of the potential borders of a Pax Americana knit together by baseball, Japan stood as the nation they most coveted for inclusion as well as the rival they most feared. C. J. North, the Department of Commerce analyst who compiled a trade bulletin on the Far East, asserted that "the Japanese, . . . in imitation of western athletic ideas and almost entirely as a result of occidental influence, have developed into a great athletic nation." So great, in fact, had Japan become that it rivaled the United States for baseball commerce and baseball influence in many parts of the Pacific Rim. The analysts who assessed the Japanese market for American baseball imports noted that high tariffs designed to protect domestic makers of sporting goods made the sale of U.S. balls, bats, and gloves quite difficult. At the same time Japan offered inexpensive baseball equipment to other nations, threatening to undermine U.S. efforts to spread American hegemony through the American national pastime—a pastime they shared with the Japanese.[146]

Department of Commerce files on Japan reveal that in spite of the tariffs and trade wars over baseball, Japanese and American firms sometimes sought partnerships. In one case, an Osaka firm, Yoshioka Gomei Kaisha, reached out to find American firms it could partner with in selling baseball equipment in Japan.[147] In another case, an obscure American corporation, the Tennessee Overall Company, tried to get information about the feasibility of selling Japanese-made baseballs in the United States.[148]

The developing interest in the baseball trade led the Department of Commerce in 1935 to issue a foreign market bulletin on the "Japanese Sport Goods Industry and Trade." Federal officials shipped the bulletin to major American sporting goods manufacturers associations and trade journals, particularly those that pushed baseball equipment, including the Athletic Goods Manufacturers Association of New York, the American Sporting Goods Association of Chicago, the *Sporting Goods Journal* of Chicago, and the *Sporting Goods Dealer* of St. Louis.[149] They also sent one to the small company that had sparked the creation of the trade survey, the Tennessee Overall Company.[150]

Industry magnates reacted with glee at the Department of Commerce's detailed information on Japanese markets. H. Boardman Spalding, chief executive officer of A. G. Spalding & Brothers and the chair of the Athletic Goods Manufacturers Association, solicited an additional thirty-seven copies of the pamphlet to send to his organization's members.[151] The president of Wilson-Western Sporting Goods of Chicago gushed his gratitude to the federal agents for their help in identifying trade opportunities in Japan.[152] The editors of Chicago's *Sporting Goods Journal* and St. Louis's *Sporting Goods Dealer* promised to print detailed information about Japanese commercial prospects in upcoming issues.[153] An updated version of the trade bulletin that appeared in 1940—as U.S.-Japanese relations deteriorated—drew similar outpourings of interest.[154]

Of course, the history of the rivalry between the United States and Japan in the near future doomed the grand vision of a pacific, and Pacific, league of nations united by baseball. The Japanese attack on Pearl Harbor would convince many Americans, as historian Richard Crepeau has ably demonstrated, that the "gift" of baseball to Japan had been a huge mistake and that the Japanese had failed to grasp the true meaning of the game for fomenting world peace and global democracy.[155] Confronted by the curve of history, baseball diplomacy struck out.

Even before December 7, 1941, signs appeared that the government's map of a baseball-governed Pax Americana might not have been an accurate guide to global political realities. After the former big-league outfielder turned baseball missionary Leslie Mann had led the American national pastime onto to the Olympic stage in Berlin, the plans of his International Baseball Congress quickly unraveled. Japan did not play a "World Series" against the United States in Tokyo in 1937 nor in Honolulu in 1939. The best that Mann could muster was a 1938 "World Series" between the United States and Great Britain in London and a 1939 "World Series" between the United States, Cuba, and Nicaragua in Havana—events that Japan and the rest of the world ignored. Even the American press paid little attention to those so-called World Series.[156] The great global tournament scheduled for the 1940 Tokyo Games also evaporated, chased into oblivion by the menacing clouds of world war.[157]

What if the seemingly inevitable war had not come? In a world with the United States and Japan existing, if not as friends then at least not engaged in total war, would baseball have become a serious rival to the rise of soccer as the world's game? Would titles such as the 2005 tome sponsored by the Brookings Institution, *National Pastime: How Americans Play Baseball and the Rest of the World Plays Soccer,* have become more than slight exaggerations? Would much more of the rest of the world now play baseball, even if they also adored soccer? During the 1920s and 1930s the trade analysts and foreign diplomats of the U.S. Departments of Commerce and State believed that such a future, though difficult, might be possible. Without the benefit of hindsight their position did not seem entirely delusional.[158] Even with hindsight some still maintained their faith. More than thirty years after World War II, former Bowdoin College baseball player Bill Shaw, a member of the "U.S. Olympics"[159] that demonstrated the American national pastime in Berlin in 1936 before what was then the largest crowd ever to witness a game, recalled the hopes of his teammates and managers. If World War II had not intervened, Shaw imagined, "baseball would now be as much a part of the regular Olympic program as soccer is."[160]

Such ruminations make the bleak report wired by Department of Commerce operatives in Japan to Washington in the wake of the cancellation of the Tokyo Olympic Games all the more haunting. The report noted that Tokyo merchants were dismayed at Japan's withdrawal from commitments to host the 1940 Olympic Games—and also from the 1940 World's Fair. In a "confidential addendum," the U.S. agents in Japan insisted "that the Japanese people in general are very sorry to see the cancellations of these projects, particularly the 1940 Olympics." Japan had invested great hope in the Olympics, the analysts argued. They concluded the confidential section of their report to Washington with ominous news: "A number of recent measures, such as the prohibition of the uses of leather for baseball equipment, and recent utterances by Government officials decrying foreign sports have all contributed to foster a loss of interest in athletics." The Japanese government, they warned, had turned its back on baseball and had commanded the people to revert to the "old native Japanese sports" designed to nurture martial fury.[161] On such shoals foundered the U.S. government's efforts to use the American national pastime to unite humankind in a baseball-inspired league of nations.

NOTES

1. The 125,000 claim came from Leslie Mann, "Report of Manager of Baseball Team," in *Report of the American Olympic Committee: Games of the XIth Olympiad, Berlin, Germany, August 1 to 16, 1936; IVth Olympic Winter Games, Garmisch-Partenkirchen, Germany, February 6 to 16, 1936,* ed. Frederick W. Rubien (New York: American Olympic Committee, 1936), 302–305, quotation from 303. The official German report on the game gave a lower, though still impressive, count. German statistics indicated 92,565 attendees. Organisationskomitee für die XI. Olympiade Berlin 1936 E.V., *The XIth Olympic Games, Berlin, 1936, Official Report,* vol. 1 (Berlin: Wilhelm Limpert, 1936), 498–99. In his history of baseball at the Berlin Olympics, M. E. Travaglini suggested that even the lower estimates made the crowd for the game at least the second largest in history, with perhaps only the 1959 World Series held in the Los Angeles Coliseum drawing a greater number of spectators. "Olympic Baseball 1936: Was es Das?," *National Pastime: A Review of Baseball History* 4 (Winter 1985): 46–55.

2. Mann, "Report of Manager of Baseball Team," 302–305; "Special Demonstrations," in Organisationskomitee für die XI. Olympiade Berlin 1936 E.V., *The XIth Olympic Games, Berlin, 1936, Official Report,* vol. 2 (Berlin, Wilhelm Limpert, 1936), 1098–99. Details of the game were provided by Dinty Dennis, the sports editor of the *Miami Herald,* who also served as the assistant manager and publicity director for the Olympic baseball team. "Out of Dinty's Dugout," *Miami Herald,* July 26, 1936, sec. D, 4.

3. Richard Mandell, *The Nazi Olympics* (Urbana: University of Illinois Press, 1987); *The Nazi Olympics: Sport, Politics, and Appeasement in the 1930s,* ed. Arnd Krüger (Urbana: University of Illinois Press, 1987).

4. The Germans chose gliding as their demonstration of an extra-Olympic national pastime. "Programmes for the Games of the XIth Olympiad and IVth Olympic Winter Games," *Official Bulletin of the International Olympic Committee* 28 (May 1935): 2; "Special Demonstrations," 1098–99.

5. "American Baseballers Play to 100,000 Bored Europeans," *Miami Herald*, August 13, 1936, 8.

6. Avery Brundage, "Report of the President," in *Report of the American Olympic Committee*, ed. Rubien, 29.

7. Quoted in Mann, "Report of Manager of Baseball Team," 303.

8. Mann, "Report of Manager of Baseball Team," 302–305; "The Games of the XIIth Olympiad," *Official Bulletin of the International Olympic Committee* 35 (October 1937): 8. The original plan for baseball in Berlin had been to pit an American versus a Japanese nine. "Programmes for the Games of the XIth Olympiad and IVth Olympic Winter Games," *Official Bulletin of the International Olympic Committee* 28 (May 1935): 2.

9. Mann, "Report of Manager of Baseball Team," 303–305; "Push Olympic Baseball," *New York Times*, August 1, 1936, 1; "16 Nations Form Baseball Group," *New York Times*, August 9, 1936, sec. S, 2.

10. As a territory of the United States, Hawaii participated in the Olympic Games as part of the American team; but the Philippines were a protectorate and beginning with the 1924 Paris Games the IOC recognized them as a participating "nation." They remained, however, a "colonial" dependent of the United States in Olympic protocol since their flag flew below the American standard and they marched behind the American squad. Myron T. Herrick, U.S. Ambassador to France, to Charles Evans Hughes, U.S. Secretary of State, Telegram on Philippine Olympic team, March 19, 1924; Joseph Grew, U.S. Undersecretary of State, to John Weeks, U.S. Secretary of War, May 20, 1924; John Weeks, Secretary of War, to Charles Evans Hughes, Secretary of State, May 22, 1924; Leland Harrison, U.S. Assistant Secretary of State, to Myron T. Herrick, U.S. Ambassador to France, May 27, 1924; State Department Decimal Files, 811.4063; Record Group 59; Foreign Relations Microfilm Files; National Archives at College Park, College Park, Maryland. (Hereafter NACP).

11. Donald Dewey and Nicholas Acocella, *The Biographical History of Baseball* (Chicago: Triumph, 2000), 261; Dave Pietrusza, Matthew Silverman, and Michael Gershman, eds., *Baseball: The Biographical Encyclopedia* (New York: Total Sports Illustrated, 2002), 702–703.

12. "Ruth in Olympic Post," *New York Times*, February 9, 1936, sec. S, 8. In 1918 when the Chicago Cubs and Boston Red Sox squared off in the World Series, Mann and Ruth faced each other. Arthur Daley, "Sports of the Times," *New York Times*, August 19, 1948, 29.

13. Given Ruth's fame in the United States, the lack of any mention of his presence on the American Olympic team in either the popular press or in Mann's own official account make it clear he did not go with the baseball team to Berlin. The standard

Ruth biography also does not mention a trip to the Berlin Games or anything else about the Olympic Games. Robert W. Creamer, *Babe: The Legend Comes to Life* (New York: Simon & Schuster, 1974).

14. Mann, "Report of Manager of Baseball Team," 304. For a brief overview of Mann's efforts and other attempts to include baseball on the Olympic program, see Peter Cava, "Baseball in the Olympics," *Journal of Olympic History* 1 (Summer 1992): 7–15. See also, Travaglini, "Olympic Baseball 1936," 46–55.

15. J. R. Hildebrand, "The Geography of Games: How the Sports of Nations Form a Gazetteer of the Habits and Histories of Their Peoples," *National Geographic* 36 (August 1919): 89–144, quotation on 89.

16. Ibid., 105–109.

17. Ibid., 144.

18. Maj. George Wythe, Capt. Joseph Mills Hanson, and Capt. Carl V. Burger, eds., *The Inter-Allied Games* (New York: Games Committee, 1919), 77–83, 196–98. For interpretations of the "Military Olympics" in American culture, see S. W. Pope, *Patriotic Games: Sporting Traditions in the American Imagination, 1876–1926* (New York: Oxford University Press, 1997), 139–55; Wanda E. Wakefield, *Playing to Win: Sports and the American Military, 1898–1945* (Albany: State University of New York Press, 1997), 35–57.

19. Richard C. Crepeau, *Baseball: America's Diamond Mind, 1919–1941,* rev. ed. (Lincoln: University of Nebraska Press, 2000), 196. On the same page Crepeau makes the case for the power of baseball in American diplomacy during that era. "It may seem farfetched to suggest a link between baseball and the foreign policy of the United States, yet as the National Pastime baseball was linked to all aspects of American life," Crepeau contends. Two other works reinforce the power of baseball in American culture in both general and specific ways. Benjamin Rader's *Baseball: A History of America's Game* (Urbana: University of Illinois Press, 2002) represents the best single-volume history of the national pastime. Daniel A. Nathan's *Saying It's So: A Cultural History of the Black Sox Scandal* (Urbana: University of Illinois Press, 2004) provides a fascinating exploration of how a particular baseball event shaped American memory and culture.

20. Materials related to these data collections can be found in several places at the National Archives and Records Administration II facility in College Park, Maryland. The U.S. Department of Commerce (hereafter USDOC) materials in the Records of the Bureau of Foreign and Domestic Commerce (hereafter BFDC), General Records of the Department of Commerce, Record Group 151, provides one set of sources. (This set of sources hereafter will be referred to as RG 151, NACP.) The U.S. Department of State (hereafter USDOS) materials in the State Department Decimal Files, 811.4063 Olympic Games, Record Group 59, provides another set. (This set of sources hereafter will be referred to as RG 59, NACP.) State Department Decimal File information can also be found in the individual country files at 811.4063, Record Group

59, Foreign Relations Microfilm Files. (This set of sources will hereafter be referred to as RG 59, FRMF, NACP.) Publications from these data include USDOC, BFDC, *European Market for Sporting and Athletic Goods: Trade Information Bulletin—No. 179* (January 21, 1924), by C. J. North, Supplement to Commerce Reports (Washington: Government Printing Office, 1924), 1–30; USDOC, BFDC, *Market for Athletic Goods in Canada and Newfoundland: Trade Information Bulletin—No. 230* (May 19, 1924), by C. J. North, Supplement to Commerce Reports (Washington: Government Printing Office, 1924), 1–13; USDOC, BFDC, *Latin American Market for Sporting and Athletic Goods: Trade Information Bulletin—No. 232* (May 26, 1924), by C. J. North, Supplement to Commerce Reports (Washington: Government Printing Office, 1924), 1–34; USDOC, BFDC, *Far Eastern Market for Sporting and Athletic Goods: Trade Information Bulletin—No. 308* (January 1925), by C. J. North, Supplement to Commerce Reports (Washington: Government Printing Office, 1925), 1–30; USDOC, BFDC, *Market for Sporting and Athletic Goods in Africa and Near East: Trade Information Bulletin—No. 319* (February 1925), by C. J. North, Supplement to Commerce Reports (Washington: Government Printing Office, 1925), 1–13.

21. "Throughout the 1920s and 1930s, liberal democratic governments remained relatively indifferent to the success or failure of their athletes in international competition, and sports administrators were happy to be free of governmental interference. Communist, Fascist, and Nazi regimes had a different view of politics to sport," argues Guttmann in his chapter on "Instrumentalized Sports." Allen Guttmann, *Sports: The First Five Millennia* (Amherst: University of Massachusetts Press, 2004), 293–306, quotation from 293.

22. For histories of government-business partnerships in the 1920s and 1930s, see William J. Barber, *From New Era to New Deal: Herbert Hoover, The Economists, and American Economic Policy, 1921–1933* (Cambridge: Cambridge University Press, 1985); Colin Gordon, *New Deals: Business, Labor, and Politics in America, 1920–1935* (Cambridge: Cambridge University Press, 1994); Robert F. Himmelberg, ed., *Business-Government Cooperation, 1917–1932* (New York: Garland, 1994); Morton Keller, *Regulating a New Economy: Public Policy and Economic Change in America, 1900–1933* (Cambridge, Mass. : Harvard University Press, 1990); Emily S. Rosenberg, *Financial Missionaries to the World: The Politics and Culture of Dollar Diplomacy, 1900–1930* (Cambridge, Mass.: Harvard University Press, 1999).

23. Hildebrand, "The Geography of Games," 105–109.

24. Walter LaFeber's *Michael Jordan and the New Global Capitalism* (New York: W.W. Norton, 1999) provides a very interesting interpretation of the role of sport in American foreign policy but, in concentrating on the post-World War II period, fails to grasp the chronological depth and breadth of these efforts.

25. For an insightful history of the connections between sport and the spread of American consumer culture, see Barbara Keys, "Spreading Peace, Democracy, and Coca Cola®: Sport and American Cultural Expansion in the 1930s," *Diplomatic His-*

tory 28 (April 2004): 165–96. For more general histories see T. J. Jackson Lears, *Fables of Abundance: A Cultural History of Advertising in America* (New York: Basic Books, 1994); Roland Marchand, *Advertising the American Dream: Making Way for Modernity, 1920–1940* (Berkeley: University of California Press, 1985); Herbet Feis, *The Diplomacy of the Dollar: First Era, 1919–1932* (Baltimore: Johns Hopkins University Press, 1950); Joan Hoff Wilson, *American Business and Foreign Policy, 1921–1933* (Lexington: University of Kentucky Press, 1971).

26. Paul A. Carter, *The Twenties in America* (New York: Crowell, 1968); Kathy J. Ogren, *The Jazz Revolution: Twenties America and the Meaning of Jazz* (New York: Oxford University Press, 1989); Emily S. Rosenberg, *Spreading the American Dream: American Economic and Cultural Expansion, 1890–1945* (New York: Hill and Wang, 1982); Robert Sklar, *Movie-Made America: A Cultural History of American Movies*, rev. ed. (New York: Vintage, 1994); Richard Butsch, *For Fun and Profit: The Transformation of Leisure into Consumption* (Philadelphia: Temple University Press, 1990); Roger Rollin, ed., *The Americanization of The Global Village: Essays in Comparative Popular Culture* (Bowling Green, Ohio: Bowling Green State University Popular Press, 1989).

27. A. B. Coffman, Secretary, National Sports Promotion Association, to Henry Morse, Chief of Specialties Division, BFDC, USDOC, July 13, 1923; Sporting Goods—Olympic Games, 1923–1931, Box 849; RG 151, NACP.

28. A. B. Coffman, Secretary, National Sports Promotion Association, to Herbert Hoover, Secretary of Commerce, USDOC, March 24, 1923; Sporting Goods—General, 1923–1931, Box 849; RG 151, NACP.

29. Hildebrand, "The Geography of Games," 103–105.

30. On Hoover, the Commerce Department, and the modernization of American economic policy, see Joseph Brandes, *Herbert Hoover and Economic Diplomacy: Department of Commerce Policy, 1921–1928* (Pittsburgh: University of Pittsburgh Press, 1962); Kendrick A. Clements, *Hoover, Conservation, and Consumerism: Engineering the Good Life* (Lawrence: University of Kansas Press, 2000); Robert K. Murray, *The Politics of Normalcy: Governmental Theory and Practice in the Harding-Coolidge Era* (New York: Norton, 1973); Joan Hoff Wilson, *Herbert Hoover: Forgotten Progressive* (Boston: Little, Brown, 1975).

31. Herbert Hoover, Secretary of Commerce, USDOC, to A.B. Coffman, Exports [*sic*] Promotion Association, April 3, 1923; Henry Morse, Chief of Specialties Division, BFDC, USDOC, to Mr. Emmet, Office of the Secretary, USDOC, March 30, 1923; Sporting Goods—General, 1923–1931, Box 849; RG 151, NACP.

32. A. B. Coffman, Secretary, National Sports Promotion Association, to Henry Morse, Chief of Specialties Division, BFDC, USDOC, July 13, 1923; Internal Memorandum from E.J. Breyere to Mr. North, BFDC, USDOC, July 19, 1923; Henry Morse, Chief of Specialties Division, BFDC, USDOC, to A. B. Coffman, Secretary, National Sports Promotion Association, July 20, 1923; Memorandum from Walter L. Miller, Foreign Service Division, to Latin American Division, BFDC, USDOC, August 1,

1923; Questionnaire No. 84, BFDC, USDOC, n.d.; Sporting Goods—General, 1923–1931, Box 849; RG 151, NACP.

33. Robert J. Phillips, Liaison Officer, USDOC, BFDC, to Wilbur J. Carr, Assistant Secretary of State, USDOS, April 10, 1930; Robert J. Phillips, Liaison Officer, BFDC, USDOC, to Wilbur J. Carr, Assistant Secretary of State, USDOS, March 28, 1930; Questionnaire No. 302, "Sports," USDOC, Bureau of Foreign and Domestic Affairs, sent from Eric T. King, Chief of the Specialties Division, Approved by the Questionnaire Committee, James W. Furness, Acting Chairman, March 25, 1930, Box 5026; RG 59, NACP. In their official report to the U.S. Congress the Commerce Department's analysts noted: "At present the division is cooperating with the American Olympic Games Committee in securing from foreign countries lists of sporting and athletic associations that may participate in the 1932 Olympic events. This, with related information, will be highly useful to exporters of athletic and kindred goods." *Eighteenth Annual Report of the Secretary of Commerce, 1930* (Washington, 1930), 133.

34. *Nineteenth Annual Report of the Secretary of Commerce, 1931* (Washington, 1931), 112.

35. Coffman to Morse, July 13, 1923; Breyere to North, July 19, 1923; Morse to Coffman, July 20, 1923; Miller to the Latin American Division, August 1, 1923; Questionnaire No. 84.

36. Chastising social theorists, especially his fellow Marxists, for ignoring sport, James contended that it was a central force in the creation of modern cultures. "A glance at the world showed that when the common people were not a work, one thing they wanted was organized sports and games. They wanted them greedily, passionately," asserted James in his withering critique of scholars who purported to study modern social relations yet had no real conception of the basic cultural question, "What do men live by?" C. L. R. James, *Beyond a Boundary* (Durham, NC: Duke University Press, [1963]1993), 152.

37. The sport data generated by foreign diplomats and trade attachés confirm what historian Bill Murray has argued, that during the 1920s and 1930s association football became beyond a shadow of doubt become "the world's game." *The World's Game: A History of Soccer* (Urbana: University of Illinois Press, 1996).

38. Report on "Sports Data in Trinidad for the Management of the Tenth Olympiad," from U.S. Vice Consul Alfredo Demorest to the USDOS, December 10, 1930, Box 5027; RG 59, NACP. See also, Report on "Sports Data for the Tenth Olympiad," from U.S. Consul General to the Bahamas Fred D. Fisher, to the USDOS, July 17, 1930; Report on "Sports Data for the Management of the Tenth Olympiad," from U.S. Consul General to Barbados, William W. Brunswick, to the USDOS, June 21, 1930; Report on "Sports Data for the Management of the Tenth Olympiad," from the U.S. Vice Consul to Bermuda, Clay Merrell, to the USDOS, May 10, 1930, Box 5026; RG 59, NACP.

39. Eduardo Galeano, *Soccer in Sun and Shadow,* trans. Mark Fried (London: Verso, 1998), 30.

40. The dominant transnational pattern that emerged from the globalization of sport was the worldwide spread of the notion of using sport to define and promote nationalism rather than the erosion of national fervor through some common fascination with sport. Mark Dyreson, "Globalizing the Nation-Making Process: Modern Sport in World History," *International Journal of the History of Sport* 20 (March 2003): 91–106.

41. See especially, Andrei S. Markovits and Steven L. Hellerman, *Offside: Soccer and American Exceptionalism* (Princeton, N.J. Princeton University Press, 2001); Franklin Foer, *How Soccer Explains the World: An Unlikely Theory of Globalization* (New York: HarperCollins, 2004); Stefan Szymanski and Andrew Zimbalist, *National Pastime: How Americans Play Baseball and the Rest of the World Plays Soccer* (Washington, DC: Brookings Institute, 2005). For an interesting critique and revision of Markovits and Hellerman, see Sean Frederick Brown, "Exceptionalist America: American Sports Fans' Reaction to Internationalization," *International Journal of the History of Sport* 22 (November 2005): 1106–35.

42. The best history of the global hegemony of modern (Western) sport is Allen Guttmann's trail-blazing *Games and Empires: Modern Sports and Cultural Imperialism* (New York: Columbia University Press, 1994). In a more recent work Guttmann has, to some degree, updated and embellished his earlier theories in *Sports* (2004).

43. Demorest to the USDOS, December 10, 1930.

44. Report, "Sports Data for the Management of the Tenth Olympiad," from the U.S. Vice Consul to the Irish Free State Edwin J. King to the USDOS, July 29, 1930, Box 5026; RG 59, NACP.

45. Memorandums dated January 24, 1924, from E. G. Holt, Acting Chief, Rubber Division, BFDC, USDOC, to Wright and Ditson; to Hillerich & Bradsby Co.; to A. J. Reach Company; Julius Klein, Director of the BFDC, USDOC, to *Sporting Goods Dealer,* January 24, 1924; E.G. Holt, Assistant Chief, Rubber Division, BFDC, USDOC, memorandums to F. Lawrence, Foreign Department, A.G. Spalding and Brothers, January 29, 1925; E. G. Holt, Assistant Chief, Rubber Division, BFDC, USDOC, to J. T. Rodgers, Hillerich & Bradsby Co., January 29, 1925; Sporting Goods—General, 1923–1931, Box 849; RG 151, NACP. Ironically, Hillerich & Bradsby were major supporters of Leslie Mann's efforts to incorporate baseball in the Olympic program. Travaglini, "Olympic Baseball 1936," 46–55.

46. *Market for Sporting and Athletic Goods in Africa and Near East;* Report on "Sports in Syria," from U.S. Vice Consul to Syria D. F. McGonigal to the USDOS, August 6, 1930; Report on "Sports Data for the Management of the Tenth Olympiad: Tangier Consular District," from U.S. Consul Horace Remillard to the USDOS, August 4, 1930, Box 5027; RG 59, NACP.

47. *Market for Sporting and Athletic Goods in Africa and Near East,* 1–13, quotation from 1.

48. On color lines in the national pastime see especially Jules Tygiel, *Baseball's*

Great Experiment: Jackie Robinson and His Legacy, rev. ed. (New York: Oxford University Press, 1997). See also Neil Lanctot, *Negro League Baseball: The Rise and Ruin of a Black Institution* (Philadelphia: University of Pennsylvania Press, 2004); Robert Peterson, *Only the Ball Was White: A History of Legendary Black Players and All-Black Professional Teams*, rev. ed. (New York: Gramercy, 1999).

49. On South African sport see John Nauright, *Sport, Culture, and Identities in South Africa* (London: Leicester University Press, 1997). See also J.A. Mangan, ed., *The Games Ethic and Imperialism* (New York: Viking, 1985). For a solid overview see the approriate chapters in Guttmann's *Sports*, "Cricket Follows the Flag," 77–88; and "Our Former Colonial Masters: African Sport," 239–49.

50. Samuel H. Day, American Commercial Attaché, Johannesburg Office, USDOC, to the Specialties Division, BFDC, USDOC, January 18, 1933; Sporting Goods—by Country, Puerto Rico to West Africa, Box 850; RG 151, NACP.

51. Samuel H. Day, American Commercial Attaché, Johannesburg Office, USDOC, to the Specialties and Motion Picture Division, BFDC, USDOC, July 10, 1935; Sporting Goods—by Country, Puerto Rico to West Africa, Box 850; RG 151, NACP.

52. Day to the Specialties Division, January 18, 1933; RG 151, NACP.

53. Eric T. King, Chief of the Specialties Division, BFDC, USDOC, to the Johannesburg Office, USDOC, February 24, 1933; Sporting Goods—by Country, Puerto Rico to West Africa, Box 850; RG 151, NACP.

54. James F. Hodgson, Manager, New York District Office, to the Specialties Division, BFDC, USDOC, March 15, 1933; Eric T. King, Chief of the Specialties Division, BFDC, USDOC, to the Milwaukee District Office and to the St. Louis District Office, USDOC, March 31, 1933; Eric T. King, Chief of the Specialties Division, BFDC, USDOC, to the Boston District Office, USDOC, March 31, 1933; F. E. Becker, Commercial Agent, Boston District Office, USDOC, to W. W. Colson, Winthrop, Massachusetts, April 5, 1933; B. P. Boykin, District Manager, Milwaukee District Office, USDOC, to George W. Levis, Madison, Wisconsin, April 6, 1933; Eric T. King, Chief of the Specialties Division, BFDC, USDOC, to the Boston District Office, USDOC, April 15, 1933; B. P. Boykin, District Manager, Milwaukee District Office, USDOC, to Specialties Division, BFDC, USDOC, April 24, 1933; F. L. Roberts, District Manager, Chicago District Office, USDOC, to Specialties Division, BFDC, USDOC, April 24, 1933; Sporting Goods—by Country, Puerto Rico to West Africa, Box 850; RG 151, NACP.

55. Samuel H. Day, American Commercial Attaché, Johannesburg Office, USDOC, to the Specialties Division, BFDC, USDOC, May 17, 1933; Sporting Goods—by Country, Puerto Rico to West Africa, Box 850; RG 151, NACP.

56. B. P. Boykin, District Manager, Milwaukee District Office, USDOC, to Specialties Division, BFDC, USDOC, May 15, 1933; Sporting Goods—by Country, Puerto Rico to West Africa, Box 850; RG 151, NACP.

57. Hugh Butler, New England Manager, Boston District Office, USDOC, to Spe-

cialties Division, BFDC, USDOC, May 23, 1933; Sporting Goods—by Country, Puerto Rico to West Africa, Box 850; RG 151, NACP.

58. T. L. Gaukel, District Manager, St. Louis District Office, USDOC, to Specialties Division, BFDC, USDOC, May 22, 1933; Eric T. King, Chief of the Specialties Division, BFDC, USDOC, to the Johannesburg Office, USDOC, May 24, 1933; James T. Scott, Acting Manager, New York District Office, USDOC, to Specialties Division, BFDC, USDOC, May 27, 1933; Harry K. Sorensen, District Manager, Philadelphia District Office, USDOC, to Specialties Division, BFDC, USDOC, July 27, 1933; King to the Johannesburg Office, USDOC, February 24, 1933; Sporting Goods—by Country, Puerto Rico to West Africa, Box 850; RG 151, NACP.

59. F. L. Roberts, District Manager, Chicago District Office, USDOC, to Specialties Division, BFDC, USDOC, August 16, 1933; George C. Payne, Commercial Agent in Charge, Chicago District Office, USDOC, to Specialties Division, BFDC, USDOC, December 5, 1933; Eric T. King, Chief of the Specialties Division, BFDC, USDOC, to the Chicago District Office, USDOC, February 24, 1933; Eric T. King, Chief of the Specialties Division, BFDC, USDOC, to the Johannesburg Office, USDOC, December 7, 1933; Sporting Goods—by Country, Puerto Rico to West Africa, Box 850; RG 151, NACP.

60. Samuel H. Day, American Commercial Attaché, Johannesburg Office, USDOC, to the Specialties Division, BFDC, USDOC, February 14, 1934; Eric T. King, Chief of the Specialties Division, BFDC, USDOC, to the Chicago District Office, USDOC, March 20, 1934; Sporting Goods—by Country, Puerto Rico to West Africa, Box 850; RG 151, NACP.

61. Day to the Specialties and Motion Picture Division, July 10, 1935; Box 850; RG 151, NACP.

62. Thomas Burke, Chief of the Specialties Division, USDOC, to *The Sporting Goods Dealer,* St. Louis, August 13, 1935; Fred E. Owens, *The Sporting Goods Dealer,* St. Louis, to Thomas Burke, Chief of the Specialties Division, USDOC, August 16, 1935; Ames A. Castle, *Sporting Goods Journal,* Chicago, to Thomas Burke, Chief of the Specialties Division, USDOC, August 20, 1935; Thomas Burke, Chief of the Specialties Division, USDOC, to Ames A. Castle, *Sporting Goods Journal,* Chicago, August 26, 1935; Thomas Burke, Chief of the Specialties Division, USDOC, to Johannesburg Office, USDOC, August 26, 1935; Sporting Goods—by Country, Puerto Rico to West Africa, Box 850; RG 151, NACP.

63. *European Market for Sporting and Athletic Goods,* 2.

64. Richard Holt, *Sport and the British* (New York: Oxford University Press, 1989).

65. *European Market for Sporting and Athletic Goods,* 16–30.

66. Report on "Sports Data for the Management of the Tenth Olympiad: Lithuania," from U.S. Vice Consul Bertel E. Kuniholm to the USDOS, July 1, 1930; RG 59, NACP.

67. T. H. Isaacs, Davega United Sport and Radio Shops, New York City, to the BDFC, USDOC, July 19, 1932; Sporting Goods—by Country, Puerto Rico to West Africa, Box 850; RG 151, NACP.

68. E. C. Ropes, Chief, Russian Section, Division of Regional Information, USDOC, to T. H. Isaacs, Davega United Sport and Radio Shops, New York City, July 21, 1932; Sporting Goods—by Country, Puerto Rico to West Africa, Box 850; RG 151, NACP.

69. *European Market for Sporting and Athletic Goods,* 16–30.

70. Arnaldo Cortesi, "Fascisti Have Won Italians to Sport," *New York Times,* February 15, 1931, sec. E, 4.

71. W. H. Mahoney, Manager of the Foreign Trade Bureau of the Merchants' Association of New York, to Eric T. King, Chief of the Specialties Division, BFDC, USDOC, March 5, 1931; Sporting Goods—by Country, Australia to Philippine Islands, Box 850; RG 151, NACP.

72. Mowatt M. Mitchell, Commercial Attaché, Rome Office, BFDC, USDOC, to Eric T. King, Chief of the Specialties Division, BFDC, USDOC, February 17, 1931; Sporting Goods—by Country, Australia to Philippine Islands, Box 850; RG 151, NACP. The closest the *New York Herald Tribune* came to such a story was a brief blurb on the Italian government sending a group of physical educators to study "American sport systems" at a Tennessee military academy. "Italy to Study Sport for Youth in America," *New York Herald Tribune,* February 17, 1931, 25.

73. Eric T. King, Chief of the Specialties Division, BFDC, USDOC, to W. H. Mahoney, Manager of the Foreign Trade Bureau of the Merchants Association of New York, March 11, 1931; Sporting Goods—by Country, Australia to Philippine Islands, Box 850; RG 151, NACP.

74. Robert Ernst, *Weakness Is a Crime: The Life of Bernarr Macfadden* (Syracuse, NY: Syracuse University Press, 1991).

75. Eric T. King, Chief of the Specialties Division, BFDC, USDOC, to Walter N. Pearce, District Manager of the Jacksonville Office, BFDC, USDOC, March 24, 1931; Sporting Goods—by Country, Australia to Philippine Islands, Box 850; RG 151, NACP.

76. Walter N. Pearce, District Manager of the Jacksonville Office, BFDC, USDOC, to Eric T. King, Chief of the Specialties Division, BFDC, USDOC, March 25, 1931; Sporting Goods—by Country, Australia to Philippine Islands, Box 850; RG 151, NACP.

77. Prentiss M. Terry, District Manager of the Louisville Office, BFDC, USDOC, to Hillerich & Bradsby Company, Louisville, Kentucky, March 21, 1931; Prentiss M. Terry, District Manager of the Louisville Office, BFDC, USDOC, to Eric T. King, Chief of the Specialties Division, BFDC, USDOC, March 21, 1931; Sporting Goods—by Country, Australia to Philippine Islands, Box 850; RG 151, NACP.

78. Eric T. King, Chief of the Specialties Division, BFDC, USDOC, to the Louisville

Office, BFDC, USDOC, March 30, 1931; Sporting Goods—by Country, Australia to Philippine Islands, Box 850; RG 151, NACP.

79. Charles Kupfer, "*Il Duce* and the Father of Physical Culture," *Iron Game History* 6 (January 2000): 3–9. The book is Thomas B. Morgan, *Italian Physical Culture Demonstration* (New York: Macfadden Book Company, 1932).

80. *Latin American Market for Sporting and Athletic Goods,* ii.

81. Ibid., 23–34, quotations from 27, 30; Report on "Sports in Ecuador," from Consul-General Harold D. Clum to the USDOS, January 26, 1931, Box 5027; RG 59, NACP.

82. Memorandums dated April 12, 1932, from Eric T. King, Chief of the Specialties Division, BFDC, USDOC, to P. Goldsmith and Sons Company; to the National Sporting Goods Manufacturing Company; to the Wilson-Western Sporting Goods Company; to the Draper Maynard Company; to A. J. Reach, Wright and Ditson, Inc.; to A. G. Spalding & Brothers; to Stall and Dean Manufacturing Company; Sporting Goods—by Country, Australia to Philippine Islands, Box 850; RG 151, NACP.

83. W. O. Leuschuier, Order Department, A. G. Spalding & Brothers, to Eric T. King, Chief of the Specialties Division, BFDC, USDOC, April 14, 1932; Sporting Goods—by Country, Australia to Philippine Islands, Box 850; RG 151, NACP.

84. Halbert E. Watkins, Commercial Attaché, Caracas Office, USDOC, to the Specialties Division, BFDC, USDOC, December 14, 1927; Sporting Goods—by Country, Puerto Rico to West Africa, Box 850; RG 151, NACP.

85. Eric T. King, Chief of the Specialties Division, Special Circular, Market for Sporting Goods in Venezuela Increasing, BFDC, USDOC, January 7, 1928; Eric T. King, Chief of the Specialties Division, Special Circular No. 434–2, Market for Sporting Goods in Venezuela Increasing, BFDC, USDOC, January 25, 1928; Eric T. King, Chief of the Specialties Division, BFDC, USDOC, to Caracas Office, USDOC, December 30, 1929; Halbert E. Watkins, Commercial Attaché, Caracas Office, USDOC, to the Specialties Division, BFDC, USDOC, December 22, 1927; Sporting Goods—by Country, Puerto Rico to West Africa, Box 850; RG 151, NACP.

86. *Latin American Market for Sporting and Athletic Goods,* 14–22.

87. Demorest to the USDOS, December 10, 1930.

88. *Latin American Market for Sporting and Athletic Goods,* 14–22.

89. Report on "Sports Data for the Management of the Tenth Olympiad," from the American Consul General to Haiti, Donald R. Heath, to the USDOS, June 12, 1930, Box 5026; RG 59, NACP.

90. *Latin American Market for Sporting and Athletic Goods,* 18–19.

91. Report on "Sports Data (Dominican Republic)," from U.S. Consul Reed Paige Clark to the USDOS, December 10, 1930, Box 5027; RG 59, NACP.

92. Alan M. Klein, *Sugarball: The American Game, The Dominican Dream* (New Haven, Conn.: Yale University Press, 1991); Rob Ruck, *The Tropic of Baseball: Baseball in the Dominican Republic* (Westport, Conn.: Meckler, 1991).

93. Roberto González Echevarría, *The Pride of Havana: The History of Cuban Baseball* (New York: Oxford University Press, 1999).

94. *Latin American Market for Sporting and Athletic Goods,* 15–16.

95. Darwin DeGolia, Assistant Trade Commissioner, San Juan, Puerto Rico Office, USDOC, to Eric T. King, Chief of the Specialties Division, BFDC, USDOC, December 10, 1929; Sporting Goods—by Country, Puerto Rico to West Africa, Box 850; RG 151, NACP.

96. *Latin American Market for Sporting and Athletic Goods,* 9; Report on "Sports Data for the Management of the Tenth Olympiad, British Honduras," from American Consul General G. R. Taggart to the USDOS, July 31, 1931, Box 5027; RG 59, NACP.

97. *Latin American Market for Sporting and Athletic Goods,* 9–10; Report on "Sport Data from Costa Rica for the Management of the Tenth Olympic Games," from U.S. Vice Consul R. W. Unckles to the USDOS, August 25, 1930, Box 5027; RG 59, NACP.

98. *Latin American Market for Sporting and Athletic Goods,* 9–13; Report on "Sports Data for the Management of the Tenth Olympiad, Honduras as a Whole," from U.S. Vice Consul R. Austin Acly to the USDOS, September 9, 1931, Box 5027; RG 59, NACP.

99. *Latin American Market for Sporting and Athletic Goods,* 12.

100. The best account of U.S. involvement in the Nicaraguan struggle is Neill Macaulay, *The Sandino Affair* (Chicago: Quadrangle, 1967).

101. Report on "Sports Data for the Management of the Tenth Olympiad," from American Consul General to Nicaragua, Christian T. Steger, to the USDOS, June 19, 1930, Box 5026; RG 59, NACP.

102. *Latin American Market for Sporting and Athletic Goods,* 12–13.

103. Merwin L. Bohan, Commercial Attaché, U.S. Legation in Guatemala City, Guatemala, to the Director, BFDC, USDOC, March 12, 1930; J. E. Dyer, Assistant Trade Commissioner, Office of the Commercial Attaché, U.S. Legation Guatemala, Guatemala City, to the Director, BFDC, USDOC, August 19, 1931; Sporting Goods—by Country, Australia to Philippine Islands, Box 850; RG 151, NACP.

104. Memorandums dated March 27, 1930, from Eric T. King, Chief of the Specialties Division, BFDC, USDOC, to A. G. Spalding & Brothers; to Alex Taylor & Company; Eric T. King, Chief of the Specialties Division, BFDC, USDOC, to Guatemala Office, USDOC, April 3, 1930; Eric T. King, Chief of the Specialties Division, BFDC, USDOC, to Guatemala Office, USDOC, April 11, 1930; Walter E. Aylor, Assistant Trade Commissioner, Office of the Commercial Attaché, Guatemala City, Guatemala, to Eric T. King, Chief of the Specialties Division, BFDC, USDOC, May 5, 1930; E. J. Breyere, Acting Chief of the Specialties Division, BFDC, USDOC, to Chicago District Office, USDOC, May 29, 1930; E. J. Breyere, Acting Chief of the Specialties Division, BFDC, USDOC, to Guatemala City Office, USDOC, July 2, 1930; James F.

Hodgson, Manager of the New York Office, USDOC, to Specialties Division, BFDC, USDOC, to New York, Chicago, and Philadelphia Offices, USDOC, September 4, 1931; William M. Park, Assistant District Manager of the New York Office, USDOC, to A. G. Spalding & Brothers, A. J. Reach Company, Rosatto-Barry-Street Company, Simmons Hardware Company, New York City, September 5, 1931; Eric T. King, Chief of the Specialties Division, BFDC, USDOC, to Guatemala City Office, USDOC, September 9, 1931; Harry K. Sorensen, District Manager, Philadelphia Office, USDOC, to Specialties Division, BFDC, USDOC, September 25, 1931; F.L. Roberts, District Manager, Chicago Office, USDOC, to Specialties Division, BFDC, USDOC, September 28, 1931; Eric T. King, Chief of the Specialties Division, BFDC, USDOC, to Guatemala City Office, USDOC, September 29, 1931; Eric T. King, Chief of the Specialties Division, BFDC, USDOC, to Guatemala City Office, USDOC, October 3, 1931; Sporting Goods—by Country, Australia to Philippine Islands, Box 850; RG 151, NACP.

105. J. E. Dyer, Assistant Trade Commissioner, Office of the Commercial Attaché, U.S. Legation to Guatemala, to G. J. Wicker, Export Department, Ken-Wel Sporting Goods, Co. Inc., October 20, 1931; J. E. Dyer, Assistant Trade Commissioner, Office of the Commercial Attaché, U.S. Legation to Guatemala, to Walter L. Miller, Chief, Foreign Service Division, BFDC, USDOC, January 11, 1932; J. E. Dyer, Assistant Trade Commissioner, Office of the Commercial Attaché, U.S. Legation to Guatemala, to Eric T. King, Chief of the Specialties Division, BFDC, USDOC, January 19, 1932; Eric T. King, Chief of the Specialties Division, BFDC, USDOC, to the New York District Office, USDOC, February 1, 1932; Sporting Goods—by Country, Australia to Philippine Islands, Box 850; RG 151, NACP.

106. Scott Thompson, Inspector General of Physical Education, Department of Education, El Salvador, to D. J. Moore, Draper-Maynard Co., September 23, 1929; Donald J. Moore, Foreign Sales Manager, Draper-Maynard Co., to Eric T. King, Chief of the Specialties Division, BFDC, USDOC, October 15, 1929; Sporting Goods—by Country, Australia to Philippine Islands, Box 850; RG 151, NACP.

107. *Latin American Market for Sporting and Athletic Goods,* 13.

108. Report on "Sports," from the American Consul General to El Salvador, A. E. Carleton, to the USDOS, May 8, 1930, Box 5026; RG 59, NACP.

109. On Mexico see Joseph L. Arbena, "Sport, Development, and Mexican Nationalism, 1920–1970," *Journal of Sport History* 18 (Winter 1991): 350–64; William H. Beezley, *Judas at the Jockey Club* (Lincoln: University of Nebraska Press, 1987); William H. Beezley, "The Rise of Baseball in Mexico and the First Valenzuela," *Latin American Popular Culture* 4 (1985): 3–23. On Canada see Colin Howell, *Northern Sandlots: A History of Maritime Baseball* (Toronto: University of Toronto Press, 1995); William Humber, *Diamonds of the North: A Concise History of Baseball in Canada* (New York: Oxford University Press, 1995).

110. *Latin American Market for Sporting and Athletic Goods,* 8–9.

111. Julius Klein, "Introduction," in *Market for Athletic Goods in Canada and Newfoundland,* ii.

112. *Market for Athletic Goods in Canada and Newfoundland,* 1–13, quotation from 8. See also, Report on "Sports Data for the Management of the Tenth Olympiad," from U.S. Vice Consul to Newfoundland, Thomas D. Bergin, to the USDOS, May 26, 1930, Box 5026; RG 59, NACP.

113. On the diffusion of baseball in the Far East see Guttmann, *Games and Empires,* 75–80, 91–96. On Australia see Bruce Mitchell, "Baseball in Australia," *Sporting Traditions* 7 (November 1990): 2–24; Bruce Mitchell, "A National Game Goes International," *International Journal of the History of Sport* 9 (August 1992): 288–301; Joe Clark, *A History of Australian Baseball: Time and Game* (Lincoln: University of Nebraska Press, 2003). On baseball in Japan see Donald Roda, "Baseball and the Quest for National Dignity in Meiji, Japan," *American Historical Review* 85 (June 1980): 511–34; Sinushe Tanada, "Diffusion into the Orient: The Introduction of Western Sports in Kobe, Japan," *International Journal of the History of Sport* 5 (December 1988): 372–76; Allen Guttmann, *Japanese Sports: A History* (Honolulu: University of Hawai Press, 2001); Robert Whiting, *You Gotta Have Wa: When Two Cultures Collide on the Baseball Diamond* (New York: Collier Macmillan, 1989).

114. Julius Klein, "Introduction," in *Far Eastern Market for Sporting and Athletic Goods,* ii.

115. *Far Eastern Market for Sporting and Athletic Goods,* 1–30, quotation from 1.

116. Ibid., 17–26.

117. Foreign Market Bulletin of the Specialties Division, No. 344–2, Sporting Goods in Singapore, USDOC, October 3, 1927, Box 850; RG 151, NACP. *Far Eastern Market for Sporting and Athletic Goods,* 1–30.

118. Richard Cashman, *Paradise of Sport: The Rise of Organized Sport in Australia* (Melbourne: Oxford University Press, 1995); Daryl Adair and Wray Vamplew, *Sport in Australian History* (Melbourne: Oxford University Press, 1997).

119. *Far Eastern Market for Sporting and Athletic Goods,* 6.

120. Bryan Stoddart and Keith A. P. Sandiford, eds., *The Imperial Game: Cricket, Culture, and Society* (Manchester: Manchester University Press, 1998); Guttmann, *Games and Empires,* 91–96.

121. *Far Eastern Market for Sporting and Athletic Goods,* 5.

122. Gai Ingham Berlage, *Women in Baseball: The Forgotten History* (Westport, Conn.: Praeger, 1994).

123. *Far Eastern Market for Sporting and Athletic Goods,* 5.

124. Mark Lamster, *Spalding's World Tour: The Epic Adventure that Took Baseball around the Globe—and Made It America's Game* (New York: Public Affairs, 2006); Peter Levine, *A. G. Spalding and the Rise of Baseball: The Promise of American Sport* (New York: Oxford University Press, 1985), 99–109.

125. H. P. Van Blarcom, Assistant Trade Commissioner, Sydney Office, USDOC,

to Eric T. King, Chief of the Specialties Division, BFDC, USDOC, November 24, 1930; Sporting Goods—by Country, Australia to Philippine Islands, Box 850; RG 151, NACP.

126. For examples of these publications see John Foster Buckingham, *How to Play the Infield and the Outfield . . . : Five Volumes Combined In One* (New York: American Sports Publishing, 1940); John Foster Buckingham, *How to Bat* (New York: American Sports Publishing, 1940); T. H. Murnane, *How to Play Baseball* (New York: American Sports Publishing, 1938).

127. Eric T. King, Chief of the Specialties Division, BFDC, USDOC, to New York District Office, USDOC, January 14, 1931; Eric T. King, Chief of the Specialties Division, BFDC, USDOC, to New York District Office, USDOC, January 30, 1931; James F. Hodgson, Manager, New York District Office, to Specialties Division, BFDC, USDOC, January 30, 1931; Sporting Goods—by Country, Australia to Philippine Islands, Box 850; RG 151, NACP.

128. Hodgson to Specialties Division, January 30, 1931; James F. Hodgson, Manager, New York District Office, to Specialties Division, BFDC, USDOC, February 2, 1931; E. J. Breyere, Acting Chief, of the Specialties Division, BFDC, USDOC, to the New York District Office, USDOC, February 10, 1931; Sporting Goods—by Country, Australia to Philippine Islands, Box 850; RG 151, NACP.

129. E. J. Breyere, Acting Chief, of the Specialties Division, BFDC, USDOC, to the Sydney Office, USDOC, February 10, 1931; Sporting Goods—by Country, Australia to Philippine Islands, Box 850; RG 151, NACP.

130. H. P. Van Blarcom, Assistant Trade Commissioner, Sydney Office, USDOC, to E. J. Breyere, Acting Chief of the Specialties Division, BFDC, USDOC, April 29, 1931; Sporting Goods—by Country, Australia to Philippine Islands, Box 850; RG 151, NACP.

131. E. J. Breyere, Acting Chief, of the Specialties Division, BFDC, USDOC, to the New York District Office, USDOC, May 29, 1931; Sporting Goods—by Country, Australia to Philippine Islands, Box 850; RG 151, NACP.

132. James F. Hodgson, Manager, New York District Office, to Specialties Division, BFDC, USDOC, June 11, 1931; Eric T. King, Chief of the Specialties Division, BFDC, USDOC, to Sydney Office, USDOC, June 20, 1931; Sporting Goods—by Country, Australia to Philippine Islands, Box 850; RG 151, NACP.

133. H. P. Van Blarcom, Assistant Trade Commissioner, Sydney Office, USDOC, to Eric T. King, Chief of the Specialties Division, BFDC, USDOC, May 1, 1931; Sporting Goods—by Country, Australia to Philippine Islands, Box 850; RG 151, NACP.

134. Eric T. King, Chief of the Specialties Division, BFDC, USDOC, to Sydney Office, USDOC, June 5, 1931; Sporting Goods—by Country, Australia to Philippine Islands, Box 850; RG 151, NACP.

135. Eric T. King, Chief of the Specialties Division, BFDC, USDOC, to Louisville, New York, St. Louis, Cincinnati, and Philadelphia District Offices, USDOC, June 9,

1931; Sporting Goods—by Country, Australia to Philippine Islands, Box 850; RG 151, NACP.

136. James F. Hodgson, Manager, New York District Office, to Specialties Division, BFDC, USDOC, June 20, 1931; Sporting Goods—by Country, Australia to Philippine Islands, Box 850; RG 151, NACP.

137. T. L. Gaukel, District Manager, St. Louis District Office, to Specialties Division, BFDC, USDOC, June 25, 1931; Sporting Goods—by Country, Australia to Philippine Islands, Box 850; RG 151, NACP.

138. Malcolm M. Stewart, Manager, Foreign Trade Department, Cincinnati Chamber of Commerce, to Eric T. King, Chief of the Specialties Division, BFDC, USDOC, June 23, 1931; J.W. Brewer, Acting District Manager, Louisville District Office, to Specialties Division, BFDC, USDOC, July 12, 1931; Eric T. King, Chief of the Specialties Division, BFDC, USDOC, to Sydney Office, USDOC, July 13, 1931; O. M. Butler, Acting District Manager, Philadelphia District Office, to Specialties Division, BFDC, USDOC, July 6, 1931; Sporting Goods—by Country, Australia to Philippine Islands, Box 850; RG 151, NACP.

139. Eric T. King, Chief of the Specialties Division, BFDC, USDOC, to Sydney Office, USDOC, June 17, 1931; Eric T. King, Chief of the Specialties Division, BFDC, USDOC, to Sydney Office, USDOC, June 30, 1931; Eric T. King, Chief of the Specialties Division, BFDC, USDOC, to Sydney Office, USDOC, July 3, 1931; Sporting Goods—by Country, Australia to Philippine Islands, Box 850; RG 151, NACP.

140. Eric T. King, Chief of the Specialties Division, BFDC, USDOC, to New York District Office, USDOC, June 30, 1931; Sporting Goods—by Country, Australia to Philippine Islands, Box 850; RG 151, NACP.

141. H. P. Van Blarcom, Assistant Trade Commissioner, Sydney Office, USDOC, to Eric T. King, Chief of the Specialties Division, BFDC, USDOC, September 26, 1931; Sporting Goods—by Country, Australia to Philippine Islands, Box 850; RG 151, NACP.

142. Eric T. King, Chief of the Specialties Division, BFDC, USDOC, to New York District Office, USDOC, October 31, 1931; James F. Hodgson, Manager, New York District Office, to Specialties Division, BFDC, USDOC, November 4, 1931; Eric T. King, Chief of the Specialties Division, BFDC, USDOC, to New York District Office, USDOC, November 11, 1931; Sporting Goods—by Country, Australia to Philippine Islands, Box 850; RG 151, NACP.

143. H. P. Van Blarcom, Assistant Trade Commissioner, Sydney Office, USDOC, to Eric T. King, Chief of the Specialties Division, BFDC, USDOC, January 27, 1932; Eric T. King, Chief of the Specialties Division, BFDC, USDOC, to New York District Office, USDOC, March 16, 1932; M. L. Wilson, Alex Taylor & Co., Inc., New York City, to Eric T. King, Chief of the Specialties Division, BFDC, USDOC, April 28, 1932; Eric T. King, Chief of the Specialties Division, BFDC, USDOC, to Sydney Office, USDOC, May 6, 1932; Eric T. King, Chief of the Specialties Division, BFDC, USDOC, to New

York District Office, USDOC, November 11, 1931; Sporting Goods—by Country, Australia to Philippine Islands, Box 850; RG 15, NACP.

144. Gerald R. Gems, "The Athletic Crusade: Sport and Colonialism in the Philippines," *International Journal of the History of Sport* 21 (January 2004): 1–15.

145. *Far Eastern Market for Sporting and Athletic Goods,* 14.

146. Ibid., 1–5, 27–30, quotation from 1.

147. Shirl H. Blalock, District Manager, Seattle District Office, USDOC, to BFDC, USDOC, December 13, 1932; Eric T. King, Chief of the Specialties Division, BFDC, USDOC, to the Tokyo Office, USDOC, January 5, 1933; Sporting Goods—by Country, Australia to Philippine Islands, Box 850; RG 151, NACP.

148. B. H. Wilkins, President, Tennessee Overall Co., to the BFDC, USDOC, November 10, 1934; Thomas Burke, Chief of the Specialties—Motion Pictures Division, BFDC, to B. H. Wilkins, President, Tennessee Overall Co., November 14, 1934; Thomas Burke, Chief of the Specialties—Motion Pictures Division, BFDC, USDOC, to the Tokyo Office, USDOC, November 14, 1934; Sporting Goods—by Country, Australia to Philippine Islands, Box 850; RG 151, NACP.

149. Thomas Burke, Chief of the Specialties—Motion Pictures Division, BFDC, USDOC, to the Sporting Goods Journal, Chicago, November 22, 1935; Thomas Burke, Chief of the Specialties—Motion Pictures Division, BFDC, USDOC, Athletic Goods Manufacturers Association, New York, November 22, 1935; Thomas Burke, Chief of the Specialties—Motion Pictures Division, BFDC, USDOC, to the American Sporting Goods Association, Chicago, November 22, 1935; Thomas Burke, Chief of the Specialties—Motion Pictures Division, BFDC, USDOC, to the Sporting Goods Dealer, St. Louis, November 22, 1935; Sporting Goods—by Country, Australia to Philippine Islands, Box 850; RG 15, NACP.

150. Thomas Burke, Chief of the Specialties—Motion Pictures Division, BFDC, USDOC, to B. H. Wilkins, President, Tennessee Overall Co., November 23, 1935; Sporting Goods—by Country, Australia to Philippine Islands, Box 850; RG 151, NACP.

151. H. Boardman Spalding, Secretary, Athletic Goods Manufacturers Association, New York, to Thomas Burke, Chief of the Specialties—Motion Pictures Division, BFDC, USDOC, November 23, 1935; Thomas Burke, Chief of the Specialties—Motion Pictures Division, BFDC, USDOC, to H. Boardman Spalding, Secretary, Athletic Goods Manufacturers Association, New York, November 27, 1935; Memorandums dated December 6, 1935, from Thomas Burke, Chief of the Specialties—Motion Pictures Division, BFDC, USDOC, to H. Harwood and Sons, Incorporated, Natick, Massachusetts; to Acushnet Process Sales Company, New Bedford, Massachusetts; to Bancroft Racket Company, Pawtucket, Rhode Island; to E. Kent Estate, Pawtucket, Rhode Island; to M. Denkert and Company, Johnstown, New York; to J. de Beer and Son; to Pederson Manufacturing Company, Mount Vernon, New York; to The Kroydon Company, Maplewood, New Jersey; to Lyon, Incorporated, Nashville, Tennessee;

to Wilson Sporting Goods Company, Chicago, Illinois; E. C. Conlin, Sales Manager, Golf Ball Department, United States Rubber Products, Inc., New York, to Thomas Burke, Chief of the Specialties—Motion Pictures Division, BFDC, USDOC, January 13, 1936; Thomas Burke, Chief of the Specialties—Motion Pictures Division, BFDC, USDOC, to United States Rubber Products, Inc., New York, January 14, 1936; E. C. Conlin, Sales Manager, Golf Ball Department, United States Rubber Products, Inc., New York, to Thomas Burke, Chief of the Specialties—Motion Pictures Division, BFDC, USDOC, January 15, 1936; Sporting Goods—by Country, Australia to Philippine Islands, Box 850; RG 151, NACP.

152. L. B. Icely, President, Wilson-Western Sporting Goods Co., Chicago, Illinois, to Thomas Burke, Chief of the Specialties—Motion Pictures Division, BFDC, USDOC, December 9, 1935; Sporting Goods—by Country, Australia to Philippine Islands, Box 850; RG 151, NACP.

153. C. T. Felker, Editor, *Sporting Goods Journal,* St. Louis, Missouri, to Thomas Burke, Chief of the Specialties—Motion Pictures Division, BFDC, USDOC, December 10, 1935; Thomas Burke, Chief of the Specialties—Motion Pictures Division, BFDC, USDOC, to C. T. Felker, Editor, *Sporting Goods Journal,* St. Louis, Missouri, December 12, 1935; Ames A. Castle, Editor-in-Chief, *Sporting Goods Journal,* Chicago, Illinois, to Thomas Burke, Chief of the Specialties—Motion Pictures Division, BFDC, USDOC, December 19, 1935; Thomas Burke, Chief of the Specialties—Motion Pictures Division, BFDC, USDOC, to Ames A. Castle, Editor-in-Chief, *Sporting Goods Journal,* Chicago, Illinois, December 24, 1935; Sporting Goods—by Country, Australia to Philippine Islands, Box 850; RG 151, NACP.

154. Fred J. Bowman, Secretary, Athletic Goods Manufacturers Association, Chicago Illinois, to H. B. McCoy, Chief of the Specialties Division, BFDC, USDOC, January 15, 1940; H. B. McCoy, Chief of the Specialties Division, BFDC, USDOC, to Fred J. Bowman, Secretary, Athletic Goods Manufacturers Association, Chicago Illinois, January 17, 1940; Sporting Goods—by Country, Australia to Philippine Islands, Box 850; RG 151, NACP.

155. Richard C. Crepeau, "Pearl Harbor: A Failure of Baseball," *Journal of Popular Culture* 15 (Spring 1982): 67–74. See also, Robert J. Sinclair, "Baseball's Rising Sun: American Interwar Baseball Diplomacy in Japan," *Canadian Journal of the History of Sport* 16 (December 1985): 44–53.

156. The *New York Times,* for instance, did not bother to cover the 1938 contests in Great Britain. A year later, as a prelude to a round-robin tourney between the United States, Cuba, and Nicaragua in Havana, the newspaper made a brief reference to John Moore Trophy that England had won in 1938 for defeating the United States, which would be presented to the winner of 1939 World Series. The *New York Times* published minimal coverage of the 1939 series. Cuba won the series by winning three times against the United States and three times against Nicaragua. While they were swept by Cuba, Nicaragua swept the U.S. team. The United States lost all

six of their games. "American Team in Cuba," *New York Times,* August 11, 1939, 23; "Cuba Beats Nicaragua," *New York Times,* August 13, 1939, sec. S, 4; "Cubans Rout U.S. Nine," *New York Times,* August 14, 1939, 21; "Cubans Triumph, 9 to 1," *New York Times,* August 25, 1939, 21; "American Nine Bows, 2–0," August 16, 1939, 31; "Cuban Nine Victor, 3–2," *New York Times,* August 18, 1939, 12; "Cubans Defeat U.S. Nine," August 20, 1939, sec. S, 3; "Nicaraguans Beat U.S.," *New York Times,* August 21, 1939, 18; "Cubans Triumph, 9 to 1," *New York Times,* August 25, 1939, 21; "Americans Bow Twice," *New York Times,* August 27, 1939, sec. S, 2. The John Moore Trophy was named for the founder of the English Baseball Association. For details of the 1938 series in London, won by England four games to one, see Peter C. Bjarkman, *Diamonds around the Globe: The Encyclopedia of International Baseball* (Westport, Conn.: Greenwood, 2005), 416–17.

157. As late as May 1938, Mann was still working toward his goal of an Olympic baseball tourney in Japan, setting up a selection process for naming a 1940 American Olympic baseball team. "Semi-Pros Barred in Olympic Play," *New York Times,* May 9, 1938, 21. Japanese officials canceled the 1940 Games in July 1938. Sandra Collins, "Tokyo/Helsinki 1940," in *Encyclopedia of the Modern Olympic Movement,* ed. John Findling and Kimberly Pelle (Westport, Conn.: Greenwood, 2004), 115–24.

158. Indeed, in the midst of World War II when Leslie Mann joined the USO, the press announcement noted that he had organized the International Amateur Baseball Federation and "put the game on the Olympic roster." "Mann Joins USO Work," *New York Times,* February 1, 1943, 20.

159. Shaw batted third and played first base for the Olympics. "Special Demonstrations," 1099.

160. As quoted in Travaglini, "Olympic Baseball 1936," 55; Cava, "Baseball in the Olympics," 11.

161. Donald W. Lamm, Clerk to the Commercial Attaché, Tokyo Office, USDOC, Tokyo—E. & T. Note 17—Postponement of the 1940 World's Fair and Cancellation of the Olympics Implored by Merchants, September 17, 1938; Olympic Games 1932–1938, Box 849; RG 151, NACP.

BENJAMIN G. RADER

"MATTERS INVOLVING HONOR"

REGION, RACE, AND RANK IN THE VIOLENT LIFE OF TYRUS RAYMOND COBB

On May 15, 1912, in an American League baseball game between the New York Highlanders and the Detroit Tigers, the New York fans heckled Ty Cobb unmercifully.[1] Among the loudest and most offensive of the hecklers was Claude Lueker, a fan who in a printing accident had lost one hand and three fingers on the other hand. After having failed to get Lueker removed from the ballpark for his obnoxious remarks, Cobb, according to one account, shouted back "an insult about Lueker's sister." Lueker may have responded by screaming that Cobb was a "half-nigger"[2] or, according to another report, yelling: "Hey Cobb! You're nothin' but a yellow-bellied bastard!"[3] Cobb's own teammates needled him, asking him in effect what he planned to do about the offender.

Finally, Cobb could stand it no longer. He vaulted over the railing and shoved his way through a crowd of surprised spectators. Upon reaching Lueker, Cobb struck him in the face with powerful blows from each fist, sending him sprawling out of his seat and onto his back. He then kicked Lueker in the arms and legs. A nearby fan yelled that Lueker was handicapped. Allegedly Cobb shouted back: "I don't care if he has no feet."[4] According to the *Philadelphia Public Ledger,* Lueker's physical handicap left him "unable to defend himself properly against Cobb's swift blows."[5] The flabbergasted New York fans could not believe what they had just seen. As Cobb retreated from the stands, they arose in a rage. To protect the Detroit superstar from their wrath, Cobb's teammates lined up along the edge of the field brandishing baseball bats. In the meantime, umpire Silk O'Loughlin thumbed Cobb out of the game. News of Cobb's assault soon swept across the nation. Never before, at least according to the newspapers, had a player climbed into the stands and beaten up a fan, let alone one who was physically handicapped. Ban Johnson, the American League president who happened to have witnessed the incident personally, immediately suspended Cobb from further play.

Ty Cobb sliding into Frank "Home Run" Baker at third base, August 24, 1909. Cobb's high-flying spikes caught Baker's arm, causing a slight laceration. Recoiling in pain, Baker dropped the ball. Connie Mack, the normally soft-spoken manager of the Philadelphia Athletics, was furious. He exclaimed that Cobb was "the dirtiest player in the history of baseball." Courtesy National Baseball Hall of Fame Library, Cooperstown, NY.

The assault on Lueker was only one of many in the violence-strewn life of Ty Cobb. Even as a youngster Cobb got into his share of fights. As a lad of five, he allegedly held his own with his fists against a much bigger boy of nine, and, when engaged in a spelling bee between the boys and the girls in the fifth grade, he struck a schoolmate with his fists for spelling a word incorrectly. The misspelled word caused the boys to lose the contest; to Cobb, his classmate's failure had brought shame on him and his male peers. Throughout his long career in baseball, opponents charged that, while running the bases, Cobb regularly and deliberately sought to inflict injuries on opposing infielders with his sharpened spikes. The austere, mild-mannered owner-manager of the Philadelphia Athletics, Connie Mack, once called Cobb "the dirtiest player in the history of baseball."[6]

Apart from the on-the-field brawls in which he participated, table 1 documents twenty-four other times in which Cobb landed bodily blows on a fellow human being. In at least two of these instances, had the revolver that he nearly always carried with him fired properly, he might have killed his antagonists.

The most popular way of understanding Cobb's violent life, one offered by his teammates, opponents, and journalists who knew him, was simple: Cobb was insane. His violent disposition arose from internal demons over which he ultimately had no control. In the wake of Cobb's assault on Lueker, *The Sporting News,* the self-proclaimed "Bible of Baseball," called Cobb "a natural insurrectionist . . . [who was] pre-disposed to take the law into his own hands." The time has now come, the sporting sheet added, "for Caesar to be dealt with."[7] Many years later, one of Cobb's biographers, Al Stump, as well as the movie based on Stump's biography, presented the Detroit superstar as a man given to irrational outbursts fueled by psychotic rage and rampant personal insecurities. Stump put the matter bluntly: "Was Ty Cobb psychotic throughout his baseball career? The answer is yes."[8]

The pursuit of a psychological understanding of Cobb's behavior has led Stump, even to some degree Cobb himself, and baseball historians (including myself) to look for personal hobgoblins that might have warped his personality. In doing so they have given special weight to the death of Cobb's father; his father, whom young Ty both feared and revered, perished from two shotgun blasts fired by Ty's own mother. As sportswriter Paul Gallico once wrote: "Cobb's admission that he never got over his father's death is all any modern psychiatrist would ask for in plumbing the cause of [his] illness."[9]

TABLE 1. A SUMMARY OF THE VIOLENT LIFE OF TYRUS RAYMOND COBB

Date	*Place*	*Victim/Combatant*	*Notes*
ca. 1891	Royston, GA	Joe Cunningham	Allegedly bloodied the nose of a boy four years older than himself.
ca. 1898	Royston, GA	Fifth grade boy	Struck a classmate for failing to spell a word correctly in a boys versus girls spelling contest.
1905	Augusta, GA	George Rucker	Fought with teammate over the use of a shared bathtub.
1905	NA	Andy Roth	Rough and tumble fight with a teammate.
Oct. 6, 1906*	St. Louis, MO	Ed Siever	Floored his teammate with a punch.
Mar. 16, 1907*	Augusta, GA	Bungy Davis	Slapped a black groundskeeper and choked the groundskeeper's wife.
Mar. 18?, 1907*	Meridian, MS	Charles Schmidt	Fought Schmidt, a teammate who intervened in the dispute with a black groundskeeper. Sources disagree on whether Cobb was beaten.
June 1908*	Detroit, MI	Fred Collins	Knocked a black construction worker down with his fists.
Sept. 3, 1908*	Cleveland, OH	George Stansfield	Slapped a black elevator operator and fought with a black night watchman.
1908	Cleveland, OH		Kicked a black chambermaid in the stomach and knocked her down a flight of steps.
1909	Detroit, MI		Slapped a black waiter.
1911	Chicago, IL		In a dispute over a room assignment, punched the desk clerk of a hotel.
May 15, 1912*	New York, NY	Claude Lueker	Climbed into the stands and assaulted a physically handicapped heckler.
Aug. 11, 1912*	Detroit, MI		Fought and chased away three assailants, the only instance in which it appears that Cobb was not the main perpetrator of the violence. That Cobb's pistol failed to fire may have saved the life of one of the assailants.

Date	*Place*	*Victim/Combatant*	*Notes*
1912	Detroit, Mich.		Punched a policeman.
Mar. 1913	Spartanburg, SC	Rutledge Osborne	In an exhibition match, struck Osborne, a Wofford College student-coach, in the face with his fists.
June 20, 1914*	Detroit, Mich.	William Carpenter/ Harold Harding	Fought both black men over twenty cents worth of meat; beat one of them with his pistol.
Mar. 31, 1917*	Dallas, Tex.	Buck Herzog	Vicious "rough-and-tumble" fight in Cobb's hotel room.
Sept. 24, 1921*	Washington, D.C.	Billy Evans	A vicious fight with an umpire under the stands.
1922	San Francisco, Cal.	Steamboat Johnson	Struck the umpire in the face with his fists.
Sept. 27, 1923	Not known	Ray Francis	Fought with Francis in the dugout.
1924	Philadelphia, Penn.	Not known	Punched a black groundskeeper.
1927	Philadelphia, Penn.	Emmett Ormsby	Shoved and punched an umpire.
1929	Princeton, NJ	Ty Cobb Jr.	For failing grades at Princeton, beat his adult son with blacksnake whip.

*These instances are the best documented. Several of the others depend on Cobb's or someone else's memory. With the exception of the last item, Cobb's continuing assaults on others during his retirement years (1928–1961) are not included here.

Source: See Note 1.

What I propose here, however, is to relegate psychological speculation, which tends to be ahistorical and to impose alien moral values and present understandings on the past, to a subordinate role in explaining Cobb's violent behavior. While acknowledging that Cobb may have had severe mental problems, especially at particular moments in his life, this essay looks at his violent life first and foremost in terms of the history of the Southern uplands in which Cobb was born and reared. Frank Navin, the principal owner of the Detroit Tigers, understood this perspective when he sought to explain Cobb's confrontational disposition to a local newspaper in 1910. Navin reportedly said that Cobb "comes from a section of the country where pride is strong."[10] It was a region in which men frequently saw force as a legitimate and even a necessary response to any insult or slight that compromised one's reputation, the reputation of one's family, or the reputation of one's region. Not only did Cobb grow up in a regional culture that endorsed personal violence, but he was also caught up in the vortex of rapidly changing social circumstances

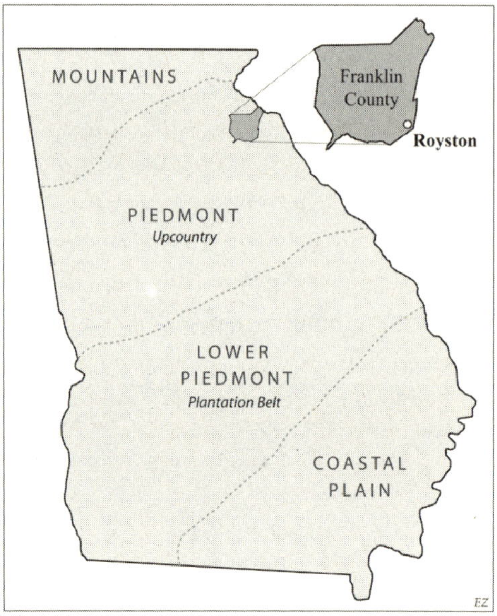

Map of Georgia regions. Ty Cobb grew up in the Piedmont, a region of rolling hills in North Georgia. During his childhood, this region underwent a radical economic and social transformation. Map courtesy Ezra Zeitler.

involving race, rank, and family. To Cobb, understanding and responding to incidents arising from these circumstances frequently entailed matters of honor. Once he perceived consciously or unconsciously that honor was at stake, he reacted the only way he thought appropriate—violently. As Cobb himself explained to U.S. Congressman Robert H. Clancy in 1927: "The *honorable* . . . Cobb blood . . . never will be subjected. It bows to no wrong nor to any man. . . . The Cobbs have their ideals and God help anyone who strives to bend a Cobb away from such."[11]

Cobb came of age in Georgia's Upper Piedmont, a region of rolling hills and expansive valleys located between the mountains to the north and the flatter lands leading out to the seacoast to the south. No other cultural region in the United States equaled the southern upcountry, or backcountry as it is sometimes called, in its proclivity for violence and personal vengeance.[12]

Comprised mostly of peoples whose ancestors had migrated from northern England, Scotland, and Northern Ireland (the Scots-Irish), the first upcountry settlers brought with them a warrior tradition acquired through England and Scotland's centuries-long border wars. Their warrior ethos was then reinforced by the harsh circumstances of the American frontier, where they fought almost continuously—with Native Americans, with the French and Indians in the intercolonial wars, with the British in the American Revolution and the War of 1812, and with the South and sometimes the North in the American Civil War. The settlers fought one another as well. With public authority held in low esteem and weak in fact, they routinely spilled blood to settle private quarrels.

At the center of the backcountry's violent society was the concept of honor.[13] As in other more traditional societies where human relationships are mostly face to face, no aspect of honor was more important than a person's good name. Personal reputation could not be taken for granted; it was a form of property that rested first of all on one's inner conviction of self-worth, but such self-appraisals meant nothing unless validated by others. As Bertram Wyatt-Brown, who has pioneered in the study of honor in the antebellum South, has observed: "One's neighbors serve as mirrors that return the image of one's self."[14] For someone to have honor, others must acknowledge its possession. Since honor had to be continuously ratified by public opinion, its possession was always tenuous and in jeopardy. It compelled one, at least the men, to assert and prove repeatedly their worth in public settings. It demanded that men be more self-assertive, aggressive, and competitive than they otherwise might have been.

At the same time that the nineteenth-century North was seeking to, and to a degree succeeding in, criminalizing all violence, traditional forms of private violence remained the ultimate resolution of matters involving honor throughout much of the American South. In the lowlands of the antebellum plantation South, otherwise irresolvable affairs of honor among the elite were likely to be settled by a highly formalized duel. While the planters valued cool restraint, those white men dwelling in the upcountry, as well as those from the lower social ranks throughout the South, inverted the upper rank's insistence on a dispassionate, antiseptic duel to resolve issues of honor. They engaged in no-holds barred, rough-and-tumble forms of personal combat, including fistfights, wrestling, kicking, knives, choking, and sometimes gouging (pulling the eye out of its socket with a finger).

A confluence of new economic and social circumstances in the post-Civil War era Southern uplands made regional, racial, rank, and family honor even more tenuous and problematic than it had been before the war. Unlike Georgia's downstate Cotton Belt, the Upper Piedmont had no "Aristocracy," explained Archibald T. Burke, a young slave-owning lawyer before the Civil War.[15] Neither did upstate Georgia have many slaves. It was comprised almost entirely of small, self-sufficient white farmers. But after the war, newly built railroads transformed the region; cotton production boomed. The railroad first entered Cobb's home town of Royston in 1878, the next year the town incorporated, and by the 1890s Royston had three busy cotton gins and a population of nearly six hundred. Cotton brought with it growing inequalities in wealth and more African Americans. The ordinary white residents in the Upper Piedmont now found themselves caught up in a contradiction. While on the one hand they were taught to think themselves the equal of any person, in short, as possessing the same honor as the rich white planter, on the other, they increasingly found themselves threatened from below by the presence of newly freed African Americans and from above by those with new wealth.

In the flux of the rapid transformation of the Upper Piedmont, racial identity took on an added importance. In the antebellum era, throughout the slaveholding areas of the South and beyond, slavery and the ownership of slaves had provided a clear-cut basis for social distinctions. The enslavement of African Americans had offered all whites a sense of superiority, but the ending of slavery with the war left this most obvious social marker in disarray. To stabilize or establish order in such a world, many whites sought to construct new boundaries grounded in racial identities. These whites insisted on a more absolute racial separation, one that strengthened their claims to superior status and honor. Such demands encouraged in the 1880s and afterward the passage of more rigid segregation laws and a soaring increase in the incidence of racial lynching. During Cobb's lifetime, his home county of Franklin itself witnessed at least four and possibly seven lynchings; four of these seven were in Royston, the town in which Cobb spent most of his youth. Yet racial segregation was never impermeable; it was ultimately contingent, fragile, and uncertain, especially in its "muddled middle" where the races—by necessity as much as choice—mixed.[16]

As a youngster, Cobb himself had to contend with this muddled middle. In his autobiography (published in 1961), he vigorously denied that he had ever held any prejudice against African Americans. Indeed, he countered such insinuations by declaring that he had had "a Negro 'mammy' as a child . . . and had lived most peacefully with colored folk for years."[17] Yet, perhaps unwittingly to Cobb, the much-ballyhooed and lovable black mammy figure of southern lore had emerged in Cobb's own lifetime as one of the region's most cherished signifiers of racial difference. The black mammy may have contributed, as Grace Elizabeth Hale has argued, to countless white children learning at firsthand the importance of race in the construction and maintenance of the South's new social order.[18] As a thirteen-year-old, Cobb also encountered the muddled middle of racial mixing when his father demanded that he assist African Americans in plowing the fields of his father's farm. His father "had Negroes to work [the farm]. . . . ," explained Cobb, "and also a son whom he saw needed some comeuppance." To keep a "certain young lady [who] had attracted [his] attention" from seeing him "in overalls doing manual labor" with black men, Cobb remembered, "I picked the lowest spot on the field I could find. I'd hide out until she had passed."[19]

As a participant in the wider process of making whiteness a source of personal identity, Cobb was particularly sensitive to situations in which African Americans might behave as though they were his equal. Cobb may have believed that blacks understood only the language of violence; a legal expert, Thomas R. R. Cobb, with whom Ty claimed to be a relative, had written in the antebellum era that a slave "can be reached only through his body."[20] When Cobb moved north to play baseball, he may have encountered African Americans who were more assertive of their equality than those with whom he was familiar in the South. In any case, Cobb interpreted any behavior by a black that was less than absolutely subservient as threat to his honor (which can also be read as synonymous with his "identity") as a white man.

The examples are many. In June 1908, Cobb inadvertently stepped on some newly laid asphalt on a Detroit street. Fred Collins, a black construction worker, yelled at him "what the——are you doing there?" Years later Cobb recalled: "I was insulted."[21] He grabbed Collins and hurled him to the ground. Charges were filed against Cobb for assault and battery. Through his attorney, Cobb later agreed to a seventy-five dollar settlement bestowed upon Collins. "When a man is insulted," Cobb told a Detroit newspaper, "it is worth $75 to get satisfaction." The newspaper went ahead to report that "Cobb was determined to fight it out, regardless of the cost."[22] The next year in Cleveland he assaulted a black elevator operator, George Stansfield, whom he described as being "insolent." In another instance, reported by a black newspaper, the *Chicago Defender* but not in the white press, he allegedly kicked a black maid in the stomach and knocked her down the stairs after she objected to being called "nigger."[23] Also on at least two occasions he apparently struck African American waiters.

Apart from Cobb's lifelong use of racist language and his numerous run-ins with African Americans (see table 1), nothing was more revealing of his contribution to the rising importance of racial identity in the United States than his relationship with the Tiger team mascot, a black man named Alexander George Washington Rivers. It was Cobb who discovered Rivers in New Orleans and brought him to Detroit. For eighteen seasons, Rivers served as the team mascot as well as Cobb's personal "bat man" and assistant. Among the superstitious ballplayers, including Cobb himself, Rivers's chief duty was to "massage good luck into Tiger bats."[24] In his relationships with Cobb and his teammates, Rivers served not only as an unambiguous inferior but also as a caricature of African Americans. He could be likened to a family's pet animal. As with the spectacle of lynching and the black minstrel shows of the day, Rivers's role as the team mascot made him a public performer who conspicuously fore-grounded race as a fundamental division in American society.

Along with the explosive mixture of uncertainties flowing from race and rank in Georgia's Upper Piedmont of the late nineteenth century, the legacy of the Civil War helps to explain Ty Cobb's proclivity for violence. To Cobb, as with countless other white Southerners, the war was what historian W. Fitzhugh Brundage has called "the crucible of southern identity."[25] More than anything else, it was a historical experience that defined for white Southerners the South's regional distinctiveness, and the war more than anything else deepened the region's self-consciousness. While defeated, white Southerners interpreted the bravery of the Confederate soldiers as a successful defense of the region's honor. Still, defeat was a bitter blow; it was an embarrassment that intensified objections to any behavior suggesting or hinting that Southern men had in any way acted in less than an honorable manner during the war or afterward.

The war loomed large in the life of Ty Cobb. As a youngster, he surely heard stories of how the flank of Gen. William T. Sherman's Union army had smashed its way across Cobb's home county of Franklin in 1865. An old-timer in the 1930s recalled: "The Yankees came through Franklin and Hart counties, and just tore up everything as they came along. They took all the cows, horses, and mules. They killed the hogs in the pens, and carried them off for their own food. They went through the houses and took whatever they wanted."[26] Cobb had a special admiration for his male ancestors who had resisted the likes of Sherman. Cobb's maternal grandfather, Caleb Chitwood, had served as a captain in the Confederate army, but Cobb esteemed more his paternal grandfather, John Cobb. While opposed to slavery, John Cobb, according to family lore (a lore that may have been for the most part false) fought with the Confederacy and achieved some renown from having suffered a wound in battle.[27] While a youngster, Ty spent nearly every summer at his grandfather's home across the Georgia border in the Blue Ridge Mountains near Murphy, North Carolina. According to Cobb's memory, his grandfather regularly regaled him with stories of hunting, fighting, and heroism. In a ritualistic gesture that may have signified the passing on of a backcountry warrior tradition from grandfather to grandson, John Cobb gave Ty his first pocket knife, a pearl-handled knife that Ty so treasured that he still retained it among his possessions to his dying day.

Alexander George Washington Rivers. Discovered and patronized by Ty Cobb, Rivers was a personal bat boy and longtime mascot of the Detroit Tigers. Courtesy *Detroit News.*

In addition to region and race, rank was equally—or in the end perhaps even more—important in understanding Cobb's truculence. Membership in the upper class, if class is understood merely in terms of wealth or income, was not sufficient for an ambitious young man born in the South of the late nineteenth century. To have standing in that society, one must have rank, and rank ultimately depended on family lineage. Cobb claimed a distinguished ancestry. "The Cobbs were people of position and property in the South," he wrote in his autobiography. "We had status."[28] He even went so far as to try to link his family with the far better known and more illustrious Cobbs of downstate Georgia, a relationship which was at best distant and tenuous.

In truth, the Cobbs of Franklin County were of far more modest origins than the downstate Cobbs. It was not his grandfather but his father, William Herschell Cobb, who was mainly responsible for the superior standing of Ty's family. As a young man, "W. H." moved out of the mountains across the state line of North Carolina into Georgia's Upper Piedmont where he struggled to make ends meet while teaching in one-room schools. Eventually he earned a college degree from North Georgia Military College in Dahlonga, but perhaps above all it was marriage to twelve-year-old Amanda Chitwood, Caleb Chitwood's daughter, in Narrows, Georgia, that helped him to get started on a path of upward social mobility. By local standards, "Captain" Chitwood was a successful planter; he owned several hundred acres of cotton land which were worked by tenant farmers. Soon after his marriage, W. H., or "Professor Cobb" as he was now known locally, began to stake out a successful career for himself. He was elected commissioner of schools for Franklin County, served as the third superintendent of the Royston Baptist Church Sunday School, owned and edited a local newspaper, and owned or leased one hundred acres of cotton bottomland. By the time Ty reached adolescence in Royston, W. H. was one of the town's most prominent residents.

Professor Cobb was known to be unusually bookish. He had a particular love of ancient history, which led him in 1886 to name his first-born son, Tyrus, after the city of Tyre in Asia Minor. As intended by W. H., the first name had a special meaning. In the fourth century B.C., the people of Tyre, in a fashion similar to the resistance of the American South during the Civil War, had bravely defended their city-state's honor and freedom by offering seven months of heroic opposition to the invading forces of Alexander the Great. It is likely that Professor Cobb also related to his son epic tales of Homeric heroism. While interested in the life of the mind, W. H. was no effeminate intellectual. He nurtured in young Ty a strong will. According to Cobb's memory, W. H. proffered explicit advice about how to respond to those who might impugn one's good name. He warned young Ty "to give as much as [one] took [from the offender]—and something more," and he frequently quoted a passage from Hamlet: "Beware of entrance into a quarrel; but being in, bear't that the oppos'd may beware of thee."[29]

Ty was expected not only to honor his father but also at all costs to avoid diminishing the family's reputation. This was not an easy requirement to meet. W. H. distanced himself physically and emotionally from his son. He withheld "acceptance of me as the man I yearned to be," recalled Cobb many years later in his autobiography. "He was critical, very strict, and I couldn't reach him."[30] Ty called W. H. "Father," not the more familiar "Pa," "Papa," "Dad," or "Daddy." The absence of parental affection and emotional support from his father may have accounted for what his mother described as young Ty's "fits of attitude." As an adolescent, Ty had what he himself later called "a vying nature." In a letter to his sixteen-year-old son in 1902, W. H. warned him: "Conquer your anger and wild passions that would degrade your dignity and belittle your manhood. . . . Starve out and drive out the demon that lurks in all human blood and [which is] ready and anxious and restless to arise and reign."[31] If Ty was indeed subject to spells of anger and wild passion, then even as a youngster he was already exhibiting behaviors that would characterize his entire life.

During Ty's boyhood, the family's social position was at stake in the single-most important conflict between father and son, that concerning a proper career for young Ty. Professor Cobb wanted Ty to substantiate and add to the family's luster by pursuing a military career; he "scheduled" Ty for West Point or Annapolis, "but . . . the military life seemed like total bondage" to the youngster.[32] Professor Cobb suggested other careers—in law, medicine, or as a planter, any of which might have helped to retain or enhance the family's social standing. None of these proposed careers appealed to his son.

Nothing absorbed Ty's passion as much as playing baseball. While it was not unusual for the sons of southern patriarchs to risk a family's good name by taking up a "dissolute" life of sport, gambling, and drinking, Professor Cobb was horrified. Reflecting an ages-old bias against mere shopkeepers and workers found in traditional societies,[33] W. H. did everything he could to dissuade his son from becoming a professional ballplayer. "Never [before] in my life had I had an argument with my father," Cobb remembered in 1926. "Boys in my section of the country accepted family discipline as a matter of course. We were supposed to respect our father's wishes without whining or quibbling."[34] Finally, after a long discussion and amidst an abundance of tears, W. H acquiesced. He let Ty as a mere seventeen-year-old try his hand at becoming a professional ballplayer. Yet, in words that could hardly have relieved the youngster's anxiety, he warned Ty: "Don't come home a failure."[35] With such an admonition, it was perhaps little wonder that Cobb later wrote: "My overwhelming need was to prove myself as a man."[36]

Yet nothing, not even Ty's failure to adopt a suitable career path, threatened the Cobb family's honor as much as the circumstances of his father's death. It entailed nothing less than the possibility that W. H. was a cuckold, which, if true or even reputed to be true, was the ultimate source of shame for a man in an honor culture. In order to verify his young (she was nearly twenty years younger than her husband) and beautiful wife's indiscretions, it may have been that W. H. prepared an elaborate ruse. In any case, according to his wife, Amanda, on the evening of August 9, 1905, W. H. unexpectedly announced that he had to leave town for a few days on business. Just after midnight, Mrs. Cobb awakened to see the outline of a figure attempting to enter her bedroom window from the porch roof. According to her own testimony, Amanda Cobb then seized a nearby shotgun and fired two shots, killing her husband almost instantly. W. H. had a six-shot revolver stuck in his side pocket. To avenge the shame to his family, W. H. may have been prepared to kill both his wife and her lover. In any event, the next day a coroner's jury ordered Amanda's arrest on the count of voluntary manslaughter. She posted a stiff seven thousand dollar bail; and, with the assistance of Ty, who had returned to Royston from Augusta, where he was playing ball, hired a battery of prominent attorneys to defend her. Almost a year later, a jury found Amanda not guilty.

There is no evidence to suggest that Ty ever doubted his mother's innocence. "This isn't the kind of people Cobbs are," he reputedly said at the time. While he was not close to his mother—he mentions her only three times in his autobiography—he did come to her defense in the trial and surface relations between mother and son remained amicable throughout her life. Indeed, for a time his mother and younger sister even lived with Ty in a house that he had purchased in Detroit. In defense of Amanda, Cobb biographers have also noted that she never remarried. Upon her death at sixty five, Ty had his mother buried in Royston next to his father.

Yet there is reason to speculate that from Ty's perspective the jury's decision failed to vindicate fully the Cobb family's good name. For years afterward rumors persisted in Royston and beyond that Amanda had had a paramour. This gossipy, private, word-of-mouth assault on the family's reputation apparently gnawed at Ty throughout his life. Stump reported that

The Royston Reds. Ty Cobb is seated at the far left side of this photo taken in about 1901. Even in his early teens, Cobb played with a fierce determination. Courtesy Special Collections and Archives, Georgia State University Library.

Cobb as an old man said, "I didn't get over that. I've never gotten over it." By taking up a career against the wishes of his father and being away when his father's death occurred, Cobb himself may have in some sense felt responsible for the tragedy. In any case, a determination to acquit his family's honor apparently refueled his fierce determination to succeed on the field of play. According to Stump, Cobb told him: "I did it for my father, who was an exalted man. . . . I had to fight all my life to survive. They were all against me. . . . but I beat the bastards and left them in the ditch."[37] Nonetheless, in terms of explaining Cobb's propensity for violence we must be careful about attributing too much significance to the death of his father. Well before the family tragedy, young Ty had already exhibited an unusual competitiveness, a hair-trigger temper, and a tendency to respond violently to any slight that he saw as a challenge to his honor.

Upon joining the Detroit Tigers in 1905 at the tender age of eighteen, "matters involving honor"[38]—Cobb's own words—shortly got him into trouble with his own teammates. His fellow players had little in common with the young Georgian. They were Northerners; only one was from as far south as Missouri. "He [Cobb] came up from the South, you know, and he was still fighting the Civil War," recalled a teammate. "As far as he [Cobb] was concerned, we were all damned Yankees before he even met us."[39] It surely did not help the rookie's disposition when the brass band in Detroit's Bennett Park sometimes struck up "Marching Through Georgia" as Cobb came up to bat.[40]

The clash of cultures extended beyond war and region to ethnicity and religion. While Cobb was of English and possibly Scots-Irish origins and had been reared a Baptist, more than half of his teammates were Irish Catholics. In his personal habits, Cobb was initially far more abstemious than his fellow players; he did not smoke, chew, drink, curse, or patronize brothels, though these behaviors would shortly change. In addition, the rookie had an off-putting, cocky attitude; unlike any other player of the day, he came to the batting circle swinging three bats, when fielding the ball from his centerfield position he frequently dashed in front of his teammates, and he ran the base paths with a reckless abandon. Not only did all of these behaviors irritate his teammates, but Cobb also threatened to beat a popular veteran player, Matty McIntyre, out of his starting position.

Even more central to his conflict with teammates was Ty's refusal to participate in a traditional ritual, the hazing of rookie ballplayers. As with many other all-male social groups, the veteran ballplayers required as a condition

Detroit Tigers outfielders. The Tiger outfielders appear to be less than happy about posing together for this photograph taken in about 1909. From left to right are Bobby Veach, Cobb, and Sam Crawford. Courtesy Bettmann/CORBIS.

for full membership into their fraternity the symbolic degradation of the newcomer's self-esteem. "Every rookie gets a little hazing," Samuel "Wahoo Sam" Crawford, a teammate from Nebraska recalled, "but most of them just take it and laugh."[41] Not Cobb. While he was surely aware of this ages-old practice, Cobb responded to the hazing in the only way he knew how. "I had never understood rough kidding, had never heard some of the language used on the big league bench," Cobb recalled in 1926. "It was unbelievable to me that men could take some of the epithets and *be manly.*"[42] When "Shoeless Joe" Jackson, another backcountry Southerner (from South Carolina), but one with a far more tranquil disposition than Cobb's, joined the Philadelphia Athletics in 1907, he had an experience similar to Cobb's. Unable to withstand the rookie hazing, Jackson quit the team several times before an exasperated Connie Mack, the owner-manager of the Athletics, finally sold him to Cleveland.

The conclusions of historian Kenneth Greenberg about joking in the antebellum South are pertinent to both Jackson and Cobb. Practical jokes, Greenberg argues, had different meanings for Southerners than Northerners. Southern men frequently took offense to practical jokes; they were more likely to see them as a source of personal humiliation than as a source of shared laughter or as a stimulus for a retaliatory joke or for verbal repartee. The practical joke might in effect "unmask" a man's honor and hence subject him to shame. In such a culture, Greenberg adds, appearances, not inner reality, counted for everything.[43]

Verbal jousting, crude imitations of his backcountry southern speech, nicknames such as "The Reb" and "Cracker," teasing about losing the Civil War, breaking his bats, crushing the crown of his hat, ripping his clothes apart, shouldering him out of the box during batting practice, locking him out of the bathroom that the team shared—to these and other forms of hazing, Cobb responded angrily. Of course, his reaction only intensified the hazing. "Cobb came up with an antagonistic attitude," Crawford remembered, "which in his mind turned a little razzing into a life-and-death struggle. He always figured everybody was ganging up on him."[44] For Cobb, the razzing indeed cut to the quick; they assaulted his very identity as a white Southerner of superior social rank.

Finally, Cobb could take it no longer. He exploded. During a spring training game in 1906, he directly confronted his persecutors. He called them "cowards," which next to "liar," was the most insulting word that a man from an honor culture could employ against another man. He challenged his teammates to fight. Shocked at Cobb's tirade, they backed off; some of them laughed nervously. Cobb interpreted their refusal to exchange blows as a sign of weakness. Yet, fearful that his fellow players might retaliate for remarks that he saw as insulting, Cobb purchased a pistol, which he carried or kept close at hand for the remainder of his life. He had as little to do with his teammates as possible. On road trips he sat alone, ate alone, and roomed alone. The stress and social isolation may have been too much for him. In July, Cobb disappeared from the lineup. Club officials, who were trying to trade him to another team, reported that he was being treated for a stomach disorder, but Stump concludes that in fact Cobb had suffered from a "nervous breakdown." In September, he rejoined the team. "I never quit on anything in my life, even when it looked like a smart play," he remembered many years later. "Matter of honor. I rested up . . . and pulled out of it."[45]

On the next-to-the-last day of the season, October 6, 1906, Cobb failed to catch a fly ball in a game in St. Louis. Upon returning to the team bench at the end of the inning, Ed Siever, the Detroit pitcher, victimized by what he thought was Cobb's poor play, said something to Cobb; perhaps he cursed him. Cobb challenged him to a fight on the spot. According to Cobb's recollection, he yelled at Siever: "Get up! Get on your feet!" He explained later that "where I came from, men had been killed for saying what Siever did."[46] But Siever remained seated, insisting that he had to finish pitching the game. That evening, in the Planter Hotel lobby, Siever apparently yelled a curse or an epithet at Cobb. Cobb did not hesitate; he retaliated by flooring Siever with a punch and then, while Siever was sprawled on the floor, kicking him in the head. Finally, Tiger teammates pulled Cobb off of Siever.

The war between Cobb and his teammates continued into the next season. Less than a week into spring training in 1907, Cobb slapped a black groundskeeper, who had apparently attempted to shake his hand. According to Cobb, the groundskeeper had been drinking; regardless, handshaking signified equality between the two men. By threatening to cross the racial boundary, the groundskeeper's behavior challenged a core ingredient in Cobb's very identity as a white man. When the groundskeeper's wife tried to intervene on behalf of her husband, Cobb reportedly either choked her or slammed her to the ground. "GEORGIA PEACH DEFENDS THE HONOR OF THE SOUTHLAND," read a headline in the *Augusta Herald*.[47] Implicit in the headline was the idea that Cobb had not only defended regional honor but also, at a critical time in Southern history, defended race as a fundamental way of distinguishing between the nation's peoples.

However, Charlie "Boss" Schmidt, Detroit's huge catcher, who was also from the South (Arkansas) and had joined the team the previous season, saw

Cobb's behavior differently. He pulled Cobb away from the hapless woman and allegedly said to him: "Whoever does a thing like that is a coward." If Schmidt did call Cobb a coward, it stung the young man deeply. Accounts vary on what happened next, but Schmidt may have given Cobb a severe beating. In any case, according to biographer John McCallum, who interviewed several of Cobb's teammates about the event, "Ty would not quit, even when Schmidt begged him to give up" the fight.[48]

Later that spring, an Atlanta newspaper reported that Cobb could whip Schmidt or anybody else on the Detroit team. Cobb denied responsibility for the piece, but Schmidt may have seen his own honor at stake. Upon learning about Cobb's alleged remarks, he called for a fight. In a ritual similar to that of the Southern elites when fighting a duel, the two men agreed to observe the Marquis of Queensberry rules for boxing. In front of his teammates, Cobb took the most brutal beating in his life. He suffered a broken nose and two black eyes. In the meantime, the Detroit ownership continued without success to try to deal Cobb to another team.

The thorough thrashing at the hands of Schmidt was something of a turning point in the young ballplayer's relationship with his teammates. Never again would he be subjected to the same degree of relentless hazing by his fellow players. Exactly why is uncertain. In part, it was probably due to the departure from the team of his main nemesis, Matty McIntyre, in 1910. Furthermore, Cobb's magnificent performance on the field plus his unquestionable bravery in fighting the biggest and strongest man on the team surely won him some respect. Equally plausible is the possibility that, even in defeat, Cobb had effectively intimidated his teammates. They may have concluded that the most sensible course of action when dealing with Cobb was simply to keep one's distance from the hot-tempered young man.

What is equally clear and perhaps more pertinent in understanding Cobb's new relationship with fellow ballplayers was his gradual—though never complete—acceptance and internalization of the prevailing values and behaviors of the early twentieth-century players' culture. Eventually he even came to some understanding of the rite of hazing rookie ballplayers. "I didn't understand [at the time] that these things were not meant as insults, [that they] were joking terms," he explained in his 1926 autobiography.[49] While continuing throughout his long career an extraordinarily prickly relationship with nearly all of the people—players,[50] umpires, and owners alike—involved in the baseball world, he shortly took up such typical player behaviors as smoking, drinking, and cursing. Cobb himself became a notorious participant in the common player practice of hurling verbal insults at opposing players; he particularly abused Babe Ruth, who challenged him as the most outstanding player in the game.

Nothing was more indicative of Cobb's partial assimilation into the wider baseball culture than Detroit's decision to employ him as team manager in 1921. Only a decade earlier the same management, led by Tiger owner Frank Navin, saw Cobb as such a disruptive force that they had attempted to trade or sell him to another club. Despite his growing unpopularity among his players and the Tigers record of winning barely half of their games, Cobb held onto his managerial post for five seasons. Upon Cobb's dismissal as manager, Connie Mack, who had years earlier described Cobb as the dirtiest player in the game, signed him to a contract with the Philadelphia Athletics. He played his final two seasons—those of 1927 and 1928—with Mack's Athletics. Cobb had planned to retire at the end of the 1926 season, but when accusations surfaced that he, along with Tris Speaker, had wagered on a game in 1919, he reasoned that his honor could only be restored by continuing to play. Playing for two additional seasons, as he later wrote to Mack, was "my vindication to the public."[51]

There is also reason to believe that baseball became for Cobb a separate universe, a world apart from that of his upstate Georgia heritage. In baseball he constructed a new reality, one governed not only by its formal rules but also by its many informal conventions and customs. In time, he felt more "at home" in this world. After all, understandings of what constituted success, rank, race, and manliness in baseball were far less ambiguous than they were in the Georgia Piedmont of his day. Batting averages, stolen bases, runs scored—these statistics and others offered manifest evidence of one's standing, or to put it in one of Cobb's favorite words, "honor." Furthermore, his world of baseball included neither African Americans nor women on the field. In part, the early-twentieth-century world of baseball was of Cobb's own making. Until the arrival of Babe Ruth, he was the game's premier player and a central figure in establishing the ascendancy of the one-base-at-a-time tactics of the day. Hence, we can understand the degree of shock that Cobb experienced when Ruth entered the game. By elevating esteem for the home run, Ruth was constructing a new baseball universe, one in which respect for Cobb's baseball world suffered a sharp decline.

Within his world of baseball—in situations far too numerous to recount here—Cobb ferociously defended his honor. An illustrative case is his much-publicized rough-and-tumble fight with Charles "Buck" Herzog of the New York Giants and his subsequent confrontation with the renowned John J. McGraw, the manager of the Giants. On March 31, 1917, the Giants and Tigers met for a spring training game in Dallas, Texas. In the morning prior to the game, Cobb played eighteen holes of golf. When he appeared on the field that afternoon only a few minutes before an exhibition match was to start, Herzog and several other Giant players began to heckle him; they called him a "swell head," "showoff," and apparently other words not considered fit to print by the newspapers of the day. This form of name calling cut Cobb deeply, perhaps in part because his tardy appearance at the ballpark suggested that he thought that he should receive special treatment. In fact, Cobb was something of a prima donna; for example, several times during his career he capitalized upon his star status to show up late for spring training. The taunts by the Giants implied that Cobb was in reality something other than what he represented himself as being. In other words, in an honor culture, the Giants were in effect calling Cobb a liar.

Cobb retaliated physically. When Cobb singled in the first inning, he yelled to Herzog from first base that he was coming down. On the first pitch, Cobb tore off for second base. The throw from the catcher was well ahead of Cobb, but Cobb slid in high. One of his spikes ripped Herzog's pants and cut the Giant infielder slightly. The two men scuffled, rolling in the dirt, before being pulled apart by teammates. The umpire threw Cobb out of the game, but permitted Herzog to continue playing.

That evening at the Oriental Hotel in Dallas, where both teams were staying, Herzog and Cobb arranged for a fight in Cobb's room. What is particularly noteworthy about this fight in terms of honor is its similarities to the rituals associated with "gentlemen's" duels. Not only was the time and place set beforehand, but Herzog and Cobb also brought along seconds, assigned a referee, and agreed on the method of fighting—not pistols or boxing but a rough-and-tumble fight. Unlike the duels of the Southern elites, it was a no-holds-barred fight (but without weapons) preferred by lower-class and backcountry Southerners. Trying to get a glimpse of the brawling players, members of both teams crowded around the hotel room doorway. With Cobb apparently pummeling Herzog at will, the referee finally stopped the fight.

The matter did not end there. The next morning, McGraw, the rotund, five-feet- seven-inch, forty-four-year-old manager of the Giants, confronted Cobb, whose six-feet-one-inch-tall frame was in excellent physical shape. No one knows for sure precisely what words were exchanged, but Cobb allegedly told McGraw that if the Giants manager were a younger man he would kill him. Then, according to Cobb's recollection many years later, he pulled McGraw's nose. In the antebellum Southern culture of honor, nose-pulling or tweaking was an act of momentous meaning. It was a manifest insult. According to historian Kenneth Greenberg, "It was the ultimate contempt toward the most public part of a man's face, an extreme expression of disdain for a man's projected mask."[52] McGraw may have been aware of the deeper meaning of nose-pulling in honor cultures; at least according to John McCallum, "John J., to his dying day, never forgave Cobb for that."[53] Cobb surely understood the act as a serious insult. Whereas physically assaulting the older and smaller man would not have vindicated Cobb's good name, pulling the diminutive Giants manager's nose was another matter. In defense of one's honor, it could be seen as a symbolic gesture of retaliation equal to a physical assault in its effectiveness.

Apparently, however, the Giants had the last word in hurling insults. After the Herzog fight and McGraw's nose-pulling, Cobb refused to play the Giants again in exhibition matches. When the Giants and Tigers finally split up in Kansas City and went their separate ways, the McGraw men sent Cobb a telegram: "It's now safe to rejoin your team." It seems safe to say, as McCallum later wrote, that this was "the only safe manner in which to have the last word with Cobb."[54]

Not as insanity but as defense of his honor and the honor of the baseball world itself—this was the way that nearly all contemporaries interpreted the Georgia Peach's assault on Claude Lueker in the incident described at the outset of this essay. "I believe every fair-minded person who has a spark of manhood in him will admit the right of a ballplayer or any other individual," Cobb told the Detroit *Free Press,* "to avenge his personal *honor* when he is not given the protection that should be accorded him by persons in authority."[55] Even in New York City itself many of the fans believed that Cobb had responded appropriately when he climbed into the stands and struck Lueker for name calling. *The New York American* took a poll: "Was Cobb within his rights, or should fans be free to express themselves?" The fans voted 3,013 for Cobb, and 1,167 against him,[56] suggesting that even Northern fans may have justified Cobb's response not only in terms of the star's personal honor but also as a defense of the universe of baseball's own honor. In protest of Cobb's suspension from play by Ban Johnson, Cobb's fellow Tigers, even though they thoroughly disliked their teammate personally, called for the first team strike in baseball history.

Fellow Georgians, of course, saw Cobb's response as matter of defending both manly and regional honor. Georgia's entire congressional delegation—two senators and ten representatives—wired Cobb: "As Georgians we commend your action in resisting the uncalled-for insult in New York."[57]

Atlanta's mayor, Courtland S. Winn, praised Cobb for defending "the principles that have always been taught to Southern manhood," and the city's police commissioner added that, if Cobb had not "licked that man as he should, he would have lost the respect of every decent man in the country."[58] In recalling the incident many years later, Cobb summed up his defense: "Now no man could have stood the abuse heaped on me that day."[59]

Cobb employed his understanding of honor in rearing his own children. In 1912, according to an article in *Baseball Magazine* by F. C. Lane, Cobb instructed his five-year-old son, Ty Jr., that, when one's honor had been slighted, one must defend oneself with physical force. "This boy insulted you and if you don't go out and lick him, then I will lick you," Lane reported Cobb as saying. Lane added that "Little Ty lived up to the reputation of his dad in a strenuous manner and since then there has been no doubt whatever of his wish to insist on his rights."[60] According to what Cobb told Stump many years later, he did in fact lick his first-born son—not when he was a five-year-old but when he was a twenty-two-year-old man! Upon learning that Ty Jr. had flunked out of Princeton, in 1929 Ty Sr. immediately packed and boarded a train to New Jersey. Upon arriving at Ty Jr.'s room, he pulled out and unfurled a long blacksnake whip from his suitcase. "I went to work on the boy pretty hard," he told Stump. "I put him on the floor and kept it up . . . tears and some blood were shed, but Tyrus never again . . . never . . . failed in his grades."[61] Whether Cobb did in fact brutally beat his adult son cannot be known, but we can surmise that, if not, when he later recalled the failure of his son to obtain passing grades, he wished that he had done so.

After all, Ty Jr.'s behavior put at risk not only the Cobb family's honor, but also perhaps more importantly all that Ty Sr. had worked for and achieved. It threatened the Cobb family's hard-earned social position, the quest for which had intensified Ty Sr.'s concerns with matters that he understood in terms of honor. From his baseball salary, endorsement earnings, and early investments in General Motors and Coca-Cola, he was well on his way to becoming a multimillionaire. He had married well; biographer Charles Alexander speculates that for Cobb to win the hand of Charlie Marion Lombard of Augusta, Georgia, he "probably had to work at breaking down the common prejudice among genteel folk against ballplayers and theater people."[62] He hobnobbed with the rich and the famous, including presidents of the United States. In the spacious house that he purchased on Williams Street in the upscale section of Augusta in 1913, he entertained—among others—such

Ty Cobb's family in Hawaii. None of the family members except Ty seem to be happy about their arrival in Honolulu. Courtesy National Baseball Hall of Fame Library, Cooperstown, NY.

notables as Georgia Governor Joseph Mackey Brown, Congressman Carl Vinson, golf's Bobby Jones, college football coach Knute Rockne, composer John Philip Sousa, sportswriter Grantland Rice, and Coca-Cola president Robert Woodruff.

Cobb further buttressed his and his family's claim to gentility by cultivating the traits of the downstate Georgia planters rather than those of his upstate heritage. True, Cobb once described himself as a "snarling wildcat."[63] (Backcountry brawlers typically referred to themselves in terms of ferocious animals.) But at the same time he exuded, as sportswriter Bob Broeg once put it, "a southern gentleman's charm and generous side."[64] Broeg's testimony does not stand alone. Many others found him affable, civil, and charming. As with the plantation gentry, Cobb was well known for his exceptional hospitality. He was a gracious host to visitors in both his Detroit and Augusta residences. In his final years, he became something of a philanthropist as well. He sent checks to several impoverished former ballplayers, in 1950 he contributed one hundred thousand dollars for the building of Cobb Memorial Hospital in Royston, and in 1953 he created the Cobb Educational Foundation for needy college students in Georgia.

Cobb embraced another important characteristic of many of those at the apex of a rank-ordered society, namely an unquenchable enthusiasm for hunting. "Cobb is a genuine crank on out-door life and is an expert cook as well as hunter," reported *Sporting Life* as early as 1906.[65] The assumption of additional family responsibilities by way of marriage and children by no means chilled Cobb's ardor for hunting (though it did contribute to his stormy marriage and eventual divorce from Charlie Lombard). In both fall and winter of baseball's off season, he spent days and even weeks on extended hunting trips with male companions. He frequently hunted in a special preserve located about seventy miles from Augusta where there was a small lodge with sleeping quarters for three men.

That Cobb savored hunting should occasion no surprise. The core values involved in southern hunting complemented the region's notions of gender and rank. While the Southern lower classes—both blacks and whites—hunted for food and pelts, it was only men of means who had the leisure time to engage in long, expensive hunting trips and to hunt for sheer pleasure. Perhaps killing animals also confirmed for Cobb and other Southern men their mastery of the animal kingdom and of death, and at least symbolically hunters could imagine having bested a worthy opponent—the hunted animal—in a life and death struggle (for the lesser animal). Hunting was a manly enterprise; women never or rarely hunted. Proficiency in riding, hunting, and shooting, it had been long claimed by southern writers, distinguished the manly men of the South from their more effeminate male counterparts of the North.

Above all, success on the killing field helped to affirm one's superior rank.[66] The hunters brought home the trophies they had killed; the more the carnage, the more the glory. Upon returning from one trip, for example, Cobb proudly displayed his kill of two deer and more than a hundred squirrels. He preferred to kill big animals; he had a trophy room filled with the mounted heads of bears, mountain lions, and moose that he had killed. One of his chief regrets in life was not finding the time or companions to hunt in Africa; he dreamed of killing huge rhinos, lions, and elephants. He also liked to hunt quail and wild turkey. He purchased and bred an assortment of pedigreed bird dogs and delighted in entering them in show competition. Appropriately for this essay, Cobb named his prize hunting dog "Honor."[67]

To recapitulate: Ty Cobb's low threshold for behaviors by others that he thought required violent responses should be considered not only as evidence of possible psychic disorders, but also in terms of family, race, and rank in a particular time and place, that of Georgia's Upper Piedmont in the late nineteenth and early twentieth centuries. His unusual propensity for violence should also be considered in the context of his own world of baseball, one in which he came to feel more at home than that of the Georgia uplands. As a product of that world and of a particular regional culture, Cobb interpreted the sudden and unsettling changes swirling around him in terms of honor. Defense of honor required a willingness to fight, to employ physical force against those who impugned one's good name, the reputation of one's family, the honor of one's region, and the integrity of one's special world (that of baseball). At the same time, it drove Cobb's determination to succeed in baseball, hunting, and other forms of manly competition.

Cobb's years after retirement from baseball suggest the inadequacy of his use of honor as a way of understanding and coping with the world in which he found himself. Aging failed to tame Cobb's truculence. He married and divorced twice, and was eventually estranged from all of his five children. In his final years, if biographer Stump reported correctly, Cobb drank to excess, continued to squabble with and assault others with startling frequency, suffered from insomnia, and periodically sank into bouts of dark melancholy.

Ty Cobb and hunting companions. This photo, probably taken in the 1930s, of Curt Downing, Cobb, Max Wilde, and Tris Speaker (from left to right) suggests the special value placed on hunting by upwardly mobile Southern men. Courtesy Bettmann/CORBIS.

NOTES

1. Ty Cobb with Al Stump, *My Life in Baseball: The True Record* (New York: Doubleday, 1961; Lincoln: University of Nebraska Press, Bison edition, 1993), 113. While Cobb was in his final days, Stump, a journalist, assisted him in doing this autobiography. As critics have observed, it is an unusually good sports autobiography. Apart from its general candor, my research indicates that it is nearly always reliable factually. An earlier, shorter autobiography of Cobb first appeared as installments in the *New York Evening News* in 1926. Recently rediscovered, it has been reprinted as Ty Cobb, *Memoirs of Twenty Years in Baseball,* ed. William R. Cobb (Marietta, GA: William R. Cobb, 2002). It contains important facts and opinions not included in Cobb's later autobiography nor in the only fully documented biography of Cobb, that of Charles C. Alexander, *Ty Cobb* (New York: Oxford University Press, 1984). While without footnotes, John D. McCallum's *The Tiger Wore Spats: An Informal Biography of Ty Cobb* (New York: A.S. Barnes and Co., 1956), and *Ty Cobb* (New York: Praeger Publishers, 1975), especially the latter, have value because McCallum knew Cobb personally and apparently did in-depth interviews with him as well as his associates. More recent biographies include Dan Holmes, *Ty Cobb: A Biography* (Westport, CT: Greenwood Press, 2004) and Richard Bak, *Peach: Ty Cobb in His Time and Ours* (Ann Arbor, MI: J.W. Edwards, 2005). Al Stump's *Cobb: A Biography* (Chapel Hill, NC: Angonquin Books of Chapel Hill, 1994) is both the fullest and most negative. During Cobb's bout with terminal cancer, Stump interviewed and lived with Cobb for extended periods of time. Stump also apparently had access to extensive Cobb memorabilia (since destroyed). For advice on this paper, I would like to thank especially Maria Luisa Venegas Laguens, William Thomas III, Elliott Gorn, and members of the University of Nebraska — Lincoln reading group.

2. Alexander, *Ty Cobb,* 105.

3. McCallum, *Ty Cobb,* 83.

4. Quotations in Alexander, *Ty Cobb,* 105.

5. Quoted in Holmes, *Ty Cobb,* 59.

6. Quoted in Bak, *Peach,* 61. According to Cobb, Paul Krichell "had a vicious habit of hooking my leg when I slid into the plate and flipping me over so that I scraped up dirt with my face. . . . I advised him 'Don't ever do that again.' Krichell gave me the hook once more, and this time I scissored my legs, caught him under an arm and almost detached it from his body. The arm was forced back and badly torn at the shoulder. Krichell's career ended right there, after only two major league seasons. 'I'm sorry about it,' I told the St. Louis players, 'but I warned him.'" Cobb, *My Life in Baseball,* 94. See also John Erardi, "Hostile Side of Ty Cobb Still Lingers in Memory: A Few of His Remaining Contemporaries Don't Think 'Georgia Peach' Was So Peachy, Especially on the Field," *Baseball Digest* 44 (August 1985): 66–72.

7. Quoted in Alexander, *Ty Cobb,* 107.

8. Stump, *Cobb,* 12. The feature-length movie, *Cobb* (1994) was directed by Ron

Shelton and produced by Warner Brothers. Tommy Lee Jones played Cobb while Robert Wuhl played Cobb's biographer Al Stump. Relying mainly on Stump's biography, the film deals almost exclusively with Cobb's final days.

9. Quoted in Stump, *Cobb*, 6. For other examples of a psychological interpretation, see Benjamin G. Rader, *Baseball: A History of America's Game*, 2nd ed. (Urbana and Chicago: University of Illinois Press, 2002), 106–109, and Rader, "Ty(rus) Raymond Cobb," Arnold Markoe, ed., *The Scribner Encyclopedia of American Lives: Sports Figures*, vol. 1 (New York: Charles Scribner's Sons, 2002), 174–76. In his sympathetic biography, Bak, *Peach*, 205–08, commenting on Cobb's sudden and violent mood changes, speculates that Cobb might have suffered from a "bipolar disorder."

10. *Detroit Free Press*, August 7, 1910, quoted in Alexander, *Ty Cobb*, 94.

11. Quoted in Stump, *Cobb*, 386. Italics added for emphasis.

12. See Elliott J. Gorn's pioneering essay, "'Gouge and Bite, Pull Hair and Scratch': The Social Significance of Fighting in the Southern Backcountry," *American Historical Review* 90 (February 1985), 18–43, as well as David Hackett Fischer's *Albion's Seed: Four British Folkways in America* (New York: Oxford University Press, 1989).

13. See especially Gorn, "'Gouge and Bite.'" For the South more generally, especially in the antebellum era, there is a burgeoning literature on the importance of honor in understanding the high incidence of violence in the region. The classic work is Bertram Wyatt-Brown, *Southern Honor: Ethics and Behavior in the Old South* (New York: Oxford University Press, 1982), but see also Edward L. Ayers, *Vengeance and Justice: Crime and Punishment in the 19th-Century South* (New York: Oxford University Press, 1984); Kenneth S. Greenberg, *Masters and Statesmen: The Political Culture of American Slavery* (Baltimore: Johns Hopkins University Press, 1985); Steven M. Stowe, *Intimacy and Power in the Old South: Ritual in the Lives of the Planters* (Baltimore: Johns Hopkins University Press, 1987); Kenneth S. Greenberg, *Honor & Slavery: Lies, Duels, Noses, Masks, Dressing as a Woman, Gifts, Strangers, Humanitarianism, Death, Slave Rebellions, the Pro-Slavery Argument, Baseball, Hunting, and Gambling in the Old South* (Princeton, NJ: Princeton University Press, 1996). See also Wyatt-Brown, *The House of Percy: Honor, Melancholy, and Imagination in a Southern Family* (New York: Oxford University Press, 1994); Wyatt-Brown, *The Shaping of Southern Culture: Honor, Grace, and War, 1760s-1880s* (Chapel Hill: University of North Carolina Press, 2001); Robert F. Pace, *Halls of Honor: College Men in the Old South* (Baton Rouge, LA: Louisiana State University Press, 2004). Ted Ownby, *Subduing Satan: Religion, Recreation, and Manhood in the Rural South, 1865–1920* (Chapel Hill: University of North Carolina Press, 1990), argues that the honor culture of the rural South was fundamentally male and was at odds with evangelical and female values. Evangelicals sought to bring men closer to the behavior presumed to be typical of women and children. Wyatt-Brown, *Shaping of Southern Culture*, 85, on the other hand, paints a more complex picture: "The interconnection of honor and moral conscience, along with shame and its relation to a sense of guilt, encouraged the Southern Christian to balance the two ethi-

cal systems or even make them one." Supplementing and perhaps to some degree complementing the historical literature on honor is that on manliness and masculinity. It may be, as one scholar has suggested, that the growing popularity of the term "manliness" in the mid to late nineteenth century represented the *embourgeoisement* of the concept of honor. In any case, rather than on men in the more rural and traditional South, the students of manliness have focused on men in the North, men who were concerned about what they perceived as a growing softness, effeminateness, and effeteness in modern life. Encouragement of a more aggressive manhood could allegedly counteract these undesirable tendencies. Yet the northern conception of manliness differed in one key respect from that of southern honor. It did not call for immediate, violent, personal, and extralegal responses to insults. Instead, it valued the expression of a "manly" physicality in sports, outdoors activities, and warfare, in short, a manhood ultimately restricted by laws, rules, or conventions of self-restraint. See for example Gail Bederman, *Manliness and Civilization: A Cultural History of Gender and Race in the United States, 1880–1917* (Chicago: University of Chicago Press, 1995), esp. 16–20; and E. Anthony Rotundo, *American Manhood: Transformations in Masculinity from the Revolution to the Modern Era* (New York: Basic Books, 1993). Making a case for a strong correlation of an honor culture with the high incidence of violence in the contemporary American South is Richard E. Nisbett and Dov Cohen, *Culture of Honor: The Psychology of Violence in the South* (Boulder, CO: Westview Press, 1996).

14. Wyatt-Brown, *Southern Honor,* 15.

15. Quoted in Steven Hahn, *The Roots of Southern Populism: Yeoman Farmers and the Transformation of the Georgia Upcountry, 1850–1890* (New York: Oxford University Press, 1983), 138. In addition to Hahn, see *History of Franklin County, Georgia* (Carnesville, GA: Franklin County Historical Society, 1986), esp. chap. vii, and Robert Preston Brooks, "The Agrarian Revolution in Georgia, 1865–1912," *Bulletin of the University of Wisconsin* 3 (1914): 393–524, for the economic and social transformation of the region.

16. See especially Peter Kolchin, "Whiteness Studies: The New History of Race in America," *Journal of American History* 89 (June 2002): 154–73, and Grace Elizabeth Hale, *Making Whiteness: The Culture of Segregation in the South, 1890–1940* (New York: Pantheon Books, 1998). According to W. Fitzhugh Brundage, *Lynching in the New South: Georgia and Virginia* (Urbana and Chicago: University of Illinois Press, 1993), 270, in the 1880 to 1930 era Franklin County witnessed two lynchings (in 1885 and 1886), a rate of lynching considerably below that of the downstate Georgia counties which had larger percentages of African American residents. Brundage, however, apparently missed a lynching in Royston in 1904 as well as murders of African Americans there in 1925 and 1926 that may have been the equivalent to lynchings. There is also a widely circulated photograph of the 1936 lynching of Lint Shaw in Royston. See "Lynchings in America," http://www.liu.edu/cwis/cwp.library/african/2000/lynching.htm.

17. Cobb, *My Life in Baseball,* 94.

18. Hale, *Making Whiteness,* 98–104. For a quasi-autobiographical account of an African American woman who challenged the "mammy" stereotype of the day, see [Negro Nurse], "More Slavery in the South," *Independent* (January 25, 1912): 196–200.

19. Cobb, *My Life in Baseball,* 33.

20. Quoted in Greenberg, *Honor & Slavery,* 48.

21. Cobb, *My Life in Baseball,* 94.

22. *Detroit Free Press,* June 22, 1908, quoted in Holmes, *Ty Cobb,* 38–39.

23. Harold Seymour, *Baseball: The Golden Age* (New York: Oxford University Press, 1971), 110. As reported by Seymour, the *Defender* plausibly "asserted that the white press and baseball officials suppressed the story because of Cobb's prominence and that the woman was quietly paid off in exchange for dropping a $10,000 damage suit." Frank Navin, the principal owner of the Tigers, paid a Cleveland law firm $1,200 for representing Cobb in the Stansfield case. In a letter to Cobb, Navin added that he hoped the incident "will prove a good lesson to you." Quoted in Alexander, *Ty Cobb,* 88.

24. Patricia Zacharias, "Ty Cobb, The Greatest Tiger of Them All," *Detroit News Rearview Mirror,* http://info.detnews.com/history/story/index.cfum?id=92&category-sports (accessed October 17, 2005). Cobb did not acknowledge the existence of Rivers in either of his autobiographies. Neither do any of Cobb's biographers mention Rivers.

25. W. Fitzhugh Brundage, *The Southern Past: A Clash of Race and Memory* (Cambridge, MA: Belknap Press of Harvard University Press, 2005), 2.

26. Quoted in Hahn, *Roots of Southern Populism,* 138.

27. According to a memoir by a neighbor, because John Cobb was found to be "physically unfit for active duty on the front," he served in the Confederate army only for "a month or so," and apparently saw no military action. Cobb then joined and served for the duration of the war in what became known as the "Home Guard," a quasi-military group that was supposed to apprehend deserters and maintain local order. Leonora Grey (Nora Cobb Spencer), "Cobb Creek: An Account of the Cobb Family and Pioneer Days," typewritten manuscript copied and bound by the Southwestern North Carolina Genealogical Society, May 1982 (copies in Murphy Public Library, Murphy, NC, and the Cobb Museum, Royston, GA), 39. Grey does not mention any injuries that Cobb might have received in his Civil War duties. I thank Steve Bullock for finding and calling this document to my attention.

28. Cobb, *My Life in Baseball,* 21, 32. Compare Cobb and other Southern men to a Northerner, Abraham Lincoln. Lincoln essentially cut himself off from both his maternal and paternal ancestry and denied their role and importance in his life and his achievements. See Kenneth J. Winkle, *The Young Eagle Takes Flight: The Rise of Abraham Lincoln* (Dallas: Taylor Trade Publishing, 2001).

29. Quoted in Stump, *Cobb,* 129.

30. Cobb, *My Life in Baseball,* 43.

31. Ibid, 280; W. H. Cobb to Tyrus Cobb, January 5, 1902, Cobb Letters Folder, Ty Cobb Collection, National Baseball Hall of Fame Library, Cooperstown, NY. Quoted in Holmes, *Ty Cobb,* 3.

32. Cobb, *Memoirs,* 15.

33. See Pieter Spierenberg, "Masculinity, Violence, and Honor," in Spierenberg, ed., *Men and Violence: Gender, Honor and Rituals in Modern Europe and America* (Columbus, OH: Ohio State University Press, 1998), 11.

34. Cobb, *Memoirs,* 18.

35. Cobb, *Memoirs,* 21.

36. Cobb, *My Life in Baseball,* 37.

37. Quotations in Stump, *Cobb,* 26–27.

38. Cobb, *My Life in Baseball,* 113.

39. Sam Crawford in Lawrence S. Ritter, ed., *The Glory of Their Times: The Story of The Early Days of Baseball Told by the Men Who Played It* (New York: Macmillan, 1966), 62.

40. Bak, *Peach,* 77.

41. Crawford in Ritter, *Glory of Their Times,* 62.

42. Cobb, *Memoirs,* 55. Italics added for emphasis.

43. Greenberg, *Honor & Slavery,* 12–13.

44. Ritter, *Glory of Their Times,* 62.

45. Quoted in Stump, *Cobb,* 129.

46. Cobb, *My Life in Baseball,* 25.

47. As quoted in Bak, *Peach,* 18.

48. As quoted in McCallum, *Ty Cobb,* 48.

49. Cobb, *Memoirs,* 55.

50. Some photos support this point. A team photograph of the 1908 American League champion Detroit Tigers shows Cobb sitting on his haunches on the far right end, next to team manager Hughie Jennings; he is the only player not touching another player or the manager. Notice a similar physical relationship of the players and Cobb in a photograph of American League all-stars taken in 1917; Marc Okkonen, *The Ty Cobb Scrapbook* (New York: Sterling Pub. Co., Inc., 2001), 29, 124. Notice, however, that Cobb is in the center of a photograph of the American League champion Tigers of 1907; Cobb, *My Life in Baseball,* 193.

51. Ty Cobb to Connie Mack, Feb. 22, 1955, Cobb Letters Folder, Ty Cobb Collection, National Hall of Fame Baseball Library, Cooperstown, NY.

52. Greenberg, *Honor & Slavery,* 16. See also Wyatt-Brown, *Shaping of Southern Culture,* 77–78.

53. McCallum, *Ty Cobb,* 107.

54. McCallum, *Ty Cobb,* 108.

55. Quoted in *Detroit Free Press,* May 21, 1912, reprinted in Okkonen, *Ty Cobb Scrapbook,* 228. Italics added for emphasis.

56. Cited in Stump, *Cobb,* 211.

57. Quoted in the *Washington Post,* May 19, 1912. Representative William Schley Howard also observed that, had he not signed the telegram, he would never be able to return to Georgia.

58. Quotations in Alexander, *Ty Cobb,* 107.

59. Cobb, *My Life in Baseball,* 43.

60. Quoted in Stump, *Cobb,* 237.

61. Ibid., 405.

62. Alexander, *Ty Cobb,* 63.

63. Quoted in Joseph Durso, *The Days of Mr. McGraw* (Englewood Cliffs, NJ: Prentice Hall, 1969), 20.

64. Quoted in Holmes, *Ty Cobb,* ix.

65. Quoted in Alexander, *Ty Cobb,* 49.

66. Cobb was an avid golfer and, for a time, before the Detroit ownership dissuaded him, he raced fast cars. For a classic essay on manly competition among the Virginia gentry in the colonial era, see T. H. Breen, "Horses and Gentlemen: The Cultural Significance of Gambling among the Gentry of Virginia," *William and Mary Quarterly* 33 (1977): 239–57. On hunting as a facet of Southern honor culture, apart from Greenberg, *Honor & Slavery,* Wyatt-Brown, *Southern Honor,* and Ownby, *Subduing Satan,* see also Stuart A. Marks, *Southern Hunting in Black and White: Nature, History and Ritual in a Carolina Community* (Princeton, NJ: Princeton University Press, 1991); Dickson Bruce Jr., *Violence and Culture in the Antebellum South* (Austin, TX: University of Texas Press, 1979), chap. 9; and Scott C. Martin, "Don Quixote and Leatherstocking: Hunting, Class and Masculinity in the American South, 1800–40," *International Journal of the History of Sport* 12 (December 1995): 61–79.

67. See esp. McCallum, *Ty Cobb,* 100. See also a photograph taken in 1926 of the kill of Cobb and three companions. Bak, *Peach,* 124.

ABOUT THE CONTRIBUTORS

RICHARD C. CREPEAU, Professor of History at the University of Central Florida, and a former president of the North American Society for Sport History, is the author of *Baseball: America's Diamond Mind* (1980).

MARK DYRESON, Associate Professor of Kinesiology and History at Pennsylvania State University, and former president of the North American Society for Sport History, is the author of *Making the American Team: Sport, Culture, and the Olympic Experience* (1998).

DANIEL A. NATHAN, Associate Professor of American Studies at Skidmore College, where he teaches courses on twentieth-century cultural history, is the author of the award-winning *Saying It's So: A Cultural History of the Black Sox Scandal* (2003). He also contributed to volume 40 in the Webb Lecture Series, *Lights, Camera, History: Portraying the Past in Film* (Texas A&M University Press, 2007).

BENJAMIN G. RADER, James L. Sellers Professor of History at the University of Nebraska–Lincoln, is the author of *Baseball: A History of America's Game* (3rd. ed., 2007).

SAMUEL O. REGALADO, Professor of History at California State University, Stanislaus, is the author of *Viva Baseball! Latin Major Leaguers and their Special Hunger* (1998), and the co-author of *Mexican Americans and Sports* (Texas A&M University Press, 2007).

STEVEN A. RIESS, Bernard J. Brommel Distinguished Research Professor of History at Northeastern Illinois University, is the author of several books on American sport history including *Touching Base: Professional Baseball and American Culture in the Progressive Era* (rev. ed., 1999).

DAVID VAUGHT is an Associate Professor of History at Texas A&M University. His two great passions are history and baseball, though the essay in this volume constitutes his first effort to combine the two.

ISBN-13: 978-1-60344-023-3
ISBN-10: 1-60344-023-2